2007

STATE of EMERGENCY

Also by Patrick J. Buchanan

Where the Right Went Wrong

The Death of the West

A Republic, Not an Empire

The Great Betrayal

Right from the Beginning

Conservative Votes, Liberal Victories

The New Majority

STATE of EMERGENCY

The Third World Invasion and Conquest of America

Patrick J. Buchanan

Thomas Dunne Books
St. Martin's Griffin ⋈ New York

THOMAS DUNNE BOOKS.
An imprint of St. Martin's Press.

www.thomasdunnebooks.com
www.stmartins.com

Library of Congress Cataloging-in-Publication Data

Buchanan, Patrick J. (Patrick Joseph), 1938–
    State of emergency: the third world invasion and conquest of America/Patrick
J. Buchanan.
            p. cm.
    Includes index.
    ISBN-13: 978-0-312-37436-5
    ISBN-10: 0-312-37436-4
        1. Illegal aliens—United States.   2. Illegal aliens—Government policy—United
States.   3. United States—Emigration and immigration.   I. Title.

JV6483.B83 2006
325.73—dc22   2006043721

First St. Martin's Griffin Edition: October 2007

10   9   8   7   6   5   4   3   2   1

Contents

Acknowledgments

For the idea and title of *State of Emergency,* I am indebted to my editor-publisher, Tom Dunne, who convinced me a book on America's immigration crisis might be more relevant and timely than my take on the fall of the British Empire. To Fredi Friedman, my agent, editor of five of my books, and my ambassador to the world of publishing, my thanks for her diplomacy in making this a reality.

For fifteen years, in speeches, columns, books, on television and radio, on panels and in debates, I have addressed the immigration issue. Today, the West, at long last, seems to have awakened to what many of us regard as an existential crisis of our civilization. Whether we shall address it with the resolution required remains an open question.

But if we fail it will not be the fault of the writers and reformers who kept this issue before the nation. In the van are my friends, the late columnist Sam Francis, whom we buried beneath Lookout Mountain in the winter of 2005, and Peter Brimelow, author of *Alien Nation* and founding father of the indispensable Web site *VDARE.com*. Others from whom *State of Emergency* has benefited include *VDARE.com* columnists Edwin Rubenstein, Allan Wall, James Fulford, Joe Guzzardi—and Steve Sailer, half a dozen of whose columns are cited here and who was most generous with his time. Editors Tom Fleming of *Chronicles,* Scott McConnell and Kara Hopkins of *The American Conservative,* Terry Jeffrey of *Human Events,* Jerry Woodruff of

Middle American News, and ex-editor John O'Sullivan of *National Review* have been indispensable in letting neither the country nor the conservatives forget the perilous consequences of ignoring this issue.

Over these years I have appeared beside many of America's bravest immigration reformers. Among them are Roy Beck of NumbersUSA, Mark Krikorian of the Center for Immigration Studies, Dan Stein of the Federation for American Immigration Reform, and Phyllis Schlafly of Eagle Forum, the First Lady of American Conservatism. From the writings and research of them all, this book has greatly benefited.

Four other women have served this cause of country and culture with distinction: the syndicated columnists Michelle Malkin and Georgie Anne Geyer, Heather Mac Donald of Manhattan Institute, and my sister, "Bay" Buchanan, who heads TeamAmerica.

Finally, my thanks to James Antle of *The American Conservative,* James Fulford of *VDARE.com,* Steve Camarota of CIS, and columnist Lowell Ponte for their comments; my copyeditor, Ann Adelman, for the weeks she invested; and Dr. Frank Mintz, the history researcher and writer-editor who worked on *A Republic, Not an Empire* and made the weekly run in from West Virginia with his commentary on successive drafts of *State of Emergency.*

The one absolutely certain way of bringing this nation to ruin, of preventing all possibility of its continuing to be a nation at all, would be to permit it to become a tangle of squabbling nationalities . . .

—THEODORE ROOSEVELT, the Knights of Columbus, 1915

You cannot become thorough Americans if you think of yourselves in groups. America does not consist of groups. A man who thinks of himself as belonging to a particular national group in America has not yet become an American.

—WOODROW WILSON, Address to New Citizens, 1915

1

How Civilizations Perish

Why was the border guard so thin? Did the Romans
not notice . . . that their way of life was changing forever?[1]
—THOMAS CAHILL, 1995

Civilizations die from suicide, not by murder.[2]
—ARNOLD TOYNBEE

Civilizations, Arnold Toynbee believed, arose when "creative minorities" devised solutions to the great crisis of the age. They perished when they failed to resolve that crisis.

After the collapse of the Roman Empire and the barbarian invasions, Toynbee concluded, the Catholic Church had solved the crisis of the age: disunity and chaos. It had done so by creating a new religious community out of which grew a new civilization and culture.

Thus began the history of Christendom.

From the fifteenth to the twentieth centuries, the West wrote the history of the world. Out of the Christian countries of Europe came the explorers, the missionaries, the conquerors, the colonizers, who, by the twentieth century, ruled virtually the entire world. But the passing of the West had begun.

Spain's empire was the first to fall. America delivered the coup de grâce in 1898. But it was the Thirty Years' War of 1914–1945, the Civil War of Western Civilization, that inflicted the mortal wounds.

By 1918, the German, Austro-Hungarian, and Russian empires had collapsed. World War II bled and broke the British and French. One by one, after war's end, the strategic outposts of empire—Suez, the Canal Zone, Rhodesia, South Africa, Hong Kong—began to fall. Within three decades, Europe's headlong retreat from Asia and Africa was complete.

From 1989 to 1991, the Soviet Empire fell and the Soviet Union split into fifteen pieces, half a dozen of them Muslim nations that had never before existed. Now, the African, Asian, Islamic, and Hispanic peoples that the West once ruled are coming to repopulate the mother countries.

By the Toynbeean concept of challenge and response, the crisis of Western civilization consists of three imminent and mortal perils: dying populations, disintegrating cultures, and invasions unresisted.

History repeats itself. After the Roman republic spread out from the town on the Tiber to rule Italy and "the Middle Sea of Earth" from Spain to Jerusalem, from Carthage to Hadrian's Wall, the conquered peoples made their way to the imperial capital. Rome became a polyglot city of all the creeds and cultures of the empire. But these alien peoples brought with them no reverence for Roman gods, no respect for Roman tradition, no love of Roman culture. And so, as Rome had conquered the barbarians, the barbarians conquered Rome. In the fifth century, beginning with Alaric and the Visigoths in 410, the northern tribes, one after another, invaded and sacked the Eternal City. And the Dark Ages descended.

And as Rome passed away, so, the West is passing away, from the same causes and in much the same way. What the Danube and Rhine were to Rome, the Rio Grande and Mediterranean are to America and Europe, the frontiers of a civilization no longer defended.

In *How the Irish Saved Civilization,* Thomas Cahill writes: "To the Romans, the German tribes were riffraff; to the Germans, the Roman side of the river was the place to be. The nearest we can come to understanding this divide may be the southern border of the United States. There the spit-and-polish troops are immigration police; the hordes, the Mexicans, Haitians, and other dispossessed people seeking illegal entry."[3]

In his *Fall of the Roman Empire: A New History of Rome and the Barbarians,* Oxford's Peter Heather challenges previous historians and attributes the fall of the empire to Rome's refusal to block a great horde of refugees that arrived at its border late in the fourth century:

"In 376 a large band of Gothic refugees arrived at the Empire's Danube frontier, asking for asylum. In a complete break with established Roman policy, they were allowed in, unsubdued. They revolted, and within two years had defeated and killed the emperor Valens—the one who had received them—along with two-thirds of his army, at the battle of Hadrianople."[4]

At first, "this sudden surge of would-be Gothic immigrants wasn't seen as a problem at all," writes Heather. "On the contrary, Valens happily admitted them because he saw in this flood of displaced humanity a great opportunity."[5] The Roman historian Ammianus wrote of how warmly the Goths were welcomed: "The affair caused more joy than fear and educated flatterers immoderately praised the good fortune of the prince, which unexpectedly brought him so many young recruits from the ends of the earth. . . ."[6]

What Valens had done was the Christian thing to do, but it had never been the Roman thing to do. Valens has his modern counterpart in George W. Bush. For in May 2006, Republican senators at Bush's urging joined Democrats to offer a blanket amnesty to 12 million illegal aliens and permit U.S. businesses to go abroad and bring in foreign workers. Senators had been shocked by the millions of Hispanics marching in America's cities under Mexican flags. And as was the emperor Valens, President Bush was hailed for his compassion and vision.

Just as Rome's time came, so today comes the time of the West. From Algeria, Tunisia, Morocco, Mauritania, and the old French colonies of the sub-Sahara, they cross the Mediterranean. From the mandated lands Europe tore from the Ottomans, an Islamic invasion is mounted that is changing the character of the Old Continent. And the future the militant imams have in mind for Europe is not the same as that dreamed of by the bureaucrats of Brussels.

In 2005, there came a fire bell in the night. Children of Arab and African peoples France once ruled burned and looted the suburbs of Paris and three hundred cities. Prophets without honor had warned of what was coming.

In 2005, 750,000 more Russians disappeared from the face of the earth, bringing Russia's population down to 143 million. Due to an anemic birth rate and early deaths, another 10 million will vanish in the next ten years. Meanwhile, Chinese workers and traders in the thousands annually cross the Amur and Ussuri rivers to work and live, slowly repossessing the lands lost to the czars and the world's last great storehouse of natural resources: Siberia and the Russian Far East. In the Caucasus and Central Asia, holy warriors take up arms to drive Mother Russia back whence the Cossacks came centuries ago.

And, above all, it is happening here. In the eighteenth century, America began her restless, relentless drive to dominance from the Atlantic seaboard over the mountains to the great river. In the age of Jackson and Polk, the United States tore Florida away from Spain, and Texas, the Southwest, and California away from young Mexico. By century's end, we had annexed Hawaii, Guam, Puerto Rico, and the Philippines. In 1900, U.S. Marines marched beside British imperial troops to Peking to crush the Boxer Rebellion. In the first half of the twentieth century, America invaded Mexico, built the Panama Canal, intervened in the Caribbean and Central America, smashed Japan's empire, and conquered the Pacific and East Asia.

Now the tape has begun to run in reverse. In 1960, there were perhaps 5 million Asians and Hispanics in the United States. Today, there are 57 million. Between 10 percent and 20 percent of all Mexican, Central American, and Caribbean peoples have moved into the United States. One to 2 million enter every year and stay, half of them in defiance of America's laws and disdain for America's borders. No one knows how many illegal aliens are here. The estimates run from 12 to 20 million.

This is not immigration as America knew it, when men and women made a conscious choice to turn their backs on their native lands and cross the ocean to become Americans. This is an invasion, the greatest invasion in history. Nothing of this magnitude has ever happened in so short a span of time. There are 36 million immigrants and their children in the United States today, almost as many as came to America between Jamestown in 1607 and the Kennedy election of 1960. Nearly 90 percent of all immigrants now come from continents and countries whose peoples have never been assimilated fully into any Western country.

Against the will of a vast majority of Americans, America is being transformed. As our elites nervously avert their gaze or welcome the invasion, we are witness to one of the great tragedies in human history. From Gibbon to Spengler to Toynbee and the Durants, the symptoms of dying civilizations are well known: the death of faith, the degeneration of morals, contempt for the old values, collapse of the culture, paralysis of the will. But the two certain signs that a civilization has begun to die are a declining population and foreign invasions no longer resisted.

Europe, having embraced what Pope John Paul II called a "culture of death," is far down the Roman road to ruin. For death has embraced Europe back. Not one European nation save Muslim Albania has a birth rate among its native-born that will enable it to survive the century in its present form. Birth rates below replacement levels have been the mark of all the great nations of Europe for decades. In many, the population has ceased to grow and begun to die.

Here in America, the self-delusion about what is happening and the paralysis in the face of the crisis have no precedent. What can be said for a man who would allow his home to be invaded by strangers who demanded they be fed, clothed, housed, and granted the rights of the firstborn? What can be said for a ruling elite that permits this to be done to the nation, and that celebrates it as a milestone of moral progress?

We are witnessing how nations perish. We are entered upon the final act of our civilization. The last scene is the deconstruction of the nations. The penultimate scene, now well underway, is the invasion unresisted.

2

The Invasion

The American Southwest seems to be slowly returning to the
jurisdiction of Mexico without a shot being fired.[1]
—*EXCELSIOR*, JULY 20, 1982, Mexico's national newspaper

Demographically, socially, and culturally, the *reconquista* of
the Southwest United States . . . is well underway.[2]
—SAMUEL HUNTINGTON, Harvard University, 2004

On August 12, 2005, Governor Bill Richardson of New Mexico declared a state of emergency on the Mexican border, claiming the region had been "devastated by the ravages and terror of human
smuggling, drug smuggling, kidnapping, murder, destruction of
property and the death of livestock."[3]

Three days later, Governor Janet Napolitano of Arizona declared
a state of emergency on her southern border. By March 2006,
Napolitano was moving National Guard to the border while assuring the people of Arizona, "We are not at war with Mexico."[4]

But the state of emergency is not confined to the Southwest. Our
state of emergency is a national one. America is being invaded, and if
this is not stopped, it will mean the end of the United States.

The Southwest is being overrun by illegal aliens who cross in the
thousands every day in an endless trek north as they repopulate
America. The trafficking in narcotics and people is a human rights

outrage and a national disgrace. Even more so is the failure of the government of the United States to enforce our laws and protect our borders, stretches of which have become a hell on earth. On September 20, 2004, *Time* magazine described what is happening on the Mexican border:

> When the crowds cross the ranches along and near the border, they discard backpacks, empty Gatorade and water bottles and soiled clothes. . . . They turn the land into a vast latrine, leaving behind revolting mounds of personal refuse and enough discarded plastic bags to stock a Wal-Mart. Night after night, they cut fences intended to hold in cattle and horses. Cows that eat the bags must often be killed because the plastic becomes lodged between the first and second stomachs. The immigrants steal vehicles and saddles. They poison dogs to quiet them. The illegal traffic is so heavy that some ranchers, because of the disruptions and noise, get very little sleep at night.[5]

It testifies to the moral rot in both parties that our leaders are so terrified of being called "nativist," "xenophobic," or even "racist" that they blind themselves to the rampant criminality along our southern frontier.

Who Are the Invaders?

On November 28, 2005, President Bush, speaking in Tucson, conceded that in five years 4.5 million aliens had been caught attempting to break into the United States. Among that 4.5 million, Bush admitted, were "more than 350,000 with criminal records."[6] One in every twelve illegal aliens the U.S. Border Patrol had apprehended was a criminal.

That is 70,000 felons apprehended each year, 200 felons every single day for five years, trying to break into our country to rob, rape, and murder Americans. Of the millions who succeeded on Bush's watch, how many came for just such purposes? How many Americans have been robbed, assaulted, or murdered because the president failed in his duty to defend the borders of the United States?

Nearly 8 million foreigners did enter during those five years, 3.7 million of them illegally. If one in twelve was a criminal, 300,000 felons slipped in during Bush's tenure. This is an historic dereliction of presidential duty.

There are today 36 million foreign-born in the United States, almost three times as many people as the 13.5 million here at the peak of the Great Wave in 1910. And it is among these tens of millions of foreign-born that illegal aliens find sanctuary. As James Edwards of the Hudson Institute writes, legal and illegal immigration are two sides of the same coin. If we fail to control the one, we cannot control the other. As a rule, he notes, when legal immigration rises, illegal immigration soars. Mexicans account for perhaps 30 percent of all the foreign-born population in the United States today, and more than half are here illegally. And while illegals made up only 21 percent of the foreign-born in 1980, they constitute 28 percent today.[7]

To measure the immensity of the immigrant cohort, let us go back to John F. Kennedy's *A Nation of Immigrants*, published in the run-up to the 1960 election. In it, the future president marvels at how many had come to these shores:

The gates were now flung open, and men and women in search of a new life came to these shores in ever-increasing numbers—150,000 in the 1820's, 1.7 million in the 1840's, 2.8 million in the 1870's, 5.2 million in the 1880's, 8.8 million in the first decade of the 20th century. . . .

Between 1830 and 1930, the period of the greatest migration

from Europe to the United States, Germany sent six million people to the United States—more than any other nation. . . .

Italy has contributed more immigrants to the United States than any other country except Germany. Over five million Italians came to this country between 1820 and 1963.[8]

Using Kennedy's numbers, there are as many illegal aliens in the United States today as all the German and Italian immigrants who ever came, the two largest immigrant groups in our history. Our foreign-born population today is almost equal to the 42 million who came over the three and a half centuries from 1607 to 1965.[9] The Border Patrol catches as many illegal aliens *every month* as all the legal immigrants who came to America in the 1820s. Today's numbers are of a different order of magnitude.

No nation has ever attempted to assimilate 36 million foreigners in a generation. Yet, each year, 1.5 million more are added to the number, half of them illegals, 90 percent of them from Third World countries whose people have never before been assimilated into our population. In the New York and San Francisco metropolitan areas, immigrants account for more than 25 percent of the population. In the Los Angeles and Miami-Dade metro areas, the respective figures are 32 percent and 36 percent.

The *Time* magazine investigation, "Who Left the Door Open?", concluded: "It's fair to estimate . . . that the number of illegal aliens flooding into the U.S. this year will total 3 million—enough to fill 22,000 Boeing 737–700 aircraft, or 60 flights every day for a year."[10]

In January 2005, a Bear Stearns study maintained: "The number of illegal immigrants in the United States may be as high as 20 million people."[11] If near the mark, we have millions more illegal aliens in the United States today than the sum total of all the Germans,

Italians, Irish, and Jews who ever came to America in the four hundred years of our history on this continent.

In a January 2006 *New Republic* essay, "Border War," John Judis writes that "over the course of a year, almost two million will make it, sometimes after several tries, and enter the underworld of undocumented migrants. . . ."[12]

In *Whatever it Takes*, Congressman J. D. Hayworth notes: "At *minimum*, almost 4,500 people cross into Arizona illegally *each day* without getting caught. . . ."[13] By Hayworth's estimates, 1.6 million illegals come through Arizona alone, every year. And as Professor Glynn Custred, cofounder of the California Civil Rights Initiative, writes, the attitude and the character of the intruders crossing the California desert has changed radically.

> Eventually the temper of the illegal aliens changed. They became more aggressive, more brazen, more dangerous. In some cases, instead of asking for food or water, they would kick down doors to get it. Meanwhile, dogs are poisoned or their throats cut; property is damaged and goods are stolen, cars are hijacked and residents threatened. One lady on her way to look after her neighbors' pets was waylaid by passing illegal aliens and murdered for her car. People in east San Diego County now often go armed as they do along the Arizona border.[14]

In 2005, 687 assaults on U.S. Border Patrol agents were recorded, near double the number of the previous year. In the San Diego and Tucson sectors, Border Patrol agents reported being fired upon forty-three times, more than twice the number of shooting incidents as in the previous year.[15]

America faces an existential crisis. If we do not get control of our borders, by 2050 Americans of European descent will be a minority in the nation their ancestors created and built. No nation has ever undergone so radical a demographic transformation and survived.

By 2050, the Hispanic population will have tripled to 102 million, or 24 percent of the nation. Most will be of Mexican ancestry and concentrated in a Southwest that Mexican children are taught was stolen from their country by American aggressors a century and a half ago.

As early as 2010, it is estimated that in the regions surrounding the cities of Miami, Houston, Los Angeles, San Francisco, and Washington, D.C., Americans of European descent will have become a minority. In the Washington metro area between 2000 and 2005, the white population grew by 2.5 percent, the black population by 5.3 percent. But the Asian population shot up 21.5 percent and the Hispanic population grew by almost 28 percent.[16]

In California and Texas, Americans of European descent are already a minority and their share of our population falls every year. Hispanics account for 34 percent of our two most populous states and their numbers are surging. During the 1990s, for the first time since it came into the Union, California's white population fell by 2 million as its native-born sons and daughters packed and left for Nevada, Idaho, Arizona, and Colorado to live out their lives in places more like the Golden State they grew up in. The *reconquista* of Alta California by Mexico is well advanced and the great question is now on the table.

Will the American Southwest become a giant Kosovo, a part of the nation separated from the rest by language, ethnicity, history, and culture, to be reabsorbed in all but name by Mexico from whom we took these lands in the time of Jackson and Polk? Chicano chauvinists and Mexican agents have made clear their intent to take back through demography and culture what their ancestors lost through war.

Who Is That at the Door?

"The one absolutely certain way of bringing this nation to ruin, of preventing all possibility of its continuing to be a nation at all, would be to permit it to become a tangle of squabbling nationalities," said Theodore Roosevelt. We are becoming what T.R. warned against: a multilingual, multiracial, multiethnic, multicultural Tower of Babel. To the delight of anti-Americans everywhere and the indifference of our elites, we are risking the Balkanization and breakup of the nation.

Most of the 36 million foreign-born here came to share in the dream and be part of our national family. They are good people who seek the same things our ancestors sought: a new start, a more rewarding life, the chance to raise a family in a better and freer place than the one they left behind. They work hard, and many have risked their lives in mountains and deserts of our Southwest to be here and to work at wages five and ten times what they can earn back home. That the bodies of 2,881 migrants have been recovered by the Border Patrol since 1998, and many more remain missing, testifies to the determination and desperation of these people. Many have served in the armed forces of the United States and bled for this country and love it as much as any descendant of the *Mayflower* generation. Others come to avail themselves and their families of the benefits America provides her poor: free medical care at clinics and emergency rooms, education for their children, subsidized rents and food, welfare cash and earned income tax credits.

But millions bring no allegiance to America and remain loyal to the lands of their birth. And though they occupy more and more rooms in our home, they are not part of our family. Nor do they wish to be. They are strangers, millions and millions of strangers in our midst.

Some come for malevolent motives—to join gangs that traffic in human beings and narcotics and to make careers robbing, raping, and killing Americans, like *Mara Salvatrucha,* the infamous MS-13. Some come with hate in their heart, like the Jamaican Colin Ferguson, who shot down twenty-five people in a racist rampage against whites on the Long Island Railroad; like Angel Resendez, the rail-riding rapist-killer of nine American women, who slipped back and forth over the border for twenty-three years; like Beltway Sniper John Lee Malvo, who shot a dozen Americans for sport and eluded the death penalty, for he was only seventeen years old when he embarked upon his rampage of serial murder.

How many spies and saboteurs have been sent into our country as sleeper agents? How many Al Qaeda are here awaiting orders to bomb subways and malls or assassinate our leaders? We have no idea. Neither does the Department of Homeland Security. Border security *is* homeland security. But America has lost control of her borders and, as Ronald Reagan said, a country that can't control its borders isn't really a country anymore.

In his address in Tucson, President Bush made a startling admission. For decades, he said, the United States has had a separate policy in dealing with non-Mexicans breaking in through the 2,000-mile border with Mexico, a policy of "catch-and-release": "about four of every five non-Mexican illegal immigrants we catch are released in society and asked to return for a court date. When the date arrives, about 75 percent of those released don't show up at court. As a result, last year [2004], only 30,000 of the 160,000 non-Mexicans caught coming across our southwest border were sent home."

"This practice of catch and release has been the government's policy for decades," said Bush. "It is an unwise policy and we're going to end it."

Is this not an astonishing admission? President Bush was conceding that, in the third year following 9/11, 160,000 border crashers from nations all over the world were turned loose into our society, and only one in five turned up in court. Some 130,000 vanished into our midst. How can the president say our homeland is secure?

Further on in his Tucson speech, Bush conceded that our government and laws have been frozen in a pre-9/11 world:

Under current law, the federal government is required to release people caught crossing our border illegally if their home countries do not take them back in a set period of time. . . . Those we were forced to release have included murderers, rapists, child molesters, and other violent criminals.

"This undermines our border security" and the work "these good folks" of the Border Patrol are doing, added the president.[17]

Again, is this not astounding? President Bush was talking about releasing "murderers, rapists, child molesters, and other violent criminals" into our society, because "current law" commands it and the nations whence these criminals come refuse to take them back.

The question begs itself: With Bush and his party in power, why had they not changed "current law"? Why had President Bush not picked up a phone and told the leaders of these "home countries" that there will not be another visa issued to their country until they take back every one of their criminal felons who has broken into ours?

What is the matter with President Bush? What is the matter with us?

"Gateway for Terrorists"

Potentially the most dangerous aliens crossing our southern border are "OTMs," other-than-Mexicans. Terrorists have boasted openly of entering the United States through Mexico and a growing number of OTMs caught at the border now come from the Middle East.

In February 2006, Senator Dianne Feinstein confronted national intelligence director John Negroponte on this threat, telling Negroponte she had questioned Admiral James Loy, acting head of the Department of Homeland Security, in 2004 and had since learned that the number of OTM illegal aliens had tripled, from 49,545 caught in 2003 to 155,000 in 2005:

Last year, Admiral Loy and I discussed border security, particularly the increasing problem of penetration of other-than-Mexicans across our borders . . . and I said at that time I felt it was a major gateway for terrorists to access the United States. . . . Do you have any on-going intelligence efforts to prevent this from happening?

Negroponte replied that the tripling of OTMs caught crossing the U.S. border was "an issue that we're sensitive to." The U.S. government, he added, is watching the border "very, very carefully."[18] Charles Allen, chief of intelligence at DHS, volunteered that his agency, too, is "very sensitive" to this matter. Negroponte did not deny that in the third and fourth year of the war on terror the number of OTMs from Africa, Asia, and the Middle East caught breaking into our country had tripled.

Again, how can they say our country is secure from terrorists?

In 1818, to halt Indian attacks on Americans in South Georgia out of Spanish Florida, James Madison sent Andrew Jackson to eradicate the nests of villainy. Jackson stormed in, killed and routed the renegades, hanged two British spies for abetting the Indians, and put the Spanish governor and his garrison on a boat to Havana. To secure our border, Old Hickory had risked war with two of the world's greatest empires.

When Pancho Villa crossed the border in 1916, burned Columbus, New Mexico, and murdered U.S. citizens, Wilson sent General

Pershing and 12,000 troops 300 miles into Mexico to pursue the terrorist bandit.

In 1954, when Eisenhower discovered a million Mexicans here who did not belong, without apology he ordered them sent home in "Operation Wetback." They went. Had Vicente Fox's regime colluded in an invasion of the United States, as it has for the last six years, those presidents would have regarded and treated it as an act of war.

What explains the paralysis of the present White House?

George Bush has taken an oath to see to it that the laws of the United States are faithfully executed. The immigration laws are clear. Businesses that hire illegal aliens break U.S. law and are subject to sanctions. Yet, as the columnist John O'Sullivan writes, "in the [Clinton] years 1995, 1996 and 1997 there were between 10,000 and 18,000 work-site arrests of illegals annually. In the same years about 1,000 employers were served notices of fines for employing them. Under the Bush administration, work-site arrests fell to 159 in 2004 where there was also the princely total of three notices of intent to fine served on employers."

"In this dramatic relaxation of internal enforcement" under George W. Bush, O'Sullivan concludes, "is the explanation of the rapidly rising estimate of immigrants living and working illegally in this country."[19]

Can anyone say that, with this record, President Bush has faithfully executed the immigration laws of the United States?

Twice, President Bush took an oath to "preserve, protect and defend the Constitution of the United States." Article IV, Section 4, reads: "The United States shall guarantee to every State in this Union a Republican Form of Government, and shall protect each of them against Invasion."

Yet, with perhaps 4 million illegal aliens having broken in during Bush's five and a half years in office, and our border states being daily breached by thousands more, can anyone say President Bush has protected the states of this Union against that invasion? In an earlier America, this dereliction of constitutional duty would have called forth articles of impeachment.

But who are these people walking across our borders in the millions and forever changing the character of our country?

3

Coming to America

What does it mean that your first act on entering a country—your first
act on that soil—is the breaking of that country's laws?[1]
—PEGGY NOONAN, 2005

[N]o society has a boundless capacity to accept newcomers, especially when
many are poor and unskilled.[2]
—ROBERT SAMUELSON, economist and *Newsweek* columnist, 2005

"Man down on Edsall Road!" came the night call to paramedic
Lieutenant Jason Jenkins. Jenkins described what he found at the
scene as "the most inhumane act of violence I've ever seen." The
sixteen-year-old was lying on his back holding up his mutilated
hands. The fingers had been severed by a machete.

The May 2004 attack occurred in Alexandria, Virginia. The victim was a member of the South Side Locos, second largest gang in
northern Virginia, with 1,500 members.[3] His attackers belonged to
Mara Salvatrucha, MS-13, the largest and most violent gang in
northern Virginia, with 3,500 members, whose savagery—mutilations,
stabbings, shootings, executions, rapes—rivals the Mafia in its hey-
day. But unlike MS-13, the Mafia never had 6,000 members in the
Washington area.

A year before the Edsall Road atrocity, the body of Brenda Paz,
eighteen, stabbed repeatedly, her head almost severed from her

torso, was found on the banks of the Shenandoah. Brenda had agreed to testify against MS-13 and was in a federal witness protection program. She was a victim of "green-lighting," a gang-sanctioned killing of a "snitch" or cop.

A week after the Edsall Road mutilation, a Herndon boy, a member of the 18th Street Gang, was "pumped full of .38 caliber bullets" and his fleeing girlfriend shot in the back. "The assailant, according to a witness, had a large tattoo emblazoned on his forehead. It read MS, for Mara Salvatrucha."[4] Columnist Michelle Malkin, who lives in the Washington suburb of Montgomery County, Maryland, wrote at summer's end 2005:

> Last year, area law enforcement officials issued a warning that MS-13 was planning to ambush Montgomery County . . . cops during service calls . . . [and] intelligence from the [FBI] Norfolk, Va. division report[ed] on a similar gang order issued in the Tidewater, Va., area:
>
> "Reporting by a reliable Norfolk source indicates MS-13 members are planning to randomly attack local law enforcement officers in the Tidewater area. Threats of this nature have been termed by gang members as 'green light' notices. . . . Additional source information indicates local MS-13 members are equipped with weapons and ballistic vests."[5]

Malkin reported on a series of stabbings at county malls, knife fights in a Target store, and federal indictments of nineteen MS-13 members for crimes ranging from a beating death in a cemetery to a drive-by killing of a teenage boy, the kidnapping of two girls and murder of one, stabbings and shootings at suburban high schools, and fatal shootings of rival gang members.

Arlington and Fairfax in Virginia and Montgomery in Maryland, the suburban counties of the nation's capital, have traditionally ranked among the most affluent and finest counties in America in which to live. They are now home to the most vicious Hispanic gangs in the hemisphere.

Mara Salvatrucha

What is *Mara Salvatrucha*? What is it doing in this country? How did it get here? How large is it? How dangerous?

Mara translates as "posse" or "gang," *Salvatrucha* as "street-tough Salvadoran."[6] In reviewing *The World's Most Dangerous Gang,* a documentary by Lisa Ling that aired on the National Geographic Channel in February 2006, the *New York Times's* Ned Martel wrote: "Mara Salvatrucha . . . derives its name from a Spanish term for army ants. Its organized crime ring has roots in Los Angeles but now includes an estimated 100,000 members in 33 states and 6 countries by Ms. Ling's count."[7] Members can be as young as nine and as old as thirty-five.

MS-13's origins are in the Central American civil wars of the 1980s, when President Reagan assisted El Salvador, then under attack by Cuban-trained, Sandinista-supported Marxist guerrillas of the Farabundo Marti National Liberation Front (FMLN). To escape the war, hundreds of thousands of Salvadorans fled to the United States, where they were granted asylum. There are now more than 1.1 million here. Salvadoran ambassador Rene Leon estimates that in the D.C. area alone, there are 500,000 Salvadorans, making our nation's capital a rich recruiting ground for MS-13.[8]

Where Nicaraguans were fleeing Communist Sandinistas, many of the Salvadorans were FMLN sympathizers. Gravitating to East L.A., they formed MS-13 to defend themselves from rival Latino and black gangs.

After the Rodney King riots of 1992, where thousands of thugs from Mexico and Central America were arrested marauding and pillaging our second largest city, many gang members were deported. But some MS-13 migrated to northern Virginia to muscle in on the drug trade.

According to *Newsweek*, MS-13 has 8,000 to 10,000 members in thirty-three states. In Fairfax County, it is credited with 90 percent of all gang-related violence.[9] Although some members were born in America and are citizens, Nicholas Zimmerman of *Medill News Service* reports that MS-13 is still "composed primarily of illegal immigrants from El Salvador."[10] And while the contingent in northern Virginia is the largest in the East, MS-13 roams from North Carolina to New England. At a meeting in suburban New York, 360 out of 480 school principals in attendance saw MS-13 as their greatest threat.[11] In Boston, six MS-13 members were charged with gang-raping two deaf girls, one of whom, a victim of cerebral palsy, was in a wheelchair.

This is not *West Side Story*.

It is the story of a policy of "open borders" and virtually unrestricted immigration championed by a political establishment that runs America for its own benefit, the public be damned.

Sanctuary Cities

Why is it difficult if not impossible for cities to get control of this growing crime menace of immigrants and illegal aliens? Because many cities, under pressure from the ethnic lobbies, have declared themselves "sanctuary" cities, where police are forbidden to arrest known illegal and criminal aliens. Heather Mac Donald, a Manhattan Institute scholar, writes:

In Los Angeles . . . dozens of members of a ruthless Salvadoran prison gang have sneaked back into town after having been deported for such crimes as murder, assault with a deadly weapon, and drug trafficking. Police officers know who they are and know that their mere presence in the country is a felony. Yet should a cop arrest an illegal gangbanger for felonious reentry, it is he who will be treated as a criminal, for violating the LAPD's rule against enforcing immigration law.[12]

Adopted in 1979, when Daryl Gates was chief of the LAPD, Special Order 40 prevents police from arresting MS-13 gang members who are in Los Angeles in violation of their deportation orders. New York, Chicago, San Francisco, San Diego, Seattle, Houston, and Austin have all adopted similar "sanctuary" policies, where local police are forbidden to work with federal authorities on immigration violations. "We can't even talk about it," a frustrated LAPD captain told Mac Donald. "People are afraid of a backlash from Hispanics."

"[I]f I see a deportee from the Mara Salvatrucha gang crossing the street, I know I can't touch him," said another LAPD officer, though sneaking back into the United States following deportation is a felony.

With 36 million foreign-born here, a third of them illegal, "numbers drive policy," Mac Donald concludes. She doubts the United States will ever regain control of its borders. "The nonstop increase of immigration is reshaping the language and the law to dissolve any distinction between legal and illegal aliens and, ultimately, the very idea of national borders."[13]

Her pessimism is realism.

She writes of the arrest of a Honduran visa violator in Miami for seven vicious rapes. A year earlier, cops had the man in custody for lewd and lascivious molestation, but did not check his immigration status, which would have revealed the visa violation, caused his deportation, and spared seven innocent women from an agonizing ordeal.

Mac Donald lists a few statistics that indicate the gravity of the threat to our society posed by illegal alien criminals:

- In Los Angeles, 95 percent of all outstanding warrants for homicide, which total 1,200 to 1,500, target illegal aliens.
- Two-thirds of the 17,000 outstanding fugitive felony warrants in Los Angeles are for illegal aliens.
- Some 12,000 of the 20,000-strong 18th Street Gang that operates across Southern California are illegals.[14]

The 18th Street Gang works in harness with the Mexican Mafia that dominates the California prisons. The historian Roger McGrath considers the gang "the bloodiest criminal organization in Los Angeles."

"During the '70s and '80s, black gangs—essentially the many versions of the Bloods and Crips—ruled the streets of South Central," McGrath writes. "Police tell me that the black gangs are now on the defensive."[15] The graffiti slogan that is everywhere in L.A., "Crips and Bloods Together!", is a call for African-American gang solidarity—for survival against the far more numerous Hispanic gangs.

According to *The Washington Times,* 80,000 "absconders," illegal aliens convicted of such felonies as murder, rape, drug dealing, and child molestation, who have served their prison time and been ordered deported, are now loose again on America's streets.[16]

A New Century Foundation study, *The Color of Crime,* that used FBI and Justice Department crime figures, found that while Hispanics are three times more likely than white Americans to be convicted of serious crimes requiring incarceration, they are *nineteen times more likely to belong to criminal street gangs.*[17] In an ominous development, Asian youth, who commit crimes at only one-fourth the rate of white Americans, are nine times more likely to belong to a criminal gang. The immigrant young are being assimilated into the gang culture.

In "Criminal Aliens," the Federation for American Immigration Reform reveals the magnitude of the exploding alien crime crisis:

In 1980 our federal and state prisons housed fewer than 9,000 criminal aliens. By the end of 1999, these same prisons housed over 68,000 criminal aliens. Today, criminal aliens account for over 29 percent of prisoners in Federal Bureau of Prison facilities and a higher share of all federal prison inmates. These prisoners represent the fastest growing segment of the federal prison population.[18]

The idea of sanctuary dates to the Middle Ages. From the Latin *sanctus,* meaning "holy," the sanctuary of the cathedral was the holiest place within that encompassed the altar and tabernacle. As the Church was beyond the reach of the king's agents, it became a place of refuge for those fleeing the king's law. Suspects seeking sanctuary could not be arrested until they emerged from the church. In the 1980s, some churches declared themselves sanctuaries for illegal aliens fleeing Central America's wars.

In 1989, Mayor Ed Koch made New York a "sanctuary city" when he issued Executive Order 124, forbidding city workers from informing the Immigration and Naturalization Service (INS) on illegal aliens. Under Koch's successors, David Dinkins, Rudy Giuliani, and Michael Bloomberg, Executive Order 124 remained in force. On December 19, 2002, a forty-two-year-old woman paid a price for the mayors' collusion in the wholesale breaking of America's immigration laws.

Sitting on a park bench in Queens, the woman was seized—as her boyfriend was beaten senseless—dragged into a shack near Shea Stadium, and gang-raped by five homeless men for three hours. Four of the men were from Mexico, one from Ecuador. Four had previous arrests, two for serious crimes. All five were illegal aliens. Had the INS been alerted to their earlier crimes, they might have been deported and that woman spared her horrible ordeal. But the NYPD never notified the INS.

FOX News' Bill O'Reilly, who made this act of barbarism the subject of his "Talking Points" commentary, called for citizen lawsuits against the city officials whose pandering "sanctuary" policies are leaving them at the mercy of thousands of criminal aliens who have come to America to prey upon our people.[19]

Washington, D.C., had an even more famous illegal alien who gained some notoriety in 2002. Seventeen-year-old John Lee Malvo, accompanied by surrogate dad John Allen Muhammad, shot thirteen people in the D.C. area, killing ten, in a twenty-three-day terror rampage in October 2002.

How did the Beltway Sniper get into this country? According to Malkin, the Jamaican teenager and his mother Uma James were stowaways on a cargo ship that arrived in Miami in June 2001. James and Malvo left for Tacoma, then Bellingham, Washington, where they were arrested in a custody dispute. Neither had papers proving citizenship. Border Patrol, told by James she and Malvo had been stowaway "passengers on a cargo ship that was filled with 'illegal asians [sic],' " recommended deportation of both.

The INS held them for a month, then turned them loose. Under U.S. law, "illegal alien stowaways are to be detained and deported without hearings," writes Malkin.[20] But James was released on $1,500 bond and Malvo was set free—to head east with John Muhammad to make himself almost as famous as John Dillinger, but more murderous.

September 11, the work of visa overstayers, and the Beltway Sniper serial murders both resulted from the failure of a government that refuses to enforce immigration laws and keep out of our national home people who do not belong here. As *The Washington Times* reported after his capture, "Sniper suspect John Allen Muhammad is the focus of an on-going probe into accusations that he financed his nomadic lifestyle and a sniper killing spree by smuggling illegal aliens into the United States from the Caribbean."[21]

Aliens in the United States account for 12 percent of the population, but 30 percent of the federal prison population.[22] The pool of legal immigrants is the sea in which the illegals and the criminals swim.

America's leaders claim she is the most powerful country on earth. But America has a government too morally flabby to act as decisively as Ike did to remove from our national home those who have broken in and had no right to be here. How many American women must be assaulted, how many children molested, how many citizens must die at the hands of criminal aliens and foreign terrorists before our government does its duty?

Assimilating to What?

Not to worry, we are told, what is happening now happened before. And since it all worked out then, it will all work out now. Just as the social pathology of the poor immigrant Irish, thanks to priests, nuns, and Catholic schools, was cured in a generation or two, just as Jewish ghetto children who, supposedly, could not learn, were soon being restricted from the Ivy League by quotas, just as the handful of Sicilian and Italian mobsters died or killed themselves off, so the problems with the new immigration will vanish in a generation if we are but patient.

Assimilation will happen, we are assured. Just as the Great Wave of immigrants who came between 1890 and 1920—Italians, Greeks, Jews, Poles, Balts, Czechs, Slovaks, Swedes, Armenians, Russians, and others from Southern and Eastern Europe—were Americanized in a generation or two, the tens of millions who are here and coming from Asia, Africa, and Latin America will all be singing "America the Beautiful" and reciting the Pledge of Allegiance. Columnist Michael Barone compares Mexican immigration to the Italian immigration of yesterday.

On inspection, however, the comparison collapses. Only 5 million Italian immigrants came, but four times as many Mexicans are already here, with potentially tens of millions more coming. Where the Italians came legally, half of the Mexicans are illegal aliens. Where the Italians came to stay or returned home, Mexicans come and go. Where the Italians wanted to be part of our family, millions of Mexicans are determined to retain their language and loyalty to Mexico. They prefer to remain outsiders. They do not wish to assimilate, and the nation no longer demands that they do so.

More critical, we are in the midst of a savage culture war in which traditionalist values have been losing ground for two generations. Millions of immigrants, but especially their children, who today survive on welfare are being inculcated with the values of a subculture of gangs, crime, drugs, and violence. The parents may work hard, attend church, and still carry with them the conservative and Catholic values with which they were raised in the Latin America and Mexico of yesterday. But these good people are not changing our culture. Our polluted culture is capturing and changing their children.

African-Americans who go on to college are more fully integrated than ever before into our society, economy, and culture. But the larger number who quit school after twelfth grade, or drop out before they finish high school, end up in disproportionate numbers in jails and prisons. Many are part of another culture altogether, and to that culture many Hispanic young are assimilating. That Hispanic males are nineteen times as likely to join a gang as young white males should tell us which way the wind is blowing.

"An Assembly Line of Diseases"

Because the vast majority of immigrants, legal and illegal, now come from rural areas, towns, and cities of the most impoverished nations of the hemisphere, where sanitation is often poor and health care nonexistent, they impose other costs upon the America people.

High among these is the appearance among us of diseases that never before afflicted us and the sudden reappearance of contagious diseases that researchers and doctors eradicated long ago. Malaria, polio, hepatitis, tuberculosis, and such rarities of the Third World as dengue fever, Chagas' disease, and leprosy are surfacing here. In the states that border Mexico, writes *NewsMax.com* columnist George Putnam, there is "a steady, silent, pervasive invasion of the United States by an unarmed army carrying an assembly line of diseases into the heart of America."[23]

The U.S. Centers for Disease Control and Prevention, writes author-columnist Phyllis Schlafly, "reported 38,291 California cases of tuberculosis that included Multiple Drug Resistant Tuberculosis, which is 60 percent fatal and for which treatment costs $200,000 to $1,200,000 per patient. Illegal aliens are also bringing in syphilis and gonorrhea. Bedbugs have invaded the United States for the first time in 50 years, with 28 states reporting recent infestations."[24]

In May 2006, the *New York Times* reported that one in every seven East Asian immigrants in the city, as many as 100,000 people, is a carrier of hepatitis B—an infection rate thirty-five times that of the general population. Almost all the new measles cases in America are brought in from abroad.[25]

John W. Whitehead of the Rutherford Institute cites a report by the Center for Immigration Studies entitled "Immigration's Silent Invasion, Deadly Consequences." "The invasion of illegal aliens pouring over borders of the United States is taking an ominous turn.

They are not alone! Their bodies may carry Hepatitis A, B, & C, tuberculosis, leprosy and Chagas Disease. Chagas is a nasty parasitic bug common in Latin America where 18 million people are infected and 50,000 deaths occur annually."[26]

For forty years, only 900 cases of leprosy or Hansen's disease had been diagnosed in the United States; by the first years of the twenty-first century, 7,000 cases had been discovered.[27] Some of the TB diagnosed is now the multi-drug-resistant strain. In 2002, northern Virginia reported a 17 percent surge in tuberculosis cases; in Prince William County, the increase was a staggering 188 percent. In northern Virginia, foreign-born accounted for 92 percent of all cases.[28] Three countries, all of which send immigrants and illegal aliens to America, account for two-thirds of all TB cases: Mexico, Vietnam, and the Philippines.[29]

The New York Academy of Sciences reports that "TB bacteria readily fly through the air, as when an afflicted person coughs. It's estimated that each victim will infect 10, 20, or more people—in time bomb effect."[30] Whitehead ends his "Deadly Invasion" commentary with a question: "What does this mean for America?" He answers:

> It means your children are at risk when attending school or going to the movies. It means that when a classmate from a foreign country sneezes or coughs, your child may be at risk for any number of diseases. If you eat at a fast food restaurant, a person infected with hepatitis could prepare your food. If you need a blood transfusion, the blood could be infected with Chagas Disease.[31]

The incidence of TB is ten times as high among immigrants as among our native-born. Among immigrant children it is 100 times as high.[32] The famous phrase from the 1980s report about our failing public schools, *A Nation at Risk,* has taken on an ominous new meaning.

While few illegal aliens carry health insurance, that does not mean they are denied health care. Under the Emergency Medical Treatment and Active Labor Act (EMTALA), every ER must treat any patient with an "emergency." This includes pregnant women, brought in to have babies in the United States, where the babies become instant citizens and qualify for a lifetime of entitlements. In the Spring 2005 issue of the *Journal of American Physicians and Surgeons,* Dr. Madeleine Cosman reported that "Illegal alien women come to the hospital in labor and drop their little anchors, each of whom pulls its illegal alien mother, father, and siblings, into permanent residency simply by being born within our borders. Anchor babies are citizens, and instantly qualify for public welfare aid: Between 300,000 and 350,000 anchor babies annually become citizens. . . ."[33]

One-tenth of all U.S. births are now "anchor babies," automatic citizens whose parents have immediate claims on federal, state, and local governments. Under EMTALA, any doctor or hospital that refuses to treat an "emergency" case is subject to a $50,000 fine. Between 1994 and 2003, the mandated cost of caring for illegals forced eighty-four of California's hospitals to shut down.

The first duty of government is to protect its citizens. By allowing at least 12 million illegal aliens to remain in this country, among whom rates of crime and infectious and contagious diseases are far higher than among Americans, the United States government fails in its first duty.

What Is the Benefit?

Though the crime rate of illegal aliens is high and many come in carrying diseases, we are told that on the whole they are of immense benefit to the economy. Should they all depart, the U.S. economy would collapse.

President Bush, who says illegal aliens "do jobs Americans won't do," is echoed by Geraldo Rivera, who says: "In vast sections of the country, there would not be a lawn mowed or a dish washed but for illegal immigrants."[34]

This is pure propaganda, the Myth of the Indispensable Alien, put out by ideologues and ethnic lobbyists, first among whom is Vicente Fox, who said in May 2005, "There is no doubt that Mexicans, filled with dignity, willingness and ability to work are doing jobs that not even blacks want to do there in the United States."[35]

According to John Hostettler and Lamar Smith, the chairman and ex-chairman of the House Judiciary Subcommittee on Immigration, Border Security and Claims, the economic argument for illegal aliens falls flat on close inspection. In December 2005, they wrote: "Some claim that illegal immigrants are doing jobs that Americans will not do. But when an illegal immigrant finds a job here, that does not mean that no American will take that job. In fact, 79 percent of all service workers are native-born, as are 68 percent of all workers in jobs requiring no more than a high-school education."[36]

Jeffrey Passel, the author of *Unauthorized Migrants: Numbers and Characteristics,* published by the Pew Hispanic Center, notes that illegal aliens constitute the following percentages of workers in various U.S. industries and occupations:

Industry	Illegals (percent)
Drywall/ceiling tile installers	27
Landscaping services	26
Maids and housekeepers	22
Roofers	21
Animal slaughter and processing	20

Building cleaning and maintenance	17
Private household workers	14
Accommodation industry workers	13
Food manufacturing workers	13
Construction and extraction workers	12
Food preparation and service workers	11
Production occupations	8[37]

In only two of these industries do illegals constitute a fourth of the labor force. In almost all they are only a fifth or less of the labor force. What these numbers fairly shout is that native-born Americans *are* doing and *will* do the work illegal immigrants do.

As Mark Krikorian of the Center for Immigration Studies writes:

California tomato farmers testified in the 1960s that "the use of braceros [Mexican guest workers] is absolutely essential to the survival of the tomato industry." But that labor program was ended anyway, and illegal immigrants did not immediately pick up the slack—so the farmers concluded that their investment in lobbying hadn't paid off, and instead they invested in harvest machinery. The result: a quadrupling of production over the following 30 years, and a drop in the post-inflation retail price of tomato products.[38]

But the arrival in our country of millions of immigrants every year, especially illegals who work for the wages offered, puts constant downward pressure on American wages. "A study by Harvard economist George Borjas shows that cheap immigrant labor has reduced by 7.4 percent the wages of American workers performing low-skill jobs."[39] This constitutes an injustice and a betrayal of the workingmen and women of America.

Both columnists Paul Krugman of the *New York Times* and

Robert J. Samuelson of *The Washington Post* exposed the fallacies and fraudulence of claims by President Bush that illegal aliens provide a net gain for our economy and "take jobs that Americans won't do." Writes Krugman, "[M]any of the worst-off native-born Americans are hurt by immigration—especially immigration from Mexico. Because Mexican immigrants have much less education than the average U.S. worker, they increase the supply of less-skilled labor, driving down the wages of the worst-paid Americans."

What Krugman is saying is that the mass migration from Mexico is an attack on America's poor. And he cites the authoritative study by Borjas and Lawrence Katz of Harvard showing that, were it not for immigration from Mexico, U.S. high school dropouts would be earning 8 percent more in wages. To allow mass migration of Third World poor is thus to betray black, Hispanic, and working-class white Americans without high school diplomas. "That's why it's intellectually dishonest to say, as President Bush does, that immigrants 'do jobs Americans will not do.'" Krugman adds that the millions of poor immigrants are also shredding the social safety net, especially in states like California, which are the most generous with their welfare benefits.[40]

Samuelson notes the enormous burden on the U.S. social welfare system as a consequence of our failure to halt the invasion. "Since 1980 the number of Hispanics with incomes below the poverty level (about $19,300 in 2004 for a family of four) has risen 162 percent. Over the same period, the number of non-Hispanic whites in poverty rose 3 percent and the number of blacks 9.5 percent. What we have now—and would with guest-workers—is a conscious policy of creating poverty in the United States while relieving it in Mexico."[41]

Cui bono? For whose benefit is this "conscious policy" if not for the workers of the welfare state and the businesses that seek an endless supply of cheap labor to keep costs down and profits up?

What are we doing to our people? What are we doing to the most vulnerable Americans, those 19 million adults who never got a high school degree, more than half of whom have given up looking for work? Among the 7 million of them still in the labor force, 10 percent are unemployed.

Is it any wonder African-Americans, millions of whom are forced to compete with immigrants for jobs, are the most forceful in demanding that the government get control of the border and halt the invasion?

There is another economic argument for open borders. By working at or near the minimum wage, poor immigrants and illegal aliens benefit us all by freeing Americans for more productive labor. Moreover, they keep costs down—of having our crops picked, lawns mowed, gas pumped, cars washed, food served, and children monitored. Thus, we have more to spend on consumer goods.

But there is no free lunch, and mass immigration is no free lunch. As Milton Friedman has said, "It's just obvious that you can't have free immigration and a welfare state."[42] Professor Borjas found zero net economic benefit from mass migration from the Third World. The added cost of schooling, health care, welfare, Social Security, and prisons—perhaps $400 billion a year—plus the additional pressure on land, water, and power resources exceeded the taxes immigrants contribute. In 1995, the National Bureau of Economic Research put the net price of immigration at $80.4 billion. Economist Donald Huddle of Rice University estimated that by 2006 the net annual cost of legal and illegal immigration would be $108 billion.[43] What benefit, then, justifies the risks we are taking with the health and safety of our citizens and the social cohesion of our country?

4

The Face of America: 2050

[I]f the United States becomes a hodge-podge of a score of races,
no one of which is dominant, it will lose its unity and become like
Metternich's idea of Italy, a geographical expression.[1]
—EDWARD LEWIS, *America, Nation or Confusion?* (1928)

These population dynamics will result in the "browning" of America, the
Hispanization of America. It is already happening and it is inescapable.[2]
—HENRY CISNEROS, U.S. Secretary of Housing
and Urban Development, 1993–97

Migration is the central issue of our time.[3]
—SAMUEL HUNTINGTON, 2001

In 1960, America was a nation of 180 million, 89 percent of whom
were of European ancestry, 10 percent black, with a few million
Hispanics and Asians sprinkled among us. Ninety-seven percent of
us spoke English.

Though of two races, we were of one nationality. We were all
Americans. We worshipped the same God, studied the same literature and history, honored the same heroes, celebrated the same holidays, went to the same movies, read the same newspapers and
magazines. We had endured together the same Great Depression and
war. Though the South remained segregated, culturally, we were one

people. But if present projections of the U.S. Census Bureau prove accurate, the America our grandchildren will live in will be another country, a nation unrecognizable to our parents. As Metternich said of Italy, America will have become but a "geographical expression."

By 2050, it is now estimated that there will be almost 2.5 times as many people here as in 1960: 420 million. The share of the population of European descent will be a minority, as it is today in California, Texas, and New Mexico. And that minority will be aging, shrinking, and dying. There will be as many Hispanics here—102 million—as there are Mexicans today in Mexico. Where Hispanics were 2.6 percent of our population in 1950, 4.5 percent in 1980, and 9.0 percent in 1990, today, they are 14.4 percent of a nation of roughly 300 million. By 2050, they will be 24 percent of a nation of 420 million. By nation of origin of our people, America will be a Third World country.

Our great cities will all look like Los Angeles today. Los Angeles and the cities of the Southwest will look like Juarez and Tijuana. Though we were never consulted about this transformation, never voted for it, and have protested against it in every poll and referendum, this is the future the elites have prepared for our children.

It's Academic

But if America is on her way to becoming a multilingual, multiethnic, multicultural society of 420 million, how will her minorities—all Americans will belong to minorities—rank on the socioeconomic scale?

At the top of the pyramid, excepting athletes and entertainers, will be the men and women of the knowledge industries: doctors, lawyers, bankers, investment counselors, accountants, professors, journalists, entrepreneurs, executives, engineers, scientists, judges, generals, computer programmers, writers, researchers. Keeping pace will require a college degree and often, as today, postgraduate work or the equivalent of a Ph.D. Brainpower is the key to the country clubs of the future. And we can see today who will be golfing at those clubs with guests, and who will be serving the food and drinks.

Since the Sputnik crisis of 1957 and *A Nation at Risk* during the Reagan years, Americans have read of rising dropout rates and falling test scores in public schools, of American kids unable to read or do math at world-class levels, of students who lose in academic competition whenever matched against youngsters in Europe and Asia.

But this is a simplistic and surface reading of the data.

Edwin S. Rubenstein of ESR Research Economic Consultants, who writes on immigration for *VDARE.com,* has analyzed the test scores of U.S. and foreign students. What he finds is both reassuring—and alarming. According to the Educational Testing Service, 45 percent of adult Americans cannot read or write at the high school graduate level, "and nearly half of these (20 percent) scored at a literacy level below that of a high school dropout."[4]

Appalling news. Yet Rubenstein found that, in a survey of twenty countries, the mean literacy test for Americans was 2 points above the mean for all adults. And among the seventeen nations that broke down the test scores between their native-born and immigrants, native-born Americans scored 8 points above the average of the native-born of the other sixteen nations.

Here was the shocker: U.S. immigrants scored 16 points below the average immigrant in other nations. In short, immigrants are dragging down average U.S. test scores in worldwide competitions. If only native-born Americans were taking these tests, there would be no crisis. The test scores for literacy of native-born Americans run 35 percent higher than the test scores of immigrants.

What makes this a huge and growing problem is that immigration now "accounts for virtually all of the national increase in public school enrollment over the last two decades. In 2005, there were 10.3 million school-age children from immigrant families in the United States."[5]

Rubenstein reports results with even more ominous implications: "[I]mmigration is not the only factor behind our weak literacy scores. The literacy gap between native-born whites and Asians and their Black and Hispanic counterparts ranges from 46 points, or 19 percent, on the prose and document literacy tests, to 57 points, or 25 percent, on the quantitative test."[6]

In layman's language, if whites and Asians are A students, with average grades of 90, blacks and Hispanics are C and D students, with grades between 67 and 72. This huge disparity of capabilities in literacy, writes Rubenstein, forced the Educational Testing Service to state the politically incorrect, albeit obvious:

> If we adjust the mean . . . scores for U.S. adults under age 65 to exclude all foreign-born adults as well as all native-born Blacks and Hispanics, then the mean prose and quantitative scores of the remaining U.S. adults (Asian and White, native born) would rise to 288, ranking the U.S. second highest—tied with Finland and Norway—on the prose scale and fifth-highest on the quantitative scale. . . . The findings clearly suggest that future gains in the comparative, international literacy standing of U.S. adults will require substantial improvement in the literacy proficiencies of Blacks, Hispanics, and the foreign born from all racial/ethnic groups.

Adds Rubenstein, "Or we could settle for immigration reform."[7]

Steve Sailer of the Human Biodiversity Institute has also delved more deeply into the data on school performance.

In 2003, Sailer reviewed *No Excuses: Closing the Racial Gap in*

Learning, by Stephan and Abigail Thernstrom, noting the authors' "detailed documentation of the size of the *racial gap in school performance* and of all the failed attempts to close it."[8]

As the Thernstroms starkly summarized,

> Blacks nearing the end of their high school education perform a little worse than white eighth-graders in both reading and U.S. history, and a lot worse in math and geography. In math and geography, indeed, they know no more than whites in the seventh grade. Hispanics do only a little better than African-Americans. In reading and U.S. history, their NAEP scores in their senior year of high school are a few points above those of whites in eighth grade. In math and geography, they are a few points lower.[9]

The Thernstroms found roughly the same disparity between the test scores of Hispanics and whites as between blacks and whites, but say the gap narrows if immigrant children are excluded. Yet U.S.-born Hispanic kids are still three grades behind white students when they graduate from high school. Among third- and fourth-generation Hispanics, test scores are no longer rising. They have plateaued. In these generations, half of all Hispanic children still fail to finish high school. Only 10 percent earn higher than high school diplomas. And even successful Hispanic students leave school years behind in academic achievement.

Two reports from the Department of Education support Sailer and Rubenstein. In the 2002–03 academic year, spending in D.C. schools, which are almost entirely immigrant and African-American, was $16,344 per pupil, highest in the nation after Alaska. But only 12 percent of D.C.'s eighth-grade public school students could read at eighth-grade levels in 2005, and only 7 percent could do eighth-grade math. In South Dakota and Iowa, both of which spend less than half per pupil as D.C., more than a third of eighth-graders read and did math at or above eighth-grade levels.[10]

Harvard's George Borjas, who was born in Cuba and is today the nation's foremost expert on immigration and poverty, has spoken of an education crisis: "Mexicans tend to be at a very low level of schooling. A very large proportion have less than eight years of education, and many have only three or four years. Quite a few actually have zero."[11]

Yet some immigrant children perform exceedingly well. Though the country was held in colonial captivity by Japan for generations and suffered three years of one of the bloodiest wars of the twentieth century, South Korea "has the second highest IQ in the world. . . . Its citizens have the longest work-weeks in the world. South Korean students typically score at the top of the world in international achievement tests."[12] Of 672,000 Koreans in the United States, 28 percent of adults are self-employed, the highest rate by far for any immigrant group.[13]

Two Americas, Separate and Unequal

What do these dramatic disparities portend?

As Amy Chua writes in *World on Fire: How Exporting Free Market Democracy Breeds Ethnic Hatred and Global Instability* (2002), within societies, economic inequality among racial and ethnic groups leads to turmoil and violence. And as there is an absolute correlation between education levels and success in life, America is inexorably becoming two nations, separate and unequal.

Our two largest minorities, African-Americans and Hispanics, which now number together 79 million or 27 percent of the population, are leaving school with achievement levels three, four, and five grades behind white and Asian students. We are headed toward a society and nation more dangerously polarized than the America of

1960, when minorities made up only 11 percent of a population that was far smaller than today's or tomorrow's. And back then, we had been marinated for centuries in a common culture. That is no longer true. We are already two, three, many Americas, caught up in a culture war over race, religion, and morality.

Given the huge and persistent gulf in academic achievement between Hispanics and blacks, and Asians and whites, the best jobs in the knowledge industry, and the pay and prestige they carry, are going to go to the latter overwhelmingly and indefinitely. And as the manufacturing jobs on which immigrants and minorities depended, their yellow brick road to the middle class, continue to be exported, not created, blacks and Hispanics will fall farther and farther behind.

However, as their combined share of the U.S. population—27 percent of 300 million—rises toward 40 percent in 2050, they will use their political clout to demand equality of result: racial and ethnic quotas and affirmative action in all professions. And as African-Americans no longer do the servile work their parents once did, we may expect the children of Hispanics to reject the "jobs no one else wants" that their fathers and mothers do today.

Dr. Martin Luther King, Jr., warned in that decade when America's cities burned:

> There is nothing more dangerous than to build a society, with a large segment of people in that society, who feel that they have no stake in it; who feel that they have nothing to lose. People who have a stake in their society, protect that society, but when they don't have it, they unconsciously want to destroy it.[14]

Are All Immigrants Equal?

In "Immigrants at Mid-Decade: A Snapshot of America's Foreign Born Population in 2005," Steven Camarota of the Center for Immigration Studies (CIS) alerted the nation to what America will look like tomorrow if we do not enforce, and reform, our immigration laws. Here is a glimpse at the CIS "snapshot" of the immigrants in America today.

- Of our adult immigrants, 31 percent never finished high school, three and a half times the rate of native-born Americans.
- The poverty rate for immigrants is 57 percent higher than for native-born Americans. Immigrants and their minor children constitute one in four persons in poverty.
- Among immigrants, 24 percent receive Medicaid, 29 percent use some form of welfare, 30 percent are eligible for the earned income tax credit. These are near twice the rates of native-born Americans.
- A third of all immigrants lack health insurance.
- Immigrant children accounted for nearly 100 percent of the increase in U.S. public school enrollments in the last twenty years.
- Immigrant children account for 19 percent of all students in U.S. public schools and 21 percent of children aged 0–4 about to enter those schools.[15]

The average immigrant comes to this country much poorer and far less educated than Americans and consumes far more per capita in public services. Economically, immigrants are a net burden on the nation. As Steve Sailer notes, a National Academy of Sciences study in 1997 found that each immigrant who comes with less than a high school education costs taxpayers $90,000 net over his or her lifetime. Those who bring a high school degree cost taxpayers $30,000. But immigrants with a college degree or better brought a net benefit to the U.S. Treasury of $100,000.[16]

However, not all immigrant groups are equal consumers of public services. Not all come uneducated or unprepared for school. Not all occupy the lower rungs of the social and economic ladder. Consider:

- Mexicans, Central Americans, and Caribbean peoples use welfare at more than twice the rate of native-born Americans.
- Koreans, Filipinos, Japanese, Canadians, Poles, Brits, Germans, Indians, and Italians use welfare at lower rates than native-born Americans.
- In 1995, close to half of all Cambodian and Laotian immigrants and a fourth of all Vietnamese were on welfare.[17]
- More than 50 percent of all immigrants from Mexico, Guatemala, El Salvador, and Honduras never finished high school.
- Only 5 percent or less of immigrants from South Korea, Canada, Russia, Britain, Germany, Iran, and Japan never finished high school.
- Half of all immigrants from China, Philippines, India, Korea, Russia, Iran, and Japan come to the United States with college degrees.

Some of the disparities among immigrant groups are so stark they dramatize the crisis America faces:

- Only 2 percent of Italian immigrants are on Medicaid and less than 5 percent of Italians qualify for the earned income tax credit.
- But 50 percent of the immigrants from the Dominican

Republic use Medicaid and 50 percent of the immigrants from Mexico qualify for the EITC.

The immigrant crisis is clarified when we see that Dominicans here outnumber Italians here by 2 to 1 and Mexicans outnumber Italians 28 to 1.

The core of the crisis is Mexico. Mexicans here outnumber all other immigrant groups by at least 6 to 1 and outnumber immigrants from Canada, our other near neighbor and NAFTA partner, 16 to 1.

In 2006, the U.S./Mexico Border Counties Coalition, consisting of officials of the twenty-four U.S. counties bordering Mexico, reported the findings of a two-year study. If those twenty-four counties were the fifty-first state, that state would be number one in federal crimes, due to drug and illegal immigration arrests, number two in tuberculosis cases, number three in the incidence of hepatitis and concentration of Hispanics. Remove prosperous San Diego County, and that fifty-first state would be number two in unemployment and fifty-first in per capita income and in the percentage of its population that has finished high school.[18] The border region of the United States is beginning to look less and less like America and more and more like Mexico.

What is our future?

Given that our mass immigration is coming first from Mexico, then from Central America and the Caribbean, and that these immigrants' crime and poverty rates are far higher and their average educational achievement far lower than that of Americans, the future is clear and the future is grim. We see it in our African-American population, where more young males are incarcerated than in college, and where, in some cities, 40 percent of black males between the ages of eighteen and thirty-six are in jail or prison, or on probation or parole.

As the immigrant poor from Latin America pour in, filling all the new schools we build, imposing a constantly rising tax burden on Middle America, their children will continue to pull down U.S. test scores and stress out teachers trying to bring them up to national standards—a task at which we have never succeeded and at which no one seems to know how to succeed. And our educrats will point with alarm each year to falling national test scores to berate taxpayers for not putting enough money into reducing class sizes and raising teachers' salaries. We are on a treadmill we will never get off, if we do not get control of immigration.

The only way America can stop an inexorable decline in test scores before we reach Third World status is: Halt the invasion now. We must decide ourselves who we wish to come, and from where. Then, set our policy and enforce it. Immigration must be designed to serve the needs of the nation, not the wants of the world. America, after all, is for Americans first. Immigration is not a right that belongs to anybody and everybody who wants to come. It is a privilege we Americans alone decide to confer.

To Live and Die in L.A.

If one wishes to see America's future, he need only drive through L.A. Sifting through census data from Year 2000, three writers at the *Los Angeles Times* discovered the coming America in the sprawling county that has become a polyglot nation where extremes of wealth and poverty mirror those of the Third World.

Though America had just ended two of the most prosperous decades in her history, Los Angeles had become a separate nation. During the 1990s, poverty in Los Angeles County did not remain stable or decline, but shot up 28 percent. By 2000, 1.6 million people in L.A. County lived beneath the poverty line. In Orange County, bastion of Goldwater Republicanism, the poverty rate had soared by

44 percent. In the Inland Empire of San Bernardino and Riverside counties, on the road to Palm Desert, poverty exploded by 51 percent and 63 percent, respectively.

During the Reagan decade, median income in L.A. County rose a smart 21.5 percent. But in the Clinton decade, median income sank 8 percent, from $45,600 to $42,200.[19] In the city of Los Angeles, it fell even further. And the new California poverty was mirrored in the dramatic demographic shift.

During the 1990s, the Latino population of Los Angeles County rose 27 percent, to 4.2 million; the Asian population rose by 26 percent; but the "Anglo" population fell by 18 percent.[20] White folks are fleeing California at the rate of 100,000 a year and the black middle class is following. Columnist Diana West has documented the demographic revolution in L.A.:

In 1960 non-Hispanic whites made up 82 percent of the population of Los Angeles County. Forty years later . . . the white population had dwindled to 31 percent while Hispanics . . . accounted for 44.6 percent of population. This colossal surge has made the Mexican population of Los Angeles second only to that of Mexico City.[21]

Three million people of Mexican ancestry today call L.A. County home, and half of all its residents—54 percent—speak a language other than English in their homes, up from 45 percent in 1990. When more than half the people of so vast a county do not speak English at home, do not listen to the same radio and TV programs as the rest of us, do not read the same newspapers, magazines, or books, do not share the same heroes, history, or holidays, how can we say we are all still one nation and one people?

Mexifornia

What has happened to L.A. is happening to California. According to the *Los Angeles Times,* in the 1990s Orange, Riverside, San Bernardino, and Ventura counties experienced increases of 36 to 70 percent in the number of foreign-born. As the state is repopulated, income disparities grow. While the number of Californians earning $150,000 tripled to 642,000 in the 1990s, the share of California's people mired in poverty rose by 30 percent.

High among the reasons workers' wages are stagnant or falling is the loss of industry. In L.A. County, the number of manufacturing jobs fell by 32 percent in the 1990s, from 861,000 to 587,000. Ruth Milkman, director of the UCLA Institute for Labor and Employment, says the county, whose 9.5 million people exceeds the population of many UN member nations, is "beginning to resemble much more a Third World society where a class of people are stuck at the bottom."[22]

Unless U.S. trade policy is reversed, the share of the nation's jobs that are in manufacturing, the highest-paid work for blue-collar labor, will fall below today's 10 percent, already the lowest level since before the Civil War. Most of our industrial production will have been outsourced. And as tax consumers continue to flood in from Mexico, and taxpayers flee, the state is sinking in a sea of red ink. Its bond rating has been dropped by Standard & Poor's to almost junk-bond status, lowest of the fifty states.

The Golden Land is no more. An exodus comparable to that out of the Dust Bowl in the 1930s has begun. For the first time since the Spanish came, native-born Californians have begun to depart. Fed up with rising crime rates and rising taxes to subsidize illegal aliens, they are leaving for Arizona, Nevada, Idaho, and Colorado, as the California they grew up in and loved morphs into Mexifornia.

Census 2000 revealed what many sensed: For the first time since statehood in 1849, European Americans had become a minority in the Golden State. Sociologist William Frey documented the outmigration. In the 1990s, the state grew by 3 million, but its white population dropped by almost half a million. L.A. County alone lost 480,000 white folks. The Republican bastion of Orange County lost 6 percent of its white population.[23]

"We can't pretend we're a white middle class state anymore," said William Fulton, a research fellow at USC's Southern California Studies Center.[24] State Librarian Kevin Starr sees the Hispanicization of California as natural and inevitable:

The Anglo hegemony was only an intermittent phase in California's arc of identity, extending from the arrival of the Spanish ... the Hispanic nature of California has been there all along, and it was temporarily swamped between the 1880s and the 1960s, but that was an aberration. This is a reassertion of the intrinsic demographic DNA of the longer pattern, which is a part of the California-Mexican continuum.[25]

California is going home to Mexico.

Who can deny it? With 100,000 whites leaving California each year, the Asian population soaring 42 percent in a decade, and 43 percent of all Californians under eighteen Hispanic, California is becoming—indeed, has become—a Third World state.

No one knows how this will play out, but California could become an American Quebec, demanding formal recognition of its Hispanic culture and identity, or a giant Ulster. As Sinn Fein demanded and was given special ties to Dublin, Mexicans and Mexican-Americans may demand a special relationship with the mother country, open borders, and a right to representation in the Mexican legislature as well as the U.S. Congress. These items are already on the agendas of Chicano militants and U.S. elites. And with

California holding 20 percent of the electoral votes needed to win the presidency of the United States, and Hispanic votes decisive in California, what party would shut the door to these demands?

Did Californians vote for this future?

Never. They saw it coming and resisted as best they could. As the illegals poured in by the hundreds of thousands yearly in the early 1990s, and the U.S. government refused to halt the invasion, Californians filed petitions with a million signatures to put Proposition 187 on the ballot. Prop 187 would have ended welfare benefits to people who broke our laws, broke into our country, and did not belong here. In a huge turnout that swept Governor Pete Wilson back into office and Republicans into control of both houses of the legislature, 59 percent of California voters supported 187.

Repudiated, the open-borders crowd found a federal judge to annul the voters' victory. Wilson appealed the ruling but, as the case dragged on, a new governor, Gray Davis, refused to pursue the appeal. The welfare benefits continued to flow. Said Esteban "Art" Torres, chairman of the California Democratic Party, "187 was the last gasp of white America in California."

So it may have been. Hispanic voters rewarded Davis with reelection in 2002, and California's budget continued to hemorrhage. In 2003, facing a $38 billion deficit and having signed a bill to grant driver's licenses to illegal aliens, Davis was recalled and fired by enraged Californians.

Who lost the Golden Land? The government of the United States did, when presidents failed in their constitutional duty to defend the state from an invasion that is conquering California.

5

Suicide of the GOP

[S]tupid people are generally Conservative. I believe that is
so obviously and universally admitted a principle that I hardly
think any gentleman will deny it.[1]

—JOHN STUART MILL, 1866

Since the Goldwater campaign of 1964, the Republican Party may
fairly be called the party of the white people. Of Goldwater's 27
million votes, probably 26 million came from white voters. Black
support for the GOP, a legacy since Lincoln's day, had vanished
with LBJ's authorship of and the Arizona senator's opposition to the
Civil Rights Act of 1964.

In the Nixon and Reagan forty-nine-state landslides, 96 percent
of all their votes may have come from white folks. In 2004, George
W. Bush won 58 percent of the white vote, and white voters made up
90 percent of all his voters.[2]

How can this be? Consider:

In 1960, the U.S. population was 89 percent white and 10 percent
African-American. Since black turnout was lower and blacks were
denied voting rights in the South, they accounted for probably 6
percent of the national vote. But as they voted nearly 90 percent
Democratic in every election beginning in 1964 (except 1972), the
black Republican vote would have been less than 1 percent of the

national vote. Hispanic and Asian votes in those years were only a fraction of the African-American vote.

With the shift of the black vote away from the party of Lincoln to the party of LBJ, the Wallace vote, 13 percent of the nation in 1968 and almost 100 percent white, moved to the Republican column. The only way Democrats could win back enough white votes to carry southern states and the White House was to nominate a Carter or a Clinton, a son of the South. Indeed, the only four times in eleven successive elections that Democrats have won the presidency, they have put a southern white at the top of the ticket.

But, as was evident in 2004, when President Bush nearly lost his reelection bid to a liberal Democrat from Massachusetts with a voting record indistinguishable from that of Teddy Kennedy, the Nixon-Reagan formula no longer assures victory. Reason: The white majority of the United States, which Bush carried easily, has steadily fallen as a share of the national population from near 90 percent in 1960 to 67 percent today—and will fall to less than 50 percent by 2050. The fastest growing segments of our population are Hispanics, at 14.4 percent, and immigrants, who are now at 12 percent. Given the franchise, Hispanics and immigrants vote heavily Democratic.

Thus, an era that began with Barry Goldwater in 1964 and peaked with Reagan's reelection in 1984 is coming to an end. The people who put the GOP in power are not growing in numbers nearly as rapidly as immigrants and people of color who want them out of power. The fading away of America's white majority entails an existential crisis for the GOP.

The Making of the New Majority

From 1972 until 1992, the Republican Party held a virtual "lock" on the presidency. Richard Nixon's "New Majority" and the "Reagan

Democrats" gave the GOP five victories in six consecutive elections. The Democratic Party was in quadrennial despair.

The key to victory was to add to the Republican base large segments of two huge Democratic blocs: southern white Protestants and northern ethnic Catholics. Nixon sheared these voters off from FDR's New Deal coalition through appeals to populism, patriotism, and social conservatism. His forty-nine-state landslide in 1972 gave the GOP a semipermanent hold on the presidency, anchored in a Solid South that had been the strategic base of the Democratic Party since Appomattox. In 1968, Nixon's strongest state had been Nebraska. By 1972, it was Mississippi.

Resurrected by Reagan, the New Majority seemed almost invincible. Mondale and Dukakis might sweep 90 percent of the black vote. But with Nixon taking 67 percent and Ronald Reagan capturing 64 percent in 1984 of a white vote that was 90 percent of the national vote, the GOP came out on top in a landslide.

This was the Southern Strategy the media called immoral, though Democrats had bedded down with segregationists for a century without censure. FDR and Adlai Stevenson put segregationists on their tickets. Outside of Missouri, a border state with southern sympathies, the only states Adlai carried in 1956 were former Confederate states, among them Alabama and Mississippi, which George Wallace would carry in 1968.

Neither Nixon nor Reagan ever supported segregation. Nixon's civil rights record was stronger than JFK's. His behind-the-scenes activism in winning passage of the Civil Rights Act of 1957 was lauded in a personal letter from Dr. King, who praised the vice president for his "assiduous labor and dauntless courage in seeking to make Civil Rights a reality."[3]

Except for Carter, a Georgian, who took ten of eleven southern states from Gerald Ford in 1976, Democrats could not pick the GOP lock because they could not shake the GOP hold on the white vote—until Ross Perot came to their aid in 1992, taking 20 percent of it. Aside from 1964, not for sixty years have Democrats won a majority or even a plurality of the white vote.

Yet, in 2005, the national chairman of the Republican Party, Ken Mehlman, a protégé of Karl Rove, went to the national convention of the NAACP, which had cheered insults to President Bush, to apologize for a Southern Strategy that had given the GOP five victories in six presidential contests and brought the party to national power: "I am here today as the Republican chairman to tell you we were wrong."[4]

"We have now moved from the Southern strategy we pursued for the last three decades, since Richard Nixon, to a Hispanic strategy for the next three decades," Republican pollster Lance Tarrance told *The Washington Times*'s Ralph Hallow in 2000.[5] That year Bush lost the popular vote to Al Gore.

On a personal note, this is an injustice to Richard Nixon, whose White House worked for four years after 1968 to recapture the black vote lost in 1964; by one poll, Nixon carried 18 percent of that vote nationally and 25 percent in the South, margins double what George W. Bush ever did. Nixon was a supporter of civil rights, but he did not believe in forced busing for racial balance, though he carried out every court order handed down.

Drowning the New Majority

The crisis of the GOP is demographic. The white vote that carried the party to five victories in six elections, three of them landslides, is not growing as rapidly as the minority vote—the Democratic base. Indeed, it is shrinking as a share of the electorate. Third World immigration is drowning the Republican base. Millions of immigrants who have come in the last forty years, and are still coming, have begun to vote and they are voting heavily Democratic. History may yet record that the Immigration Act of 1965 converted *The Emerging Republican Majority* of Kevin Phillips's classic work into the Lost Colony of the twenty-first century.

After the crackdown of the anti-Soviet riots in East Berlin in June 1953, the Communist playwright Bertolt Brecht famously and sarcastically quipped, "Would it not be easier . . . for the government to dissolve the people and elect another?"[6]

With the Immigration Act of 1965, the nation began to import another electorate. In the 1990s, immigrants and their children accounted for 100 percent of the population growth of California, New York, New Jersey, Illinois, and Massachusetts, and half the population growth of Florida, Texas, Michigan, and Maryland. Six of these nine states have become solidly Democratic in presidential elections and Michigan and Florida are trending that way.

Republican elites have, for decades now, supported an open-borders immigration policy certain to swamp and drown the coalition that their best political minds assembled to lead them to national power. Like Esau, the GOP is selling its birthright.

In 1996, Republican altruism was rewarded. Of the seven states containing the largest numbers of foreign-born—California, New York, Illinois, New Jersey, Massachusetts, Florida, and Texas—six went for Bill Clinton. In 2000, five went for Al Gore and Florida was dead even.

However, of the nine states with the smallest share of immigrants—Alabama, Arkansas, Mississippi, Missouri, Montana, North Dakota, South Dakota, West Virginia, Wyoming—all went for George W. Bush in 2000 and again in 2004. Of the fifteen states with the smallest shares of immigrants, Bush carried thirteen, losing only Maine and Vermont. But the warning signs are up in the red states. Between 2000 and 2005, the immigrant populations of Wyoming,

Georgia, and South Carolina grew by over 100 percent, with Mississippi seeing an increase of 149 percent. Writing after the May Day strike and boycott of 2006, William Frey, the Brookings Institution demographer, went back fifteen years to document the massive "immigrant influx to the heartland and the more rural and agrarian states . . . the growth rates are rapid: 25 states more than doubled and nine more than tripled their foreign-born population since 1990. In North Carolina, the foreign-born and Hispanic populations grew over 390 per cent and 540 per cent respectively over the past 15 years. Georgia's and Colorado's foreign born grew over 200 per cent."[7]

Among the seven states with the largest number of immigrants, only Texas remains reliably Republican; but it is beginning to resemble California. In the 1990s, the Lone Star State took in 3.2 million new residents, 60 percent of them Hispanic, raising the Hispanic share of Texas's population from 25 percent to 33 percent. Today, it is at 34 percent and rising. In El Paso, Houston, Dallas, and San Antonio, Hispanics outnumber Anglos. Where the white population of Texas was 60 percent in 1990 and 53 percent in 2000, today whites are a minority for the first time since the Alamo. Like California, Texas today is starting to look a lot like Mexico.

America is going the same way. In 1960, the U.S. population was 89 percent white; by 1990, it was 76 percent. Today, it is 67 percent. By 2050, white Americans, the most loyal voting bloc the Republican Party has, which delivers 90 percent of all GOP votes, will be just another minority because of an immigration policy championed by Republicans. When John Stuart Mill called the Tories "the Stupid Party," he was not entirely wrong.[8]

Amnesty for illegals and a fast track to citizenship may win the GOP editorial encomiums, but they will also accelerate the end of a Republican hegemony in American politics.

Importing Democrats

In 1980, Hispanics made up 6.4 percent of our population; by 1990, 9 percent. Today, they form 14.4 percent. The Census Bureau estimates that by 2050 the Hispanic population will triple, to 102 million, and constitute 24 percent of our national population. If present geographic distribution holds, the political map of 2050 will find 50 million Hispanics in California and Texas, and another 25 million in New York, Florida, Illinois, Arizona, and New Jersey.

Not only are Hispanics our largest minority now, their birth rate far outstrips that of native Americans. As Steve Sailer writes, while 56 percent of all U.S. births were to white women in 2004, 23 percent were to Hispanics. And while fertility rates among white women are now below replacement levels (2.1 babies per woman) and continue to fall, among Hispanics the birthrate is rising. Among Mexican women who have entered the United States illegally, the birthrate is soaring: 3.5 children per woman.[9] Says demographer Jeffrey Passel, "The Hispanic fertility rates are . . . at the levels of the baby boom era of the 1950s."[10]

One in every ten babies born in America is born to an illegal alien. These "anchor babies" are instantly eligible for all the benefits of U.S. citizens, for every one is a citizen at birth. That was not the intent of the Fourteenth Amendment—"All persons born or naturalized in the United States and subject to the jurisdiction thereof, are citizens of the United States." But that is the interpretation put on that amendment that our government refuses to correct. Small wonder the maternity wards of the Southwest are jammed with pregnant women who have slipped over the border.

At 43 million, Hispanics outnumber black Americans by 6 million now, but are not so solidly Democratic. Bush lost African-Americans eleven to one in 2000 and nine to one in 2004. But he lost Hispanics by only two to one in 2000 and three to two to 2004. He was fortunate in running against white-bread candidates like Kerry and Gore who lacked the charisma of Clinton.

In 1996, Clinton swept the Latino vote seventy to twenty-one. Among first-time Latino voters, his margin was ninety-one to six. Aware that immigrants can give the Democrats their own lock on the White House, Clinton's men worked to naturalize them. In the year up to September 30, 1996, the Immigration and Naturalization Service swore in 1,045,000 new Americans so quickly that 80,000 with criminal records—6,300 for serious offenses—became citizens.[11] Through the 1990s, 5.6 million immigrants became American citizens, four times as many as in the 1970s. Here are the numbers of new citizens in the five years up to the Bush-Gore election of 2000:

1996	1,045,000
1997	598,000
1998	463,000
1999	872,000
2000	898,315[12]

From 2000 to 2005, 7.9 million more immigrants arrived, legal and illegal, with Mexicans forming the largest contingent. This set an all-time record. If Republicans believe these millions of largely uneducated, unskilled, and poor people are going to rally to a party that advocates slashing the size of the government, the party is in need of a brain transplant.

California took a third of the new citizens. And as white registration fell in the 1990s, 1 million Latinos registered. At 16 percent of the California electorate, Hispanics helped give Gore and Kerry the state, with more than 1 million votes to spare.

"Both parties show up at swearing-in ceremonies to try to register voters," chuckles Democratic consultant William Carrick.

"There is a Democratic table and a Republican table. Ours has a lot of business. Theirs is like the Maytag repairman."[13] With 55 electoral votes, California—which Nixon carried on five national tickets and Reagan carried all four times he ran—has become a killing field of the Republican Party.

From 1952 through 1988, Republicans took California in nine out of ten presidential elections. Since 1988, Republicans have lost California in four consecutive presidential elections by 10 points or more.

Republicans continue to fantasize about winning the Hispanic vote. But Republicans have never won the Hispanic vote in a presidential election. Even in his forty-nine-state landslide, Reagan, despite his charisma and cowboy image, a bland opponent, and a booming economy, won only 44 percent. That was a generation ago. In every presidential election since 1984, Hispanics have voted Democratic by anywhere from 60 percent to 75 percent. The more Hispanic America becomes, the more Democratic America becomes.

Natural-Born Democrats

In 1994, Hispanics, rallying under Mexican flags, opposed Proposition 187 to end welfare to illegal aliens. In balloting on the California Civil Rights Initiative in 1996, Hispanics voted overwhelmingly for affirmative action and ethnic preferences. In 1998, Hispanics voted for bilingual education. In all three referenda, Californians voted the other way in landslides.

"The *Economist* reported that the ballot measure [Prop 187] won the support of 64 percent of white voters and 56 and 57 percent of black and Asian voters, respectively, but only 31 percent of Hispanic voters." But 78 percent of Republicans and 78 percent of conservatives backed Proposition 187, showing the potency of the immigration issue not only to the GOP base but across the spectrum of American politics.[14]

Ron Unz, father of the "English for the Children" initiative that ended state funding for bilingual education, believes that during the L.A. riots of 1992 California crossed the Rubicon on the road to Balkanization.

> The plumes of smoke from burning buildings and the gruesome television footage almost completely shattered the sense of security of middle-class Southern Californians. Suddenly, the happy "multicultural California" so beloved of local boosters had been unmasked as a harsh, dangerous, Third World dystopia . . . the large numbers of Latinos arrested (and summarily deported) for looting caused whites to cast a newly wary eye on gardeners and nannies who just weeks earlier had seemed so pleasant and reliable. If multicultural Los Angeles had exploded into sudden chaos, what security could whites expect as a minority in an increasingly nonwhite California?[15]

The militancy of the mass demonstrations of May 2006, the largest of them in Los Angeles, for amnesty for illegals, with many marching under Mexican flags, has further polarized the communities of California.

Except for refugees from Communist countries, such as Hungary in 1956 and Cuba in 1960, immigrants gravitate to the party of government. Mostly uneducated and poor, they get more back in government benefits—free education for their children, housing subsidies, free health care, food stamps, welfare checks, Supplemental Security Income, earned income tax credits—far more than they ever pay out in government taxes.

Why should they support a Republican Party that will cut taxes they do not pay rather than a Democratic Party that will grow the programs on which they depend? Like African-Americans, Hispanics benefit from and believe in government, and they vote their interests.

After Ellis Island, the Democratic Party has been the next stop for immigrants. Only when they achieve economic security and a share of prosperity do immigrants migrate toward the GOP. That process can take generations. With Third World immigrants, the mass conversion to the Republican Party has never happened. The naturalization and registration of 500,000 to 1 million immigrants each year is thus locking up the future for the Democratic Party and throwing away the key. If the GOP does not do something about immigration, immigration will do something about the GOP: Turn it into a retirement home of America's newest minority.

Mass immigration pushes politics to the left. The expanding share of the electorate that is African-American, Hispanic, and Asian has already caused the GOP to go silent on affirmative action and to mute its calls for cuts in social spending. Republicans once pledged in their platforms to abolish the Department of Education. Bush and the Republican Congress have doubled its size. As people of Third World origins become an ever larger share of the population, the agenda of America's minorities will become America's agenda. And that is not the agenda of the Reagan Revolution.

If we do not secure the border, the Southwest will soon become so Hispanicized any candidate who pledges to seal it and maintain the separate identity of the United States will be threatened with loss of all the electoral votes of California, Arizona, New Mexico, and Texas. While we are not there yet, we are moving to a tipping point where ethnic lobbyists and the Democratic Party may be able to stir up enough hostility to border control to make it impossible for a candidate to declare he (or she) will seal the border and be elected president. The intimidation factor is already present. In 2004, the entire Arizona Republican congressional delegation, led by Senators

John McCain and Jon Kyl, opposed Proposition 200, which would deny social welfare benefits to illegal aliens. Arizonans supported it in a landslide.

The Asian-Republican Myth

Some Republicans believe that Asian-Americans, our second largest immigrant group, who have solid family values and a strong work ethic, are "natural-born Republicans" who will offset the votes of immigrants who trend Democratic. This appears a forlorn hope. Though President Bush's father narrowly won the Asian vote against Bill Clinton, George W. lost the Asian-American vote by a landslide in every survey taken after the 2004 election. The only disagreement among pollsters was over the margin of the Bush defeat.

Steve Sailer analyzed a series of polls and found that in the largest survey, of 11,000 Asian-Americans in twenty-three cities east of the Mississippi—taken by the liberal Asian-American Legal and Educational Fund—Bush lost Asian-Americans in a wipeout, 74–24. In California, in the Edison-Mitofsky Poll, Bush did better. But even there he was swamped 66–34, a two-to-one rout by John Kerry. The *Los Angeles Times* gave Kerry a national victory among Asian-Americans by the same margin.

While an early Edison-Mitofsky Poll had Kerry winning the Asian vote nationwide by only 53–44, a second look dropped Bush to 39 percent.[16]

Whatever poll was used, the sole question was how large was the landslide that buried the Republican president among Asian-Americans. On the breakout figures, the news is even worse for the GOP. Among South Asians (Indians, Bangladeshis, Pakistanis), Kerry mopped up the floor with President Bush, 90–9.[17] And, as among Hispanics, Democratic identification is strongest among first-time Asian voters. When one realizes that today's champion of open borders is a president whose own party is mortally imperiled by open borders, Bush is truly the Sidney Carton of the GOP, assuring himself it is a "far, far better thing" he is doing than he has "ever done before," as the tumbrels haul him and his hapless party to the guillotine.

The Bush-Rove Strategy

From their success in Texas, Bush and Rove devised their strategy for regaining the lock on the presidency that had been the legacy of Nixon and Reagan. The Bush-Rove solution to the crisis of a shrinking white vote that is the party base, and a growing minority vote that is heavily Democratic, was to court the Hispanics. But the inherent contradictions of the Bush-Rove strategy are clear from a cursory study of political history.

The GOP is a small-government party. Its faithful are appalled by fiscal imprudence and ashamed when they indulge in it. But if President Bush, who has governed as a Great Society Republican, begins channeling Robert Taft, he will have to slash domestic spending and open himself to the charge he is "balancing the budget on the backs of the poor." There is an irreconcilable conflict between being a conservative party and being the party of Hispanics. The conflict is pulling the Bush-Rove coalition apart.

In a House vote before the Christmas break of 2005, Republicans endorsed building 700 miles of security fence along the Mexican border and tough sanctions on companies that hire undocumented workers. No issue more fires up the Republican base and working-class Democrats than America's unprotected borders and the flooding of their cities and towns by illegal aliens.

Yet Bush has refused to deal with the border crisis and denounced as "vigilantes" the Minutemen volunteers who serve in Arizona as spotters for the Border Patrol. Bush and Rove fear a hard line against illegal immigration would do to the national party what they believe Governor Pete Wilson's hard line did to the California party. Their fears are reinforced by neoconservatives like *The Weekly Standard*'s William Kristol. In April 2006, Kristol disparaged as "yahoos" four GOP congressmen, including Tom Tancredo of Colorado, chairman of the House Immigration Reform Caucus, who had denounced a Senate-proposed amnesty. Citing the Republican drought in California as proof that any tough stand against illegals is suicidal politics, Kristol wailed: "How many Republicans will have the courage to stand up and prevent the yahoos from driving the party over a cliff?"[18]

The president, Rove, and Kristol have all bought into a media myth.

Riding that illegal alien issue, Wilson, the most unpopular incumbent in California history prior to Gray Davis, came from 20 points down to win reelection with 55 percent in 1994; gained a majority in both houses of the assembly for the first time in thirty years; and carried four new GOP congressmen in with him. The only statewide race Republicans have won since Wilson was the 2003 victory of Arnold Schwarzenegger, whose strongest issue was Davis's decision to grant driver's licenses to illegals. Arnold promised to undo it and swept to victory. Every GOP senatorial, gubernatorial, or presidential candidate who has run away from the issue of illegal immigration in California has been wiped out. The reasons are twofold: illegal immigration is always among the hottest issues in the race and, like opposition to quotas and bilingual education, one of several on which Republicans can win Democratic votes.

Democrats have begun to see its potency. After Bush called the Minutemen vigilantes, Bill Richardson called them patriots. A favorite of Hispanics, as his own ancestry is partly Hispanic, Richardson is awake to the potential of the immigration issue, and was the first governor to declare a state of emergency on the Mexican border.

Hillary Clinton has, if only on rare occasions, sounded like Tom Tancredo. Yet, as the Democratic Party is the party of minorities, and cannot risk alienating its Hispanic base, Democrats will never secure the border. They may play the patriot card against Bush, but they are running a bluff.

When the immigration issue exploded in the Senate in March 2006, Bush came face-to-face with his insoluble dilemma. The GOP cannot be both the party of the Hispanics and the party that sanctions employers who hire illegal aliens, most of whom are Hispanics. If he reaches for the bird in the bush, the Hispanic vote, by supporting amnesty and a guest worker program, his party could lose the bird in the hand, the white working and middle class, to anger and apathy.

If Bush's father had secured the border and begun deporting illegal aliens in 1992, he might have won a second term, and his son and Karl Rove might not face today's dilemma. But not to decide is to decide. Either Bush secures the border now, or the Bush Republicans go the way of the Whigs.

Last Chance for the GOP

The Republican Party has one last chance. If the president will act, he may yet regain the allegiance for his party of enough Reagan Democrats to more than compensate for any Hispanic votes he may lose. Consider:

Hispanics make up 14.4 percent of the population, but, as so many are illegal and many do not vote, were only 6 percent of the electorate in 2004. White voters still constitute more than 80 percent of the electorate.[19] This means the white vote is thirteen times the size of the Hispanic vote. Adding 1 percent of the white vote is thus worth as many raw votes as gaining 13 percent of the Hispanic vote.

An increase of only 2 percent of the white vote adds more GOP votes than a 25 percent increase in the Hispanic vote. Now, which is easier for the GOP to accomplish? Raise the party's share of the white vote by 2 points, or raise the party's share of the Hispanic vote from 35 percent to 60 percent?

What these relative numbers shout is that a Republican campaign that comes down hard for border security and enforcing the law on companies that chronically hire illegals can rally far more white voters, and black voters, than any conceivable loss among Hispanics. Indeed, many Hispanics put a commonsense philosophy ahead of identity politics and are demanding the borders be protected. In Arizona, 47 percent of Hispanics voted for Proposition 200 to require proof of citizenship before welfare benefits are handed out.[20] A Pew Foundation poll found that only 7 percent of Hispanics thought there were "too few" immigrants in the United States, while 48 percent said there were "too many."[21] For it is Hispanic citizens whose jobs are threatened and whose wages are suppressed by illegal aliens. It is Hispanic citizens, among whom the illegal aliens live, who pay the greatest costs of the rising crime and delinquency rates.

Anecdotal evidence is coming in that taking a tough stand on illegal immigration is a winner, even among Democrats. In late 2005 in Boston, the legislature, 87 percent Democratic, was about to ram through a veto-proof bill to grant illegal aliens in-state tuition rates at Bay State colleges. Illegal aliens would thus be granted a privilege, worth $9,000 a year, that is denied to U.S. students from neighboring New Hampshire, Vermont, Rhode Island, Connecticut, or any other state.

The bill was gliding toward passage when, columnist Mac Johnson reports:

A small revolt began. In the crackling electromagnetic hinterlands of talk radio (conservative even in Massachusetts) people began to gather and passions began to rise. Numerous talk-show hosts, foremost among which was Howie Carr of

WRKO in Boston, took up the cause in disgust and sparked a surprisingly intense grassroots wildfire.

The legislature went reeling. In-state tuition for illegal aliens went down to defeat, 96 to 57. "America is fighting for its sovereignty today," declared Representative Marie Parente of Milford. Added Mac Johnson: "Consider how far we have come when Pat Buchanan's words begin coming out of a Massachusetts Democrat's mouth."[22]

Like Yogi said, "It ain't over till it's over."

6

Roots of Paralysis

We can't protect our own border.[1]
—DONALD RUMSFELD, NOVEMBER 29, 2005

With its resources, the U.S. government could secure the Mexican border within weeks. Why, then, is the will of the majority thwarted and the Constitution ignored? Why does President Bush refuse to deal with the state of emergency?

The people would rally to him. In June 1992, this writer, after losing primaries for four months, won almost 30 percent of the vote in the big counties of Southern California in a primary against President George H. W. Bush by calling for a fence on the border. In 1994, Governor Pete Wilson wiped out a 20-point deficit to win re-election by a double-digit margin by riding Proposition 187, which called for an end to welfare for illegal aliens, to victory. Proposition 187 carried 59 percent of the state, and sweeping majorities of Asian- and African- as well as Anglo-American Californians.

According to a May 6, 2005, Zogby Poll, 81 percent of Americans want local and state police to assist U.S. authorities in enforcing immigration laws; 56 percent oppose "the Bush administration's proposal to give millions of illegal aliens guest-worker status and the opportunity to become citizens"; 53 percent support deployment of U.S. troops on the Mexican border.[2]

Zogby found the greatest hostility to illegal aliens among

African-Americans, Democrats, women, and workers earning less than $75,000. These are the Americans directly impacted socially and economically by 12 million illegal aliens willing to work for wages below what an American family needs to survive.

In November 2005, a Rasmussen Reports survey found 60 percent of the nation supporting a fence on the border. Less than half that number were opposed. By late April 2006, the issue was so hot a Rasmussen Poll found that, in a three-way presidential race in 2008, if "a third party candidate ran . . . and promised to build a barrier along the Mexican border and make enforcement of immigration law his top priority," that third-party candidate would run dead even with the Democrat, while the Republican presidential candidate would be a distant third with 21 percent of the vote.[3]

Following a debate at NBC in Washington, as I walked to my car, a black worker drove up beside me and rolled down his window.

"Mr. Buchanan," he said, an edge in his voice. "Did I hear you say we need a fence on our border?"

"That's right," I replied, "across all two thousand miles."

"We don't need a fence," he shot back, "we need a wall!"

Why Does Bush Not Act?

With the Constitution, the law, and the politics on the side of doing his duty and securing our broken borders, why does President Bush not act? What is paralyzing the White House?

Answer: Political correctness, political cowardice, political opportunism, a sense of guilt for America's sins, and twin ideologies that have a grip on our elites not unlike a religious cult. The proud old boast, "Here, sir, the people rule!", no longer applies. We no longer live in a truly democratic republic.

Federal judges routinely throw out popularly enacted laws. Our corporate elite demands and gets an endless supply of low-wage foreign labor. Our cultural elite, contemptuous of the old America, wishes to see it drowned in wave after wave of immigrants, and tars as racists and nativists those who wish to preserve that country.

A White House that calls itself conservative sees Hispanics as its last hope to cling to power and is desperate not to offend Mexican president Vicente Fox or the ethnic lobbies. So, the reigning Republicans ignore the law. If, by 2050, America is a souk of squabbling nationalities united only by a common lust for consumer goods, the guilty men will be our unpatriotic elites who put money and power ahead of country and culture.

Truth be told, many really do not care about the other America. For they live in another country, a country of gated communities and college towns, of gentrified neighborhoods and wealthy suburbs, their children secure in private or up-scale public schools. Illegal aliens are to them the hardworking folks who mow their lawns, pick up their trash, wash their cars, clean their offices, and collect the dishes after meals at their favorite restaurants.

But to the other America, mass immigration is another experience. They see the neighborhoods, towns, and cities they grew up in changing before their eyes. They see crowds of strange men congregating on the street corners their kids pass on the way to and from school. They have neighbors now who don't speak English and won't try. They see their state income and property taxes rising to pay for schools and welfare for people who do not belong here. They see the crime rate rising again, find their kids in gang fights at school, and hear reports of knifings on playgrounds and shootings at the mall. They watch old friends move out of town and out of state to escape to an America that looks more like the country they grew up in. Nightly on cable, they see footage of the invaders sneaking through fences on the border. And they want to know why, when their sons and daughters are guarding Korea's borders and dying to secure Iraq's borders, their government will not defend America's borders.

The dividing line on the issue, writes the historian Victor Davis Hanson, is not liberal versus conservative, but elites versus the people:

Nor is the evolving debate framed so much anymore as left-versus-right, but as the more privileged at odds with the middle and lower classes. On one side are the elite print media, the courts and a few politicians fronting for employer and ethnic interests; on the other are the far more numerous, and raucous, talk-radio listeners, bloggers and cable news watchers, the ballot propositions, and populist state legislators who better reflect the angry pulse of the country.[4]

Just as enthusiasm for forced busing of public school children for racial balance was greatest among those with children in private schools, so the support for open borders is highest today among those who live in neighborhoods where the illegal aliens work but do not live.

A 2002 poll by the Chicago Council on Foreign Relations exposed the gulf between average Americans and the elites. While 60 percent of those surveyed said present levels of immigration constitute "a critical threat to the vital interests of the United States," only 14 percent of prominent Americans agreed.[5] Thus, when hundreds of citizens, many retired and elderly, went to Arizona in the spring of 2005 to serve as spotters for the Border Patrol, to public applause, they were contemptuously dismissed by President Bush as "vigilantes," as he stood beside a Mexican president who acts as though he has a sovereign right to export his misruled people to the United States.

George W. and T.R.

Like most Americans, Theodore Roosevelt welcomed newcomers to America but wanted those who wished to be part of the national family, not just those willing to do servile labor: "Never under any condition should this Nation look upon an immigrant as primarily a labor unit. He should always be looked at primarily as a future citizen. . . ."[6]

Immigrants were welcome if they meant to become citizens and patriots. No others need apply. Weeks before his death, T.R. declared of the immigrant that he or she must become

> an American and nothing but an American. . . . There can be no divided allegiance here. . . . We have room for but one flag, the American flag. . . . We have room for but one language here; and that is the English language . . . and we have room for but one sole loyalty, and that is loyalty to the American people.[7]

In T.R.'s America, there was no room for hyphenated Americans. If you wanted to keep one foot in your home country, keep both there.

This idea, that America is a home, not a hiring hall, a country, not an economy, has died among the elites. Both parties, at the bidding of the transnational corporations that finance them, have killed the dream. To see how far the party of Theodore Roosevelt and Ronald Reagan has slipped its moorings, one need only reread President Bush's East Room address on immigration in January 2004. Rallying support for his guest worker plan, Bush laid down the new principle upon which all future immigration laws must be constructed:

> [N]ew immigration laws should serve the economic needs of the country. . . .

If an American employer is offering a job that American citizens are not willing to take, we ought to welcome into our country a person who will fill that job. . . .

I propose a new temporary worker program that will match willing foreign workers with willing American employers, when no American can be found to fill the jobs. . . . This program will offer legal status, as temporary workers, to the millions of undocumented men and women now employed in the United States, and to those in foreign countries who seek to participate in the program and have been offered employment here. This new system should be clear and efficient, so employers are able to find workers quickly and simply.[8]

Under the Bush immigration plan, K Street values replace American values. Twelve million illegal aliens would be amnestied, and businesses that cheated on their competitors by colluding in mass criminality would be pardoned and rewarded by having their illegal workers declared legal.

Corporations would be empowered to go overseas and find millions more. All an employer need do is advertise jobs at pay lower than most Americans—who cannot feed, clothe, house, and raise their families on the minimum wage—could accept. When no U.S. applicant turned up, companies would be free to go abroad and hire Africans, Asians, and Latin Americans to come to the United States and take the jobs Americans could not take. Our immigration policy would be outsourced to transnational corporations for whom loyalty to country is a sentimental attachment and impediment to the maximization of profit.

The Bush plan is economic treason against the American worker. That "civil rights leaders" are silent about the dispossession of the black working class, that unions are not marching against this sell-out of blue-collar and white-collar America, only tells us that the amorality of the transnational corporation has infected both. Solidarity be damned; it is all about money now.

The Economism Cult

To Theodore Roosevelt, immigration was about America as a nation and a people. To George Bush of the Harvard Business School, immigration is about America as a giant job mart for companies that wish to be liberated from the burdens of loyalty to roam the world and hire foreign workers at the lowest possible wages to de-Americanize the U.S. labor force. This is the real K Street Project.

"The business of America is business," Calvin Coolidge declared. But Coolidge would have recoiled at a plan to permit U.S. businesses to scour the planet to round up Chinese, Indians, and Africans to take jobs Americans could not accept at Third World wages. Coolidge put country first. On the eve of enactment of the toughest immigration law in U.S. history, Coolidge declared: "America must be kept American."[9]

Scholar John Attarian gave a name to the cult that has captured the party of Goldwater and Reagan: "economism." This neo-Marxist ideology is rooted in a belief that economics rules the world, that economic activity is mankind's most important activity and the most conducive to human happiness, and that economics is what politics is or should be all about.

Economism does not just believe in markets, it worships them. The invisible hand of Adam Smith becomes the hand of God. The commands of the market overrule the claims of citizenship, culture, country. Economic efficiency becomes the highest value. We see the cult in the Republican dogma of salvation-through-tax-cuts-alone, in the willingness of the right to yield sovereignty when so ordered by the WTO, in the mockery of Middle Americans as "pitchfork-wielding xenophobes" for questioning whether, in a war against

Arab-Islamic terrorists, it is wise to consign U.S. ports to the sheikhs of Dubai.[10]

We see the cult at work in corporate executives who proudly declare that theirs is no longer an American company but a "global" company. The "multinational businessman," writes conservative scholar Roger Scruton,

> is someone who wishes to break down the distinctions between people and who does not feel at home in any city because he is an alien in all—including his own. He sees the world as one vast system in which everyone is equally a customer, a consumer, a creature of wants and needs. He is only too happy to transplant people from place to place, to abolish local attachments, to shift boundaries and customs in accordance with the inexorable demands of economic progress.[11]

To the "economite," the true believer in economism, sovereignty, independence, industrial primacy, the values of community and country, must be sacrificed, should the gods of globalism so command. Where Abraham lifted his son on an altar of sacrifice at the command of God, the economites put the nation there. To acolytes of the cult, what's good for GDP is good for America. *Washington Post* columnist Robert Samuelson is not far from the mark:

> What's the dominant religion of the past 100 years? The answer isn't Christianity with its 2.1 billion followers or Islam with its 1.3 billion. It's the idea of economic growth, the Church of GDP. . . . Getting richer is now an almost universal craving. And yet the worship of growth . . . is widely seen—especially in already wealthy societies—as morally corrupting: the mindless pursuit of empty materialism (do flat-panel TVs

really make us better off?) that drains life of spiritual meaning and also wrecks the environment.[12]

To converts to the Church of GDP, mass immigration means more workers, more consumers, bigger markets, a bigger economy. And because it is good for the GDP, it is good for America. Dissidents and skeptics are Luddite enemies of progress.

Taking a trip to the border, John Judis of the *New Republic* came home with an appreciation of what Arizonans felt that worshippers at the Church of GDP will never understand: In Arizona, "those who are most up in arms over illegal immigration are far more concerned with its sociocultural than its economic effects. They are worried about what is commonly called the 'Mexicanization of Arizona.' . . . They fret about . . . Arizona becoming a 'Third World country' or 'the next Mexifornia.' "[13]

Having risen above patriotism, economites see such sentiments as symptoms of xenophobia. Economism, writes Attarian

eventually turns everything into a commodity to be marketed at a profit. This necessarily presupposes that nothing is sacred.

Driven by a craving for maximum return at lowest cost, economites relentlessly dispense with loyalty, consideration or any other restraints. If cheaper workers or suppliers appear, the existing ones are summarily dropped. Advertisers pillage music for tunes to be converted to jingles. Animals are reduced to protein factories put here for our use; libertarian Virginia Postrel defined a cow as a " 'machine' for turning grass into protein"; they may be raised on factory farms in tiny, immobilizing pens; outrage at this is sentimental hogwash. Though hallowed by the blood of thousands, Bull Run and Gettysburg are fair game for developers seeking to build restaurants, movie theaters, and shopping centers. . . . [14]

Economism's roots may be traced to an Enlightenment that "made atheism, denial of the soul and free will, and impiety intellectually respectable," and to nineteenth-century liberals David Ricardo, James and John Stuart Mill, Richard Cobden, and Frédéric Bastiat.[15] These men of words looked to an ideal world where all the European empires had vanished, trade and travel among nations was unimpeded, borders had disappeared, and nations themselves might cease to exist as man came to know the "perpetual peace" of which Immanuel Kant had lately written. To the "Cobdenites," free trade was "God's diplomacy."

The Quaker leader of the Anti–Corn Law League, Cobden persuaded the British government to lift barriers to imported grain and embrace free trade but never denied his agenda was about more than cheap grain for Britain's poor. "Commerce is the grand panacea," he rhapsodized, "which, like a beneficent medical discovery, will serve to inoculate with the healthy and saving taste for civilization all the nations of the world."[16]

A visionary and master orator, when Cobden rose at Free Trade Hall in Manchester on January 15, 1846, the audience was so large seats in the hall had to be removed so more could be accommodated:

I believe that the physical gain will be the smallest gain to humanity from the success of this principle. I look farther; I see in the Free Trade principle that which shall act on the moral world as the principle of gravitation in the universe—drawing men together, thrusting aside the antagonism of race, and creed, and language, and uniting us in the bonds of eternal peace.[17]

Having heard enough from Mr. Cobden, Lord Palmerston, among the more tough-minded of Victorian statesmen, wrote the loquacious Quaker a letter concerning his brave new world:

It would be very delightful if your Utopia could be realized, and if the nations of the world would think of nothing but peace and commerce, and would give up quarreling and fighting altogether. But, unfortunately, man is a fighting animal, and that this is human nature is proved by the fact that republics, where the masses govern, are far more quarrelsome, and more addicted to fighting, than monarchies, which are governed by comparatively few persons.[18]

The Cobdenite vision was embraced by Woodrow Wilson, whose Fourteen Points called for global free trade as a precondition of permanent peace. In the late twentieth century, the Republican Party converted to this religion that economic patriots from Lincoln to Theodore Roosevelt to Calvin Coolidge to Robert Taft had rejected as utopian and un-American. That capitalist values are Christian values and conservative values is now defined dogma in the Church of GDP.

Forces Behind Open Borders

For decades, the Republican establishment has watched transfixed as minorities have exploded from 20 to 94 million, from 11 percent of the nation to 33 percent. Mass immigration is the cause, but the Republican Party recoils from the obvious solution: a moratorium. Instead, the GOP looks wistfully to Hispanics, our largest minority at 43 million and rising, as its only hope to retain power as Americans of European ancestry become a minority. Believing the media myth that the party lost California because Pete Wilson backed Proposition 187, the GOP is terrified of a backlash among Hispanic voters, should its leaders enforce the law, fence the border, and sanction companies that hire illegals. To enforce the immigration laws, Republicans fear, is to cut their collective throats. And in their cravenness they are buttressed by powerful forces.

Corporate America and its K Street arm, on which the GOP depends to keep the party machinery greased and its candidates flush with cash, demands a constant resupply of cheap labor to hold wages down. For the corporate elite, immigration means low-wage workers to replace high-wage Americans, while taxpayers assume the social costs—welfare, Medicaid, rent supplements, food stamps, clinics, cops, courts, prisons, and legal services for the immigrants. The Business Roundtable believes in socializing costs, while privatizing profits. To Corporate America, mass immigration is the gift that keeps on giving.

Should the Bush White House build a security fence on the Mexican border and impose sanctions on employers who hire illegals, the U.S. Chamber of Commerce and Business Roundtable could snap their checkbooks shut and the GOP would react like some trust fund baby whose father just phoned from Hobe Sound to tell him his ATM card had been canceled.

Of the one hundred largest entities on earth, half are nations and half are corporations. The executives of these corporations work ceaselessly to erase borders and diminish national sovereignty. Allied with them in the drive to circumscribe the liberty and independence of nations are scores of thousands of "international civil servants," who labor in the vineyards of the EU, the UN, the World Bank, the IMF, the WTO, the World Court, the International Criminal Court, and in thousands of NGOs, nongovernmental organizations that consider their mandates to be global and who work for a world government they and their comrades must come to dominate.

Backing up the Bush Republicans and Big Business are intellectuals like the late Robert Bartley, for three decades editorial editor of the *Wall Street Journal*. The neoconservative Bartley was an open-borders, free-trade fanatic. "I think the nation-state is finished," he reportedly told author Peter Brimelow, as his newspaper campaigned for decades for a constitutional amendment declaring, "There shall be open borders."[19] When Vicente Fox called for a North American Union modeled on the European Union, Bartley hailed him as a "visionary" and pledged solidarity: "He [Fox] can rest assured that there is one voice north of the Rio Grande that supports his vision . . . this newspaper."[20]

To utopians like Bartley and his colleagues at the *Journal,* there are not too many immigrants coming from the Third World, legal or illegal; there are not enough. In our diversity is our strength. The more who come, the stronger and better nation we become. It makes no difference what country or culture you come from. The European core of America has become irrelevant. What matters is that you contribute to the GDP.

The Democratic Party sees immigrants, legal and illegal, as future voters who will bury the Nixon-Reagan coalition. Nor are they mistaken in that hope. For the Third World poor, the vast majority of those coming, depend on the social programs that are the raison d'être of the Democratic Party. The more immigrant poor who come, the larger the Leviathan state, and the greater the number of employees needed to operate and manage it. And there are no more reliable Democratic constituencies than those who depend on government for their health, education, and welfare, or for their paychecks. Government unions are Democratic unions.

"We're going to close down Los Angeles, Chicago, New York, Tucson, Phoenix, Fresno," said Jorge Rodriguez, an official of one of the unions of the American Federation of State, County, and Municipal Employees on the eve of the May Day general strike and boycott. "We want full amnesty, full legalization for anybody who is here [illegally]."[21] If 12 million illegals are amnestied, it means hundreds of thousands of new jobs for AFSCME and its allied unions to manage the vastly expanded welfare state required to meet their social needs.

Mainline churches believe that siding with illegal immigrants fulfills the commandments of the Social Gospel. And immigrants fill up the pews emptied of the older Christians who have passed on, or who, fed up with the dilutions of doctrine, have moved on to more orthodox congregations.

The Catholic hierarchy has come out for amnesty for illegal aliens, believing this comports with Christ's admonition to feed the hungry, give drink to the thirsty, clothe the naked, and harbor the homeless. But Christ's commands are for us as individuals. They are not met by benedictions over mass demonstrations by illegal aliens marching under foreign flags or press conferences by His Eminence Cardinal Mahony demanding that the faithful finance an endless stream of social welfare benefits for people who have broken into our country, and now demand all the rights and privileges of American citizens.

Unions once opposed mass immigration as undercutting the wages of workers. They now see immigrants in the service and construction industries as replacements for the members lost to outsourcing and downsizing. By making illegal aliens legal, unions hope to organize them and restore lost union power. Around 2000, an AFL-CIO that had been losing members for decades came out for de facto amnesty.

Internationalists see a fusion of the United States, Canada, and Mexico as the logical next step to world government. Transnationals see borders as impediments to the flow of workers and goods. Alienated intellectuals and cultural elites, discontented with the America we love, are committed to open borders to alter forever a country and culture they abhor. Disraeli called them "Cosmopolitan critics, men who are the friends of every country save their own."

When Susan Sontag said, "The white race is the cancer of human history," she did not speak for herself alone at a time when it was elite campus fashion to put up posters of Ché Guevara in the dorm and march under Vietcong flags chanting: "Ho, Ho, Ho Chi Minh, NLF is going to win!" And when he leads student demonstrators across Stanford campus chanting, "Hey, Hey, ho, ho, Western Civ has got to go," Jesse Jackson means tossing out more than just required courses on Western Civilization.

Finally, there are those slush funds of sedition, the big foundations, foremost among which is the Ford Foundation, with assets of $11 billion.

Forty years ago, the League of United Latin American Citizens, or LULAC, was a patriotic organization that had as its code: "Respect your citizenship, honor your country, maintain its traditions in the minds of your children; incorporate yourself in the culture and civilization." In 1968, one militant broke away and approached Ford for money for a new Mexican American Legal Defense and Educational Fund. MALDEF was given an initial grant of $2.2 million. It has since raked in $30 million from Ford and tens of millions more from corporations to convert itself into the most powerful lobbying arm in the United States for illegal aliens and Mexico's interests. The National Council of La Raza—the advocacy and lobbying arm of Latino peoples in America—is another beneficiary of the big corporations and big foundations that finance the left in the culture wars.

With the ACLU, MALDEF leads the fight for bilingual education, for granting driver's licenses and in-state tuition rates to illegal aliens, for opening the border. When voters enact laws in statewide referenda to end social welfare benefits to illegal aliens, MALDEF and the ACLU go judge-shopping together to have the laws overturned. And through the judges and courts, minority rule replaces majority rule in America.

One MALDEF subsidiary claims to have persuaded Governor Gray Davis not to appeal a federal court decision overturning Proposition 187, which Democratic Party chair Esteban "Art" Torres called the "last gasp of white America in California." Given the exodus of whites from California since Proposition 187 was overturned, Torres may not have been entirely wrong. And as MALDEF and La Raza have moved left, LULAC has followed.

Then there is the new Hispanic media—the purveyors of films, the owners of the Spanish-language radio and TV stations, the publishers of magazines, books, and newspapers for Hispanics. Survival for these media institutions, some of the fastest growing and most politically powerful in the nation, depends on immigrants *not* converting to the English language. They will fight to the death against making America an English-speaking nation again.

These, then, are the institutions and elites with the vested interests, economic and ideological, in letting the invasion run on until there is no longer a recognizable nation, but a multilingual, multiracial, multi-ethnic, multicultural America, the first universal nation of Ben Wattenberg's utopian dream. And the country we knew will be gone and the warning of T.R. will have proven prophetic. The last best hope of earth will have become "a polyglot boarding house" for the world.

The Hidden Motive

But there is a hidden motive for what the historian and scholar Clyde Wilson calls our "fatalistic paralysis."[22] Western society is afflicted with a guilty conscience. For Europeans, the guilt is over centuries of imperial rule. For Americans, it is guilt over our ancestors' injustices to the Native Americans and two centuries of enslavement of black Americans, followed by a century of segregation.

Our ancestors were not paralyzed by guilt. Confident in their culture and civilization, they believed in their superiority over what Kipling had called the "lesser breeds without the law." We come from a different people than the people we have become. Five of our first seven presidents were slaveholders. Andrew Jackson, among the fiercest Indian fighters in history, spoke for the Jacksonians when he defended ethnic cleansing:

> What good man would prefer a country covered with forests and ranged by a few thousand savages to our extensive Republic, studded with cities, towns, and prosperous farms, embellished with all the improvements which art can devise or industry execute, occupied by more than 12,000,000 happy people, and filled with all the blessings of liberty, civilization, and religion?[23]

The Great Emancipator believed in white supremacy and favored repatriation of slaves to the African continent whence their ancestors had come. "The only good Indian is a dead Indian," said his fiercest general, Sherman, who burned Atlanta, to Sheridan, who burned the Shenandoah. It was Sherman who sent Sheridan to settle accounts with the Plains Indians and urged a "final solution" to the Sioux question: extermination.

In his *Winning of the West,* young Theodore Roosevelt spoke for his generation of imperialists in terms that are raw, racialist, and ruthless. As Peter Brimelow writes, he "presented the settling of the lands beyond the Alleghenies as 'the crowning and greatest achievement' of the 'spread of the English-speaking peoples' which he saw in explicit terms:

> . . . it is of incalculable importance that America, Australia, and Siberia should pass out of the hands of their red, black, and yellow aboriginal owners, and become the heritage of the dominant world races."[24]

Woodrow Wilson was a segregationist, who had D. W. Griffith's *Birth of a Nation* shown at the White House. Harry Truman flirted with the Klan. Lyndon Johnson, "the civil rights president," was given to using the "n" word in front of black men who worked for him.

Today, we find such views repellent. But, if racism means a belief in the superiority of the white race and its inherent right to rule other peoples, American history is full of such men. Indeed, few great men could be found in America or Europe before World War II who did not accept white supremacy as natural. Churchill surely did. In September 1943, at a White House lunch, he said to FDR, "why be apologetic about Anglo-Saxon superiority . . . they were superior."[25]

How could Ike send back all illegal aliens in "Operation Wetback" without a second thought while Bush refuses to act? Because Eisenhower's conscience was untroubled. To the Greatest Generation, America was not a racist country. Those would have been fighting words in 1950.

Growing up in the 1940s and 1950s, we did not feel any need to apologize for America's past, but took pride in all she had accomplished. African-Americans shared that pride. That there were sins in our past, no one denied. But Americans did not obsess over wrongs done by previous generations, for, compared with all other nations, America merited the gratitude of mankind. And so the world seemed to believe.

Yet, though the achievements of our civilization in art, architecture, law, literature, technology, science, and governance, and the advance of human freedom and God-given rights eclipse those of any other, there has arisen among our intellectual and cultural elites a contempt for the West. Many see our ancestors as irredeemably racist, imperialist, and genocidal. George Orwell located this self-loathing on the British Left: "England is perhaps the only great country whose intellectuals are ashamed of their nationality. In left-wing circles, it is always felt that there is something slightly disgraceful in being an Englishman and that it is a duty to snigger at every English institution."[26]

By the late 1960s, the disease had crossed the Atlantic and become an epidemic. Some American writers, scholars, and teachers now spend careers tearing down what our ancestors built up. Their contempt for America, her culture and history, has induced a paralysis that stultifies a resolute defense against enemies who can make out credentials as victims of Western crimes. And as the West is guilty of the most odious of offenses against peoples of color, some among our elite ask: Why should not the West suffer the fate of all evil empires? By the time the coming generation reaches middle age, writes John Derbyshire, "The concept that lay beneath and supported our collective consciousness until recently, the concept that white Europeans, their civilization and their bourgeois culture, were the apex of human achievement, will have been shamed, mocked, and badgered out of existence—along, of course, with the civilization and culture."[27]

Baby boomers have been marinated in guilt, indoctrinated to believe America is fatally flawed—racist, sexist, nativist, homophobic. Many were not taught to see her history as glorious but only as the shameful past of a brutal country that had enslaved one people and exterminated another. Growing up in the civil rights era, many baby boomers bought into its core doctrine: America must confess her sins, seek absolution, do penance, and make eternal restitution.

In public and private schools, colleges and universities, through Hollywood films and Broadway plays, in fiction and nonfiction, magazines and newspapers, TV documentaries and prime-time shows, this message of our oppression of minorities has been drummed so deep into the souls of this generation, many are incapable of mounting a defense when confronted by alleged victims charging America with injustice. As Clyde Wilson writes, "President Carter's refusal to enforce our laws during the *Mariel* boatlift and Congress's proposal to amnesty and reward those who have flouted them in the past would have immediately been recognized by the Founding Fathers as evidence of a deplorable fall from republican virtue. . . ."[28]

The moral paralysis seems most pronounced among progressives.

Though union leaders once damned as "scabs" and "strikebreakers" men who hired out at lower wages to take the jobs of union members, today many are silent or welcoming of illegal aliens who shoulder aside American workers.

Booker T. Washington and A. Philip Randolph demanded that immigration be curbed so black Americans could fill the openings in the booming industrial economy; today's civil rights "leaders" are mute as these jobs are taken by Third World immigrants.

And how explain the craven silence of the environmental movement?

No portion of the nation is more polluted than the southern border where the armies of the night cross, leaving their garbage and debris on the great trek north. Do the environmentalists believe the anticipated addition of 120 million people to the U.S. population by 2050, mostly Third World poor, can be accomplished without devastating impact on our air, land, and water?

This land of ours, writes columnist Chilton Williamson, who moved west to Wyoming, "is going to be overrun and despoiled in 50 or 100 years because of the folly, greed, and dishonesty with which Congress has responded to the immigrant invasion of the last 25 years."

It is the silence of the progressives that most disgusts Williamson:

It is considered "humanitarian" to fret about population growth and its effects on the natural environment at the global (which is to say, at the abstract) level; but "racist," "xenophobic," "uncompassionate," and "un-American" to worry about the population crisis as it immediately affects the United States, the only place in the world where we are in a position to be able to do anything about it.[29]

A liberal—conservatives used to joke—is someone who will not take his own side in an argument. Now the malady afflicts the right. On immigration, it translates into a reflexive denunciation as "xenophobic" or "nativist" of anyone who argues that mass migration from the Third World risks disuniting and even destroying America. Middle America, seeing its views disregarded as morally repugnant, reacts accordingly. "This is the kind of issue," says pollster Frank Luntz, "that the Silent Majority talks about in private but doesn't mention to pollsters."[30]

What Changed America?

Events of the twentieth century were the catalysts that caused the sea change in attitudes. First came the revelation of Nazi atrocities against minorities, culminating in the Holocaust. Hitler's crimes arose out of a dark and Darwinian "survival-of-the-fittest" notion of Aryan supremacy and race struggle. The awful consequences of these ideas, visited and revisited, caused a recoil of disgust in the West. In his seminal work on America's immigration crisis, *Alien Nation* (1995), Peter Brimelow rooted the present U.S. immigration policy in our reaction to Hitler's crimes:

There is a sense in which current immigration policy is Adolf Hitler's posthumous revenge on America. The U.S. political elite emerged from the war passionately concerned to cleanse itself from all taints of racism or xenophobia. Eventually, it enacted the epochal Immigration Act of 1965. And thus, quite accidentally, triggered a renewed mass immigration, so huge and so systematically different from anything that had gone before as to transform—and ultimately, perhaps even to destroy—the one unquestioned victor of World War II: the American nation, as it had evolved by the middle of the twentieth century.[31]

After the revelation of Hitler's crimes came the decolonization of Asia and Africa following generations of Western rule. The "winds of change," as Harold Macmillan heralded what was sweeping across the sub-Sahara, were welcomed by Western elites with an enthusiasm not unlike the first reactions to the French Revolution: "Bliss was it in that dawn to be alive/But to be young was very heaven!" A new world of possibility was replacing the old world of wicked empires.

In America, the formative experience for this generation was the civil rights movement, liberalism's hour, an era to which the left returns again and again in nostalgia. The civil rights revolution dethroned one moral order and enthroned another. Discrimination against people of color came to be seen as the original sin of Western man and its extirpation his highest moral duty. The end of white rule in South Africa and transfer of power to Nelson Mandela is regarded even by some conservatives as an event as epochal as the defeat of fascism and the fall of communism and the Soviet Empire.

As Catholic schoolchildren of the 1940s were instructed in the evils and temptations of impurity, American children since the 1960s have been indoctrinated in the evil of racism and moral imperative to avoid thoughts, words, or deeds that might be so construed. In public life, the charge of "racism" has become modernity's equivalent of the charge of heresy in the Inquisition. The punishment for the latter was death for the unrepentant. Modernity's punishment for remarks deemed as racist, and unrepented, is political ruin and pariah status.

"Jimmy the Greek" [Snyder], the CBS commentator who mused after a bibulous lunch about the reasons for the superior performance of black athletes, saw his career obliterated in an afternoon. Earl Butz, secretary of agriculture, was forced to resign when it was reported that he had retold a crude racial joke in private. Charles Murray, coauthor of *The Bell Curve,* who argued that intelligence is in part inherited, that it may be measured by IQ tests, that it correlates with success and failure in school and life, that it is unevenly distributed among racial and ethnic groups, paid a career price for saying in public what few of his colleagues would deny in private.

The new orthodoxy teaches as dogma that race does not matter, that to treat people of different creeds, colors, or cultures differently is immoral in principle and intolerable in practice. The crisis of the new orthodoxy is that it is rooted in an ideology few truly believe. For creed, culture, and ethnicity *do* matter, immensely. They are not everything, but they are not nothing. They are the forces tearing down empires and tearing apart nations. When we act as if they do not exist, we court disaster, as we did when we marched to Baghdad certain our democratic ideals would be embraced once the tyrant was gone, only to discover that divisions among Kurds, Shia, and Sunni over ethnicity, culture, history, and creed vanquished all our hopes.

"Liberalism is the ideology of Western suicide," wrote the geostrategist James Burnham. In *Suicide of the West,* Burnham argued that liberals, then dominant in politics, did not seek the ruin of the West; but the ideas and ideals they held dear, followed to their logical end, would disarm the West of its natural defenses and result in civilizational ruin.[32]

Burnham today might compare liberalism to the HIV virus that destroys the immune system, leaving victims unable to resist the infections that kill them. For America to assume that people of all races, cultures, and creeds are equally assimilable in a First World nation like the United States, and to declare a policy of "open borders" on that assumption, he would surely argue, is to risk national suicide. Yet the liberalism of which he wrote, introduced into the GOP as "compassionate conservatism," now informs the immigration policies of the hierarchy of both our national parties.

Afflicted with guilt over her racial sins, America did the right thing in the 1950s and 1960s: struck down laws that mandated segregation and legislated equality of legal rights. But a guilt-stricken generation went far beyond mandating equal justice under law.

In the name of justice, it established injustice. Quotas instituted to keep Jews out of the Ivy League were reintroduced to assure minorities a predetermined number of seats. When desegregation failed to achieve a level of integration that satisfied judges, children were bused across cities for purposes of racial balance. Property rights and freedom of association were sacrificed to make society conform to the commands of the new moral order. But it was the transference of this idea—that America has sinned unpardonably against equality and must make amends, no matter the cost—to immigration law that may spell the end of the United States.

From 1789 to 1960, American leaders were obsessed about who came to this country, what beliefs they brought, what their innate capacity was to become a part of the American people. Alarm about a radical change in our ethnic composition is as American as Ben Franklin. In 1751, Franklin asked aloud: "Why should Pennsylvania, founded by the English, become a Colony of Aliens, who will shortly be so numerous as to Germanize us instead of our Anglifying them. . . ?"[33] He would never find out if his fears were justified. German immigration was halted during the Seven Years' War.

After each wave of immigrants reached our shores, restrictions were imposed until the new immigrants had been assimilated. The Irish who came in 1845–49 caused a ferocious backlash, depicted in Martin Scorsese's *The Gangs of New York*. The Great Wave from

Southern and Eastern Europe, in the period 1890–1920, was followed by the most restrictive immigration laws in our history, which stayed on the books until 1965.

One reads in the last years of the Great Wave remarks by T.R. and Woodrow Wilson that would today end careers. We may call them bigoted, but they preserved the America we are losing. For there is little evidence that the scores of millions who have come in the last forty years from Asia, Africa, and Latin America are assimilating as the European immigrants once did. Nor are our elites demanding that they be assimilated.

Yet we are told that there is never again to be a letup, moratorium, time-out, or pause to Americanize those who have come not in the millions but the tens of millions. To their numbers we add more than 1 million every year. Half of them now ignore our laws and come illegally. We do not know how many are coming. We do not know how many are here.

We are conducting an experiment rooted neither in common sense nor the American experience, but in an ideology that declares, against all historical evidence, that people of every country, creed, culture, or civilization are equally and easily assimilable into America, and all have an equal right to come here.

Thus the world's finest five-star hotel, the United States of America, becomes the flophouse for the planet. We may call our ancestors racists, as we trumpet our moral superiority. But history may yet mark ours as the generation of fools that threw away the last best hope on earth.

7

A Grudge Against the Gringo

Destiny beckons us to hold and civilize Mexico.[1]
—SECRETARY OF STATE JAMES BUCHANAN, 1846

Poor Mexico! So far from God and so close
to the United States.[2]
MEXICAN PRESIDENT PORFIRIO DÍAZ, 1910

The U.S. Department of State was negotiating over a spit of land that, due to a shift in the course of the Rio Grande, seemed now to be on Mexico's side of the river. As the Americans argued into the night, the Mexican envoy imbibed. Frustrated at the U.S. refusal to concede the sliver of land, the Mexican negotiator got up, walked to a wall map, and, running his hand across the southwestern United States, blurted:

"Why are you Americans fighting over this tiny piece of land? Don't you know we will one day take all this back—by demography?"

That story was told to me by a ranking diplomat of the Reagan era. And, indeed, once, all that land did belong to Mexico, and knowing how we acquired it helps explain Mexican attitudes toward the United States.

The Amputation of Texas

"O wad some Pow'r the giftie gie us/To see oursels as others see us!" wrote the poet Burns. To understand the resentment of so many Mexicans against America, especially descendants of the Spanish who had ruled that land since Cortés came ashore in 1521, to independence in 1821, one must understand the history Mexicans are taught never to forget.

It began in 1821, when the Spanish authorities ceded a huge tract of Texas land to an enterprising Missourian named Moses Austin to settle three hundred families in the unpopulated province. As the historian Thomas Bailey writes, the triumph of the revolution that same year gave Mexico "an excellent opportunity to cancel the contract, but with the same fatal blindness as their predecessors, they legalized the arrangements."[3]

Two conditions were imposed on the settlers. They must become Catholic and must swear allegiance to Mexico. Land-hungry Americans began to take up the offer by the thousands.

In 1826, Haden Edwards, a Texas landowner, decided to run all squatters off his property. When the Mexican government sided with the squatters and canceled Edwards's contract, his brother, Benjamin, leading a party of men, rode into Nacogdoces and, on December 16, under a red-and-white flag inscribed "Independence, Liberty and Justice," proclaimed the "Republic of Fredonia . . . from 'the Sabine to the Rio Grande.'" "Our friends in the United States," boasted Benjamin Edwards, "are already in arms, and only waiting for the word."[4]

Acting on behalf of the Mexican government, Stephen Austin, at the head of a small army, rode in and snuffed out the "Fredonian Rebellion."

But, to many in Texas, the land speculator Haden Edwards was a martyr, persecuted by a tyrannical Mexican regime. To the Mexican government, however, aware of how Andrew Jackson had torn Florida away from Spain, the fear arose that Texas could be lost the same way. By 1829, an alarmed Mexico tried to cut off further immigration by outlawing slavery in Texas—most of the Americans were southerners—and by a flat prohibition in 1830 against any more Americans entering the territory.

Yet, still the Americans continued to pour in, and, increasingly, these "Texicans" became frustrated with the Mexican legal system and their lack of representation. When the Texans demanded the rights of statehood in the national legislature, they were rebuffed. Mexico's blunder, writes the historian Robert Leckie, was in not realizing that these Americans they had foolishly invited into their country were aliens with whom they had nothing in common, foreigners who had no interest in assimilating, but intended to maintain their own separate identity—inside Mexico:

> Mexico's error . . . was to encourage migration from a neighboring people who were as different from the Mexican people as these two former colonies of Protestant Britain and Catholic Spain could possibly be. These mostly Southern Americans who migrated to Texas were drawn . . . simply by the lure of land and for no other reason. When they promised to become practicing Catholics and to obey the Mexican prohibition of slavery they had no intention of doing so.[5]

Thomas Bailey is more pungent. Adventurers like Jim Bowie and Sam Houston, he wrote, never took kindly to the "greaser yoke."[6] They saw themselves as Americans living in a foreign country. Nor did they get along with the neighbors. Writes Jaime Suchlicki in his history of Mexico: "Political, religious, cultural, ethnic, and language differences accentuated tensions with Mexican settlers."[7]

In 1835, after the tyrannical General Antonio López de Santa

Anna seized power in Mexico City, the Texans—who by now out-numbered the Mexicans ten to one—fed up with loyalty oaths and fake conversions, rebelled and chased the tiny Mexican garrison across the Rio Grande.

To restore his lost province, Santa Anna led an army north, first encountering the rebels at a mission called the Alamo. When the Texans refused to surrender, Santa Anna on March 6, 1836, raised the black flag of no quarter, overran the mission, and massacred the defenders to the last man, including Davy Crockett. The general then marched to Goliad, where he executed in cold blood more than three hundred rebels who did surrender. Men, women, children, and slaves now fled toward the Sabine, Mexico's border with the United States, as Santa Anna's victorious soldiers took up the battle cry: "Exterminate to the Sabine!"[8]

But in April, at San Jacinto, Santa Anna stumbled into a trap set by Sam Houston. His army was caught at siesta and the wild Texans stormed in, howling, "Remember the Alamo!" "Remember Go-liad!" and "Death to Santa Anna!" The victory was followed, writes Leckie, by a massacre that "remains the bloodiest in the annals of American arms."[9]

Even Sam Houston had no power over this berserk mob. Rid-ing among them he could . . . hear one of his captains ha-ranguing his men. "Boys, you know how to take prisoners, take them with the butt of your guns. Club your guns, and re-member the Alamo! Remember Goliad! Club your guns right and left and knock their god damn brains out!"

They did indeed, killing more Mexicans than all the Texan-Americans who had died both at the Alamo and Goliad. Against only 9 Texan-Americans killed and 34 wounded, 630 Mexicans died, while another 200 were wounded and the re-mainder of Santa Anna's star-crossed army was taken prisoner. Only darkness ended this ghoulish sport, and the dishonorable Battle of San Jacinto came to an end.[10]

After escaping the battlefield, Santa Anna had been captured and the Texans demanded his execution. But Sam Houston had another idea. Let the butcher live, on condition he sign away Texas. Under the threat of death, Santa Anna signed the Treaty of Velasco. Texas was free and, on his last day in office in 1837, Andrew Jackson recognized the Lone Star Republic of his old comrade who had led Old Hickory's Tennesseans at Horseshoe Bend in the 1814 slaughter of the Red Sticks. Back in Mexico, as Santa Anna had anticipated, the Mexican Congress repudiated the treaty as having been signed under duress in violation of international law.

Considering Texas a renegade province, Mexico City refused to recognize the Lone Star Republic. And so matters simmered for a decade.

"Jimmy Polk's War"

The Mexicans seethed at their loss to predatory Yankees they had invited in as guests, but did nothing; and worse was yet to come. In 1844, former Speaker of the House James K. Polk pledged to the aged Jackson that, if nominated by the Democratic Party and elected, he would annex Texas and keep it out of the paws of the British Lion that Jackson feared had designs upon it. Jackson urged the delegates in Baltimore to vote for the "dark horse," Polk, although his own vice president, former president Martin Van Buren, was the front-runner for the nomination.

Polk was nominated and elected. But President John Tyler, in his final hours in office in 1845, having failed to persuade two-thirds of the Senate to ratify a treaty annexing Texas, decided to write his own page in the history books. Through a joint resolution of Congress,

Tyler effected the annexation of Texas, robbing Polk of the honor of bringing the Lone Star Republic into the Union.

As Mexico considered Texas a rebellious province, U.S. annexation was tantamount to a declaration of war. The Mexican minister demanded his passports. Diplomatic relations were broken. War loomed.

Moreover, Mexico disputed Texas's claim to all land north of the Rio Grande and west to El Paso, claiming the border of Texas had always been the Nueces River, 150 miles north of the Rio Grande. This amounted to a Mexican claim to more than half of what is today the state of Texas.

With an army of only 7,000 officers and men scattered in border posts, Polk preferred diplomacy to war and sent John Slidell of Louisiana to negotiate. Slidell was to offer a U.S. assumption of all claims against Mexico, if Mexico would agree to U.S. annexation of Texas to the Rio Grande. Slidell was also empowered to offer $25 million for New Mexico and California and go as high as $40 million. But with anti-Americanism and nationalism rampant in Mexico, the government refused to negotiate. Denied an audience with President Jose Herrera, Slidell wrote Polk: "Be assured that nothing is to be done with these people until they have been chastised."[11]

"Jimmy" Polk had come to the same conclusion. To back up U.S. claims, he now made the critical move in the crisis. Polk sent Brigadier General Zachary Taylor and 3,500 men, half of the U.S. Army, to the Rio Grande and began to draft a declaration of war. Secretary of State James Buchanan cautioned Polk to wait for an overt act by the Mexican hotheads who, by now, had overthrown Herrera.

Meanwhile, General Pedro de Ampudia had arrived at Matamoros on the opposite bank of the Rio Grande, where he ordered Taylor to withdraw from Mexican land. Taylor's response was to blockade the river. Mexican soldiers now crossed the river and fired on one of Taylor's patrols, killing or wounding a dozen of his men. Two days earlier, Mexico had declared a "defensive war" on the United States.[12] James K. Polk had his *casus belli*.

As he wrote Congress in his request for a declaration of war: "We have tried every effort at reconciliation. The cup of forbearance has been exhausted. After reiterated menaces, Mexico has passed the boundary of the United States, has invaded our territory, and shed American blood on the American soil."[13]

The nation rallied to Polk, and Congress declared war. Though the Mexican forces were six times the size of the U.S. Army and made up of stolid and brave soldiers, these were peasant and Indian conscripts who confronted a U.S. superiority in guns, equipment, officers, training, and motivation. By 1848, John Frémont had occupied Northern California and the Bear Flag Republic had been proclaimed. Taylor's army had routed Santa Anna at Buena Vista, where his ex-son-in-law, Colonel Jefferson Davis, and his Mississippians heroically broke up a Mexican cavalry charge.

Colonel Stephen Kearny had occupied Santa Fe and marched on to Los Angeles. Winfield Scott, landing at Veracruz, fought six brilliant battles in six months and led his army of 6,000 into Montezuma's City. For the first time in history, Old Glory flew over a foreign capital. Junior officers Lee, Grant, and McClellan, among others who would become legends in our Civil War, distinguished themselves. But "Sam" Grant openly questioned the morality of the cause. This is an "unholy" war, said Grant, one "of the most unjust ever waged by a stronger against a weaker nation."[14]

Nicholas Trist, a State Department aide sent to conclude the peace, ignored a Polk order to desist and return and negotiated until he brought home the Treaty of Guadalupe-Hidalgo whereby Mexico ceded Texas, the entire Southwest, and California to the United States. To ease the pain of amputation of 1.2 million square miles, more than half of their country, Congress gave Mexico City $15 million, or $12.50 for each square mile of Mexico. Polk fired Trist, but urged and won ratification of Trist's treaty rather than continue what had become an unpopular and, many now believed, an unjust war. Just or not, the fruits were undeniable. Polk had added a vast territory to the United States that rivaled Jefferson's Louisiana Purchase.

In 1853, to smooth out America's new border and acquire land for the Southern Pacific Railroad to cross the continent, James Gadsden, an agent of President Franklin Pierce, himself a veteran of the war, offered Mexico $10 million for a Mesilla Valley the size of Connecticut, Massachusetts, and Rhode Island combined. Santa Anna, again in power, accepted. The U.S. Congress, recoiling at the cost of all this empty land, refused a Mexican offer to sell all of Baja California for another $10 million.[15]

Mexican children are today taught that Texas was stolen from them by rapacious Americans when their country was young and weak, and that the war of 1846–48 was a war of Yankee aggression that cost them half their country and inheritance from Spain. These episodes are as important in Mexican history as the Civil War is in ours.

One hundred and fifty years after Chapultepec, the last battle before Mexico City fell to General Scott, President Clinton laid a wreath in honor of "Los Niños," the boy heroes of Mexico's Military College who are said to have leapt to their deaths from Chapultepec Castle on September 13, 1847, rather than surrender. Reputedly, one of the six, Juan Escutia, wrapped himself in the red, white, and green flag of Mexico rather than yield the national colors to the invading Gringos.

Most Americans have never heard of the battle or read much of the war, but the story of "Los Niños" is required reading in Mexican schools and the names of Juan Escutia and the other five boys are taught to every child. South of the Rio Grande, what to us is the Mexican War is known as the War of the Northern Invasion.

Cinco de Mayo

With America torn by civil war in 1861, France, Britain, and Spain decided to conduct a military expedition into Mexico to collect the debts on which Benito Juárez, the full-blooded Indian who had seized power, had defaulted. The European invasion was a flagrant violation of the Monroe Doctrine. But Lincoln's Union, preoccupied, did nothing. By the end of 1861, it was clear that the French emperor, Napoleon III, was after other game than collecting debts, and the British and Spanish bowed out. As Thomas Bailey writes,

> Napoleon tipped his hand shortly after a Spanish force captured Vera Cruz, in December. . . . Responding . . . to the urgings of Mexican monarchists, he was evidently planning to erect a Latin, Catholic monarchy in Mexico as a dike against the expansionist waves of the Anglo-Saxon Protestant republic to the north. Perhaps most important of all was the fact that a resurrection of France's colonial empire, which even the great Napoleon I had failed to achieve, would win applause from the glory-loving French masses.[16]

However, on May 5, 1862, at Puebla, an outnumbered Mexican army defeated a French force of 6,000, a victory still celebrated as "Cinco de Mayo." The cavalry commander and hero was Porfirio Díaz. But the defeated French did not depart, and after Napoleon had dispatched 30,000 soldiers, the French captured the capital. Lincoln did nothing. When the U.S. consul general in Paris implored Secretary of State William Seward to take some action, Seward admonished him: "We have compromised nothing, surrendered nothing, and I do not propose to surrender anything. But why should we gasconade about Mexico, when we are in a struggle for our own life."[17]

After Appomattox, however, Union veterans began to volunteer to fight alongside the Mexican rebels. Juárez wanted the victorious Union army of 900,000 to intervene, and President Johnson had begun to lean in that direction. At the urging of Grant and Sherman, he sent 50,000 troops to the border under General Philip Sheridan, while Seward sent General John Schofield to Paris with a message for the emperor: "I want you to get your legs under Napoleon's mahogany and tell him he must get out of Mexico."[18]

Napoleon got the message. The French troops departed. But Maximilian, the Hapsburg prince Napoleon had put on the throne as emperor of Mexico, refused to leave "my country." Captured by Juárez, he was put before a firing squad as a lesson to future imperialists.

Maximilian's fate had been foretold by the former queen of France and grandmother of his ambitious wife, Carlotta. The old lady had warned Maximilian, "They will murder you."[19]

U.S.-Mexican relations had never been so warm as in that time when Juárez looked to the Union to liberate his country and America was ready to play a decisive role, asking nothing in return.

Professor Wilson's Tutorials

Juárez died in office. From 1877 to 1911, Mexico was ruled by the hero of Cinco de Mayo, Porfirio Díaz, and prospered as U.S. and foreign companies invested and developed the nation's resources. But in 1911 the Díaz dictatorship, unable to contain a rising nationalism, collapsed. The old president fled and was succeeded by Francisco Madero, a visionary who in turn was overthrown in 1913 by General Victoriano Huerta, who had Madero and his vice president murdered. Shot while trying to escape was the official report. General Huerta then threw 110 members of the Mexican Chamber of Deputies into prison and installed a dictatorship. New to office, a shocked Woodrow Wilson refused to recognize "a government of butchers."[20]

Wilson was alarmed: by 1913, 50,000 Americans lived in Mexico, and the United States had investments of $1 billion, more than all other foreign nations combined. The do-nothing attitude of President William Howard Taft toward Huerta's coup and murderous regime had enraged U.S. newspapers, including the Hearst press, whose owner, coincidentally, "had inherited a ranch in Mexico larger than Rhode Island."[21]

Came then the incident that led to two U.S. interventions. On April 9, 1914, U.S. Marines on shore leave in Tampico were roughed up, arrested, and marched through the streets. They had apparently entered a restricted area. Admiral Henry T. Mayo, commander of the American flotilla, demanded and got an immediate apology. But the admiral wanted more, a twenty-one-gun salute to Old Glory. President Wilson backed him up.

Huerta agreed to salute the U.S. flag, if U.S. warships would fire a return twenty-one-gun salute to the Mexican flag. Believing this would constitute recognition of Huerta's regime, Wilson refused, and when a German ship carrying arms to Huerta was sighted off Veracruz, he ordered the Marines to occupy the port. Nineteen Americans and two hundred Mexicans died in the battle for the city. A British envoy asked Wilson what precisely U.S. policy was. Replied the president, "I am going to teach the South American republics to elect good men."[22]

By August 1914, when World War I broke out, Huerta had fallen and been replaced by one of his commanders, Venustiano Carranza, who was challenged by a former ally, Doroteo Arango, a horse and cattle thief who had taken the name "Pancho Villa." To incite a U.S. intervention he hoped would humiliate and topple Carranza, Villa stopped a Mexican train carrying eighteen American college students who had come under a safe-conduct pass to open a mine. In the massacre of San Ysabel, Villa murdered them in cold blood. He then crossed into New Mexico and, on March 15, 1916, burned Columbus and murdered another seventeen Americans. Senator Henry Ashurst of Arizona called for more "grape shot" and less "grape juice."[23]

Villa's provocations succeeded. Wilson sent General Pershing with a U.S. Army that eventually numbered 12,000 men into Mexico and called up virtually the entire U.S. National Guard, 150,000 men, and sent them to patrol the border. Though Pershing drove 300 miles into Mexico, he never captured the elusive Villa. Between 1915 and 1917, seventy U.S. citizens were slain inside Mexico.[24]

Further exacerbating relations, the German foreign minister, Arthur Zimmermann, sent a telegram to Mexico City, intercepted by the British, who delightedly turned it over to the United States. Zimmermann urged Mexico, should war break out between the United States and Germany, to seize the opportunity to "reconquer the lost territory in New Mexico, Texas and Arizona."[25]

As Henry Kissinger has observed, this was not a brilliant moment in the diplomatic history of the Second Reich. The Zimmermann telegram inflamed U.S. opinion into supporting war on Germany. But before he asked for a declaration of war, Wilson recalled Pershing to lead the U.S. Army in France. Mexico now descended into a long period of anti-Catholic and anti-American revolutionary violence. Not for a generation would the breach with the United States be healed.

In 1938, despite FDR's "Good Neighbor" policy, Mexican president Lazaro Cárdenas nationalized U.S. oil companies, a day still honored in Mexican history. Americans were paid a fraction of what the oil wells were worth. Pemex was born, a state cartel that in the Clinton era would collude with OPEC to run up oil prices to gouge the Americans who had raised $50 billion in 1995 to bail out the bankrupt Zedillo regime in Mexico City.

Good Neighbors?

The point of this brief history: Mexico has historic grievances against the United States. These are taught to its children and felt deeply by tens of millions of Mexicans who believe we robbed their country of half its land. The indoctrination has taken. A Zogby Poll in June 2002 found that when Mexicans were asked, "Do you agree or disagree that the territory of the United States Southwest belongs to Mexico?" 58 percent agreed.[26] Only 28 percent disagreed, while 14 percent, one in seven, were unsure whether California, Texas, New Mexico, and Arizona rightfully belong to Mexico or the United States.

This sense of grievance is embedded in the Mexican consciousness. And in America, there is a reciprocal sense of guilt over what our fathers did, that has been bred into schoolchildren and college students since the 1960s in the institutions that teach many of America's leaders.

Consider again the insight of historian Robert Leckie on the folly of Mexico's inviting Americans to settle in Texas: "Mexico's error . . . was to encourage migration from a neighboring people who were as different from the Mexican people as these two former colonies of Protestant Britain and Catholic Spain could possibly be."

Unlike all other immigrants, Mexicans, by far the largest bloc ever to come to the United States, have an historic claim upon American lands.

La Reconquista

What we did to Mexico, Mexico is doing to us. It is we who are now making the fatal blunder. For we are not talking about several thousand Mexicans entering Texas, but a projected 50 to 60 million people of Mexican ancestry living here by 2050, most of them in Texas, New Mexico, Arizona, and California, lands Mexico regards as stolen. In all four border states, the Hispanic share of the population has risen above 25 percent. In Texas and California, it is 34 percent; in New Mexico, 43 percent. The numbers are soaring in Utah, Colorado, and Nevada, the other states carved out of the territory detached from Mexico by the Treaty of Guadalupe-Hidalgo.

And as Mexicans move in, Americans move on. University of Michigan demographer William Frey and reporter Jonathan Tilove noted in the *New York Times Magazine* for August 20, 1995, that

> For every immigrant who arrives [in a large metropolitan area] a white person leaves. . . .
>
> The trend constitutes a new, larger form of white flight. Unlike in the old version, whites this time are not just fleeing the cities for the suburbs. They are leaving entire metropolitan areas and states—whole regions—for white destinations. And new census estimates indicate that this pattern of flight from big immigration destinations has become even more pronounced in the 90's.[27]

The U.S. Census of 2000 confirmed the findings of Frey and Tilove.

Two decades before, a Mexican writer had come to Los Angeles to marvel at the transformation. After Mexico City, he wrote, Los Angeles is the second largest Mexican city in the world. Like a latter-day Israel Zangwill, author of *The Melting-Pot,* Carlos Loret de Mola saw the future and fell in love with it: "A great region seems to be slowly returning to the jurisdiction of Mexico without the firing of a single shot." The Mexican nationalist merits quoting at length:

A peaceful mass of people, hardworking, carries out slowly and patiently an unstoppable invasion, the most important in human history. You cannot give me a single example of such a large migratory wave by an ant-like multitude, stubborn, unarmed, and carried on in the face of the most powerful and best-armed nation on earth.

The territory lost in the 19th century by a Mexico torn by internal strife . . . seems to be restoring itself through a humble people who go on to settle various zones that once were ours on the old maps.

Land, under any concept of possession, ends up in the hands of those who deserve it. All of us Mexicans should prove ourselves worthy of what we have and what we want.[28]

Paralyzed by guilt, we are inviting *La Reconquista,* the reconquest of the Southwest by Mexico, even as Ferdinand and Isabella effected *La Reconquista* of Spain in 1492 from the Moors who had invaded eight hundred years before. What Mexico's elites have in mind, what they are systematically pursuing, is a sharing of sovereignty in these lost lands and their ultimate recapture, culturally and linguistically, by Mexico, no matter which nation holds title to them.

"We Are Aztlan"

Aztlan is the mythical land out of which the Aztec people came, a millennium ago, before they began the trek south to establish their empire. In history, Aztlan is in northwestern Mexico. In Chicano lore, it is the land from Oregon to California to Texas, stolen by the Americans.

This is myth and fabricated nonsense.

As the historian Robert Ferrell writes,

One cannot stress sufficiently the point that Texas and the other northern territories of Mexico [New Mexico and California] were virtually empty lands, lacking Mexican settlers, and because of the distance lacking almost any control from Mexico City. . . .

Mexican establishments in California, like those in Texas, were pitiful in their poverty and unimportance. If in Texas, there were only about three thousand Mexicans of Spanish origin in the 1830's, there were little more than four thousand in California, a mere handful consisting chiefly of priests and monks about the missions, soldiers employed to keep the Indians submissive, and a few large landowners and cattle raisers. In California, the area of Mexican control never extended north of San Francisco, nor inland beyond the coastal area.[29]

Nevertheless, racial mythology can have consequences.

Consider the student organization MEChA, whose UCLA chapter was chaired, a few years back, by Antonio Villaraigosa, who, in 2005, became mayor of Los Angeles by carrying four out of five Hispanic votes. MEChA stands for *Moviemento Estudiantil Chicano de Aztlan,* the Chicano Student Movement of Aztlan. And what is *El Plan de Aztlan* for which MEChA exists? In its own words, MEChA aims to reclaim the land of their fathers stolen in the "brutal 'gringo' invasion of our territories."[30]

With our heart in our hands and our hands in the soil, we declare the independence of our mestizo nation. We are a bronze people with a bronze culture. Before the world, before all of North America, before all our brothers in the bronze continent, we are a nation, we are a union of free pueblos, we are Aztlan.[31]

In *El Plan*, "Aztlan belongs to those who plant the seeds, water the fields, and gather the crops and not to foreign Europeans. We do not recognize capricious frontiers on the bronze continent." The MEChA slogan is "*Por la Raza todo. Fuera de La Raza nada,*" which translates as "For the race, everything. Outside of the race, nothing."[32] The MEChA slogan seems a conscious echo of the slogan of Mussolini's Fascists: "Everything for the state, nothing outside the state, nothing above the state."

Like African-Americans who demand reparations, MEChA demands "restitution" for "past economic slavery, political exploitation, ethnic and cultural psychological destruction and denial of civil and human rights." "Political Liberation," asserts MEChA, "can only come through independent action on our part, since the two-party system is the same animal with two heads that feed from the same trough. Where we are a majority we will control; where we are a minority we will represent a pressure group; nationally we represent one party: *La Familia de Raza*."[33]

In its constitution, MEChA declares its symbol "shall be the eagle with its wing spread, bearing a *macahuittle* in one claw and a dynamite stick in the other with the lighted fuse in its beak."[34]

MEChA is a Chicano version of Aryan Nations, only it claims four hundred campus chapters across the Southwest and as far away as Ann Arbor and Cornell. With its chauvinism about a "mestizo nation," a "bronze people," "bronze culture," "bronze continent," and "race above all," it is unabashedly racist. That Villaraigosa could become mayor of Los Angeles without having to repudiate MEChA, that Cruz Bustamante could run for governor of California without having to explain his role in this racist organization at

Fresno State, testifies to a truth: America's media is morally intimidated by a minority that can make out credentials as a victim of past discrimination.

As Michelle Malkin notes, MEChA members "have rioted in Los Angeles [and] editorialized that federal immigration 'pigs should be killed, every one' in San Diego. . . ."[35] Nowhere has their ethnic intimidation been more successful than in academia. After years of disruptive MEChA protests, the University of Texas downgraded Texas Independence Day. In 2000, the university held a "private alumni fund-raising event to milk the holiday for money, while according it virtually no public recognition."[36]

A spirit of separatism, nationalism, and irredentism is alive in the barrios. During the Villaraigosa mayoral campaign of 2005, MEChA's slogan was "Los Angeles Today, Alta California Tomorrow."[37] Where MEChA seeks the return of the Southwest to Mexico, Charles Truxillo, professor of Chicano Studies at the University of New Mexico, sees a new Aztlan rising with its capital in L.A. and urges Mexicans to seek it by any means necessary. "We're recolonizing America, so they're afraid of us. It's time to take back what is ours," rants Ricky Sierra of the Chicano National Guard. Jose Angel Gutierrez, a political science professor and director of the Mexican-American Study Center of the University of Texas, told a university crowd: "We have an aging white America. They are not making babies. They are dying. The explosion is in our population. They are shitting in their pants in fear! I love it."[38]

When 500,000 Hispanics massed in downtown Los Angeles in the spring of 2006 to protest any congressional bill to secure America's borders or send illegal aliens back, Americans could have seen a close-up of their rising radicalism, had not the *Los Angeles Times* and local TV covered it up. *Slate* writer Mickey Kaus, who attended the L.A. demonstration, called the *Times*'s coverage "propagandistic." Columnist Malkin wrote on what went largely unreported:

Demonstrators gleefully defaced photos of President Bush and urged supporters to "Stop the Nazis!" Los Angeles talk show host Tammy Bruce reported that protesters burned American flags and waved placards of the North American continent with America crossed out. . . .

One of the largest, boldest banners visible from aerial shots of the rally read, "THIS IS STOLEN LAND." Others blared: "CHICANO POWER" and "BROWN IS BEAUTIFUL." Thugs with masks flashed gang signs on the steps of L.A. City Hall. . . . Young people raised their fists in defiance, clothed in T-shirts bearing radical left guerrilla Che Guevara's face and Aztlan emblems.[39]

In Mexico, Albert Tinoco, a reporter on the Televisa network, exulting over the L.A. "megamarcha," remarked, "With all due respect to Uncle Sam, this shows that Los Angeles has never stopped being ours."[40]

One of Mexico's most respected pundits, Sergio Sarmiento, seeing illegal aliens marching defiantly under Mexican flags through the streets of America's greatest cities in the scores and hundreds of thousands, wrote that

[T]he United States now has no way of turning back the clock . . . with 11 million illegal aliens in the country, it is already too late. . . . If it is true, as some have said, that Mexicans have begun the *reconquista* of the territory that the United States took by force from Mexico between 1835 and 1848, they have been able to do this, thanks to the fact that the Americans themselves have permitted it.[41]

Small wonder that *La Voz de Aztlan*, the radical and racist voice of the Aztlan movement in America, was exultant: "What does the immense success of 'La Gran Marcha' mean to Mexicanos and other Latinos? It simply means that we now have the numbers, the political will and the organizational skills to direct our own destinies and not be subservient to the White and Jewish power structures."[42]

Among the projects *La Voz de Aztlan* urged this new political force to support was Mayor Villaraigosa's "bold move to wrestle control of the [Los Angeles Unified School District] from a Jewish dominated school board and a White superintendent that are just fleecing the schools. . . ."[43]

Now, this may be Corona talk in the cantina, but authoritative voices are sounding the same notes. Mexico's consul general Jose Pescador Osuna remarked in 1998, "Even though I am saying this part serious, part joking, I think we are practicing *La Reconquista* in California."[44]

In 2001, the award-winning novelist Elena Poniatowski, who came to Mexico as a child during World War II, told an audience in Caracas:

> Mexico is recovering the territories yielded to the United States by means of migratory tactics. . . . The common people—the poor, the dirty, the lice-ridden, the cockroaches are advancing on the United States, a country that needs to speak Spanish because it has 33.5 million Hispanics who are imposing their culture . . . it fills me full of joy because the Hispanics can have an ever-greater influence all the way from Patagonia to Alaska.[45]

As Ms. Poniatowski and Mexican chauvinists were reveling in the reconquest of our Southwest, what was President Bush saying?

Addressing the Hispanic Chamber of Commerce of Albuquerque on August 15, 2001, Bush declared: "Mexico is a friend of America. Mexico is our neighbor. And we want our neighbors to succeed. . . . And that's why it's so important for us to tear down our barriers and walls that might separate Mexico from the United States."[46] For five years of his presidency, Bush would aid the *reconquista* by refusing to do his duty to defend his country from Ms. Poniatowski's "migratory" invasion.

As for Mexican migrants in the USA, why should they not have greater loyalty to the land of their birth than to a foreign country they broke into to find work? Why should patriotic Mexicans not dream of *La Reconquista*?

The New Border War

As we have seen, a few years after Americans migrated to Texas and began to outnumber Mexicans there, a struggle for control began. In 1836, it erupted into war. Today, a new border war has begun with the first signs of an "intifada" to retake control of the Southwest.

Already, the demographic sea change has engendered a new ethnic chauvinism. When the U.S. soccer team played Mexico in Los Angeles Coliseum a few years back, the crowd showered the U.S. team and its fans with water bombs, beer, bottles, and garbage. "The Star-Spangled Banner" was hooted and jeered. Mexicans bring these attitudes into the country with them, for when the U.S. team played Mexico in Guadalajara in 2004, for a spot in the Olympics, 60,000 Mexican fans chanted: "Osama, Osama," as Mexico took control of the game. The U.S. goalkeeper seemed relieved. "Since Mexico won convincingly, every fan walked out cheering," said D. J. Countess, "I've been hit with bags of urine, limes and batteries."[47]

In early 2006, Zogby International, in conjunction with a Mexican polling firm, did a survey of attitudes of 1,000 Americans and 1,000 Mexicans. Americans viewed Mexicans positively, with 78 percent saying Mexicans were hardworking and 44 percent seeing them as tolerant. Americans hold these positive views because many of us went to Catholic and public schools where Mexican-American kids were not uncommon, and where we have encountered Mexican immigrants we have found them to be a courteous, friendly, hard-working, likable people.

The Mexicans hold a markedly different view of us.

"Mexicans think Americans are neither hard workers, nor honest," wrote the Zogby authors: "They see them as racist, intolerant and moderately law-abiding." Only one in six Mexicans thought Americans are honest and one in four said we were hardworking, while 62 percent said the United States is wealthier because we "exploit other people's wealth." Three out of every four Mexicans, 73 percent, said Americans were racists.[48]

In New Mexico, a state that is 43 percent Hispanic, a resolution was introduced in the legislature in 2001 to rename the state "Nuevo Mexico," the name it carried before entering the Union. When the bill was defeated in committee, sponsor Representative Miguel Garcia told reporters "covert racism" may have been the reason, the same racism, he said, that was behind originally naming the state New Mexico.[49]

Several years ago, while George Bush was governor, the Texas town of El Cenizo declared Spanish to be its official language, ordered all documents written and town business done in Spanish, and made cooperation with U.S. immigration authorities a firing offense. El Cenizo had de facto seceded from the USA. And it is in these border towns that another battle, a shooting war, has begun.[50]

The "Colombianization" of Mexico

"As I walked out on the streets of Laredo," begins the mournful melody, "I spied a poor cowboy wrapped in white linen,/Wrapped in white linen as cold as the clay." Taken from an Irish ballad that tells a similar story, "Streets of Laredo" is known as "The Cowboy's

Lament." But the romance of Laredo is gone. For a few yards across the border is Nuevo Laredo, which less resembles the setting of a cowboy ballad than a Sunni town in Anbar Province.

Two powerful drug gangs have been conducting an all-out war over Nuevo Laredo, through which pass six thousand trucks a day and 40 percent of Mexico's exports. The gangs are battling for control of the principal entry port for cocaine and marijuana into the United States. From January 1 to October 15, 2005, 135 people were murdered in this town of 350,000.[51] The dead included police reporter Guadalupe Garcia, gunned down outside her radio station; a city council member; thirteen police officers; and the police chief, who was assassinated within twenty-four hours of his appointment.

Mexican federal authorities then moved to purge the city police. As Ted Galen Carpenter of the Cato Institute notes: "After being required to take polygraph exams, 305 of the 765 police officers [on the Nuevo Laredo force] were dismissed. Indeed, 41 of them were arrested for attacking the federal police when those units arrived in the city."[52] Thirty Americans were kidnapped or murdered in Nuevo Laredo over the same period, writes Dave Adams, Latin American correspondent for the *St. Petersburg Times,*

> April (2005) saw 11 murders, assassination attempts and a shootout . . . on the international bridge. On April 10, traffickers, armed with assault rifles and a rocket-propelled grenade ambushed a police convoy barely 10 blocks from city hall. Four policemen and a passer-by were wounded. Investigators found more than 300 shell casings at the scene.[53]

Texas governor Rick Perry rushed police reinforcements and equipment to assist Texas and Mexican authorities in the line of fire.

"I offer this plan, not because it is the state's responsibility to control the federal border, but because the state of Texas cannot wait for the federal government to implement needed border security measures," said Perry, in a stinging rebuke to the man in charge of U.S. border security, his predecessor as governor of Texas, George W. Bush.[54]

Early in 2006, gunmen blasted their way into the newsroom of *El Mañana,* the newspaper in Nuevo Laredo, and launched a grenade as they fired assault weapons. Night shift reporter Jaime Orozco was shot three times.[55] Jerry Seper, the investigative reporter for *The Washington Times* sent to cover the border war, had written in October 2005 that much of the murderous violence

> has been attributed by U.S. and Mexican authorities to a renegade band of Mexican military deserters known as the Zetas. Trained in the U.S. as an elite force of anti-drug commandos, they have since signed on as mercenaries and recruiters for Mexican drug traffickers.
>
> As many as 200 Zetas, including former Mexican police officers, are thought to be involved in the violence. Their hub . . . is Nuevo Laredo. . . . Authorities say the Zetas control the city. . . . [56]

Up to ten Zetas operate in Texas as assassins, protecting the $10-million-a-day drug trade, Seper reports. The Justice Department believes the Zetas are moving into Florida and California.

Ted Carpenter sums up the situation inside the nation with which we share one of the longest and least defended borders on earth:

> For years, people both inside and outside Mexico have worried that the country might descend into the maelstrom of corruption and violence that has long plagued the chief drug-source country in the Western Hemisphere, Colombia. There

are growing signs that the "Colombianization" of Mexico is now becoming a reality.[57]

Mexican Military Incursions

America's once sleepy border is now the scene of confrontations every day from Brownsville to San Diego. Even the Mexican army has begun to show contempt. The U.S. Department of Homeland Security (DHS) reports that, in the last decade, 216 military incursions were conducted by the Mexican army into California, Arizona, and Texas.

In 2000, two truckloads of Mexican soldiers barreled through a barbed-wire fence, pursued a Border Patrol vehicle and two officers on horseback, while firing shots. In July 2005, two Border Patrol agents were ambushed and shot near Nogales, Arizona, by assailants in black commando clothing who escaped into Mexico. Border Patrol agents believe Mexican army units and retired military collaborate with drug cartels. In January 2006, Seper reported that the Border Patrol had "warned agents in Arizona of incursions into the United States by Mexican soldiers 'trained to escape, evade and counterambush' if detected. . . . The warning to Border Patrol agents in Tucson, Ariz., comes after increased sightings of what authorities described as heavily armed Mexican military units on the U.S. side of the border."[58]

The Mexican Embassy denied its soldiers had crossed the border. But twenty-seven-year Border Patrol veteran T. J. Bonner, who heads the 10,000-member National Border Patrol Council, retorted, "Give me a break. Intrusions by the Mexican military to protect drug loads happen all the time and represent a significant threat to the agents. Why else would they be in the area, firing at federal agents in the United States?"[59]

DHS chief Michael Chertoff brushed off Border Patrol complaints, saying incursions were mistakes and reports were overblown. But late in January 2006, Texas Department of Public Safety troopers, chasing three SUVs believed to be carrying drugs, ran into ten heavily armed soldiers. According to Chief Deputy Mike Doyal of the Hudspeth County Sheriff's Office, the Mexican troops had mounted .50-caliber machine guns from their Humvees on the ground, 200 yards inside the United States. Said Doyal: "It's been so bred into everyone not to start an international incident with Mexico that it's been going on for years. When you're up against mounted machine guns, what can you do? Who wants to pull the trigger first? Certainly not us."[60]

When Mexico insisted the Americans were wrong, that it was drug traffickers who crossed the border, Hudspeth County Sheriff Arvin West was having none of it: "There is no doubt in my mind there was Mexican military involved. I have seen it too many times over the years." T. J. Bonner called for the U.S. military to be stationed on the border to deal with the intruders: "If there's an incursion, let the chips fall where they may. Let them do what they were trained to do."[61]

Late in 2005, the Department of Homeland Security alerted the Border Patrol that alien smugglers planned to hire *Mara Salvatrucha* gang members as "contract killers" to murder U.S. agents interfering in their business.[62] But rather than securing our bleeding border, U.S. soldiers secure the borders of Korea and Kosovo, where no threat exists to the United States of America.

8

The Aztlan Plot

The march of Latin America to the United States shouldn't
be understood as a wave of anger or revolutionary passion,
but more of a peaceful conquest.[1]
—FR. FLORENCIO M. RIGONI, Mexican Bishops' Conference, 1986

We're changing you into a Latin country.[2]
—GABRIEL GARCIA MARQUEZ (circa 1991)

If the border patrol agent finds you, try again.[3]
—ERNESTO RUFFO APPEL, Mexican Commissioner for Northern Border Affairs, 2001

This is a "mind-boggling concept," said CNN anchor Lou Dobbs.
It must cause Americans to think our political and academic elites
have "gone utterly mad."[4] What had detonated the mild-mannered
Dobbs?

Dr. Robert Pastor, vice chair of the Council on Foreign Relations
(CFR) Task Force on North America, had just called for erasing the
U.S. borders with Mexico and Canada and merging the three nations
into a new North American Community, stretching from Prudhoe
Bay to Guatemala. Pastor had promoted this vision before a sub-
committee of the Senate Committee on Foreign Relations.

Under the Pastor plan, the crisis of millions of aliens breaching
our border with Mexico every year would be solved by eliminating

the border and legalizing the invasion. We would give up defending the Rio Grande.

"The best way to assure security is not at our borders with Canada and Mexico," Pastor instructed the senators:

We are thinking too small. . . . What we need to do is forge a new North American Community. . . . Instead of stopping North Americans on the borders, we ought to provide them with a secure, biometric Border Pass that would ease transit across the border like an E-Z pass permits our cars to speed through tolls.[5]

In the Pastor-CFR plan, all barriers between America and Mexico would be torn down and travel made as free as it is between Virginia and Maryland. A continental customs union would be created, with a common external tariff. What Pastor and CFR seek is "economic integration" of the United States, Mexico, and Canada. North-South highways and railways would be built to weld the three countries together as the Union was welded together by the Northern Pacific, Union Pacific, and Southern Pacific, and by Eisenhower's Interstate Highway system.

The way to end illegal immigration is to stop defending the U.S. border, said Pastor, and by making "Mexico's economy grow faster than that of the U.S." Pastor conceded that creating a North American Union will require "a new consciousness" among Americans.[6]

Hearing news of the Boston Tea Party, Patrick Henry declared, "The distinctions between Virginians, Pennsylvanians, New Yorkers, and New Englanders are no more. I am not a Virginian, but an American!" Echoes Dr. Pastor: We must cease to see ourselves as Americans, and begin to see ourselves as part of a continental community: North Americans.

Toward One World

Even in economic terms, this idea seems suicidal. With 40 percent of Mexico's 106 million people earning less than $2 a day, while the U.S. minimum wage is $41 a day and $54 in California, Mexicans would pour across the border in the millions within months.

But the Pastor plan is about more than money. For generations U.S. and foreign elites have sought to diminish American sovereignty and dilute our national identity. What makes the CFR plan remarkable is that those out to abolish America are now out of the closet. The penultimate step to world government, a North American Union built on the model of the European Union—which would one day merge with it in a World Union of Nations and Peoples—is on the table.

This is where NAFTA was designed to lead us. As too few patriots appreciate, free trade—with its lure of a cornucopia of consumer goods at the cheapest possible price—is the Pied Piper to world government. For any continental common market must call into existence institutions with the power to enforce its rules. These evolve into regimes. So history teaches.

Hamilton's free trade zone, which tied together thirteen independent states in a common market, ensured the rise of a central government that displaced the states and robbed them of their independence. State sovereignty has diminished every decade since 1789. When South Carolina threatened to break free of the Union over northern protectionism and the Tariff of Abomination, Jackson called it sedition and threatened to hang the leaders of his native state—foremost among whom was his own vice president, John Calhoun. When the South seceded in 1860–61, Abraham Lincoln decided they were no longer free to go.

Bismarck's customs union, the *Zollverein*, gradually crushed the old Germany of free cities, principalities, duchies, and kingdoms, producing the Prussian-dominated Second Reich. Jean Monnet's European Coal and Steel Community evolved into the European Economic Community, then into the European Community and to-day's European Union, which is evolving into the New Europe of the faceless bureaucrats of Brussels.

Like Pastor, the Mexican regime sees the EU as its model for North America. In a 2002 speech in Madrid, Vicente Fox took note of American resistance to open borders and loss of sovereignty, and laid out his vision: "Eventually, our long-range objective is to establish with the United States . . . an ensemble of connections and institutions similar to those created by the European Union, with the goal of attending to future themes as important as . . . the freedom of movement of capital, goods, services and *persons*. The new framework we wish to construct is inspired in the example of the European Union."[7]

Fox warned his European allies that an obstacle blocked their path: "[W]e have to confront . . . what I dare to call the Anglo-Saxon prejudice against the establishment of supra-national organizations."[8]

Now, an "ensemble of connections" was how Gulliver was tied down on the beach by the Lilliputians, who then conscripted him to do their labors and fight their wars. Jorge Castañeda, the foreign minister of Mexico, rather liked the Lilliput analogy:

"I like very much the metaphor of Gulliver, of ensnarling the giant," Castañeda told Mexican journalists in a November 2002 interview. "Tying it down with nails, with thread, with 20,000 nets that bog it down: these nets being norms, principles, resolutions, agreements, and bilateral, regional and international covenants."[9]

At Madrid, Fox underscored the essential element of the post-NAFTA agenda: Absolute freedom of movement for persons, as well as goods, between Mexico and the United States. Foreign Secretary Luis Ernesto Débrez put it succinctly in April 2005. What Mexico is about is "complete integration," a merger of the two nations.[10]

A hidden motive of Fox and his collaborators is greed—to get their hands on America's wealth. For the EU mandates huge cash transfers from rich member states to poor member states. Under a North American Union, the United States would not only have to absorb tens of millions of Mexico's unemployed poor and provide them with all the social welfare benefits of U.S. citizens, but transfer scores of billions of dollars yearly to Mexican politicians for development of their country, until the standard of living of the two nations was comparable. As Dr. Pastor said, for the North American Union to work, we must make "Mexico's economy grow faster than that of the U.S."

Since Mexico's per capita GDP of $5,000 is a fraction of America's, which is more than $40,000, and the income gap between us is the largest between any two large neighbors on earth, U.S. wealth transfers to Mexico City would have to be enormous—and eternal. Mexico's politicians would be awash in U.S. foreign aid until the end of time. Fox's enthusiasm for Pastor's project is easily understood.

The Aztlan Strategy

The temptation is to think that Fox, who heads a country 46 percent of whose people say they would like to live in the United States, is but another failed Third World politician prattling on for the benefit of globalists who have been beavering away on their impossible dream for generations.

The reality is otherwise. Fox & friends are far closer than all but a few realize to making inevitable a North American Union where American sovereignty is dissipated and the republic is no more.

The great leap forward toward Fox's vision was NAFTA, the North American Free Trade Agreement that Henry Kissinger called "the most creative step toward a new world order" since World War II and the "architecture of a new international system." NAFTA removed the trade and tariff barriers between the two nations. U.S. transnationals moved swiftly to resite factories in Mexico to shed high-wage U.S. workers and exploit the low-wage labor south of the border. Economic integration of America and Mexico had begun.

NAFTA also created trinational tribunals to decide trade disputes, against which U.S. citizens and American companies would have no appeal in U.S. courts. The foundation of the North American Union was in place. As the Hudson Institute scholar John Fonte writes,

> what is envisioned by Mexican elites and their American allies is not (as some would have it) a crude attempt at *reconquista* (or a reconquest of the American Southwest), but a sophisticated and long-term strategy similar to the approach promoted by leaders of the European Union and other global and transnational elites, of slowly and steadily building a series of institutions and structures that would lead to greater and greater political integration in North America—and thus, by definition, a weakening of American constitutional sovereignty.[11]

Fonte is correct about the Fox agenda of "building a series of institutions and structures" leading to "greater political integration" of North America. He is wrong in his airy dismissal of any Mexican idea of *reconquista*. For Fox's EU strategy runs parallel to a far more ambitious strategy that Mexico has pursued for a decade.

This strategy aims directly at a reannexation of the Southwest, not militarily, but ethnically, linguistically, and culturally, through transfer of millions of Mexicans into the United States and a migration of "Anglos" out of the lands Mexico lost in 1848. In California, the project is well advanced. As native-born Californians depart, Hispanics move toward dominance. As Mexicans come in the millions—one in six is already here—they are urged to seek U.S. citizenship to advance the agenda of the mother country. The near-term goal of Mexico City is to attain that leverage over U.S. policy toward Mexico that the Jewish community has over U.S. policy toward Israel and Cuban-Americans have over U.S. policy toward Castro. Mexicans leaders have said as much.[12]

The presence in the United States of a vast diaspora that retains its emotional and blood ties to Mexico provides Mexico City with immense leverage to advance an agenda that entails the steady diminution of U.S. sovereignty and economic and political merger of the United States with Mexico. The marches against Proposition 187 under a "sea of Mexican flags," the "Grand March" of half a million Hispanics in Los Angeles for amnesty on May Day 2006, that shocked U.S. politicians with its display of Hispanic power, show how potent is the machine Mexico is building inside the United States. In Mexico, where anti-Americanism is rife, the Aztlan project has ecumenical support. As Hispanics walked off their jobs and boycotted shops and stores in the United States on May Day, 2006, thousands marched in solidarity in the streets of Mexico City:

Even Subcommandante Marcos, the leader of the Zapatista rebels who rarely emerges from his jungle hideout, joined the march through Mexico City . . . protected by a ring of Zapatista militants, some wielding machetes.

They marched alongside union workers celebrating Labor Day, radicals waving banners showing Russian revolutionary heroes Karl Marx and Vladimir Lenin, middle-class nannies and some protesters dressed in clown costumes and banging drums.[13]

On the *reconquista,* Mexicans from Chiapas rebels to Communists to conservatives are united.

The decisive step in the strategy was the decision of the Zedillo regime to change the constitution to allow Mexican-Americans to regain Mexican citizenship. This change was completed in 1998. Since then, U.S. citizens of Mexican ancestry have been encouraged to renew their ties to Mexico, become dual citizens, and participate in Mexican as well as American politics and elections.

In the early postcolonial period after 1945, Third World regimes looked on multinational companies as agents of a new imperialism, and on their young who departed for the West as defectors. Third World rulers behave more sagely today. They compete for Western investment. They provide incentives for Western companies to transfer factories and technology and to train local workers. The near-term goal is to have the First World modernize Third World industries to compete in Western markets. The long-term goal is to make the Third World the producers upon whom their former masters depend for the necessities of national life.

Regimes like Mexico's now look on citizens who leave to work or study in the United States as agents of influence, a fifth column inside the belly of the beast. Mexico's elite sees Mexican-Americans in a new light, as loyalists in exile. In 1995, Zedillo was quoted in the *New York Times* as telling a gathering of U.S. politicians of Mexican descent in Dallas, "You're Mexicans—Mexicans who live north of the border."[14]

University of Texas professor Rodolfo O. de la Garza described the purpose of the new policy: "The Mexican Government wants them [Mexican-Americans] to defend Mexico's interests here in the United States."[15] In 1997, Fonte himself wrote,

> Zedillo addressed the annual convention of the National Council of La Raza in Chicago, the first time a Mexican President spoke before a major Latino-American organization. According to the *Copley News Service*: "In a stirring address, delivered in impeccable English to a crowd of more than 2,000, Zedillo evoked feelings of patriotism and pride in Mexican roots." He told the La Raza conventioneers, "I have proudly affirmed that the Mexican nation extends beyond the territory enclosed by its borders. . . ."[16]

Carlos Gonzalez Gutierrez, head of the Institute of Mexicans Abroad, explained the new vision in the fall of 2005: "The basic concept is that the Mexican nation goes beyond the borders that contain Mexico. You can feel part of our nation without being on our territory."[17]

In short, "the Mexican nation" extends into the United States.

Vicente Fox echoed Zedillo. Visiting Chicago on June 16, 2004, the Mexican president declared, "We are Mexicans that live in our territories and we are Mexicans that live in other territories. In reality there are 120 million people that live together and are working together to construct a nation."[18] Fox sees Mexican-Americans as Mexicans first. His regime has begun a campaign to recapture their loyalty and allegiance, and the forty-seven Mexican consulates in the United States promote the Fox agenda of assuring that even in America, those of Mexican blood stay loyal to Mexico: "Each of Mexico's 47 consulates (a number that expands nearly every year) has a mandate to introduce Mexican textbooks into schools with significant Hispanic populations. The Mexican consulate in Los Angeles showered nearly 100,000 textbooks on 1,500 schools in the Los Angeles Unified School District this year alone. Hundreds of thousands have gone to school districts across the country."[19]

These history texts indoctrinate Mexican-American children in the history of the Mexican War as seen from the Santa Anna point of view. Heather Mac Donald writes, "The textbook [provided by Mexican officials] concludes by celebrating Mexican patriotic symbols, the flag, the currency, and the national anthem. 'We love our country because it is ours,' the primer says."[20]

This then is the Aztlan Strategy: endless migration from Mexico north, the Hispanicization of the American Southwest, and dual citizenship for all Mexican-Americans. The goals: Erase the border. Grow the influence, through Mexican-Americans, over how America disposes of her wealth and power. Gradually circumscribe the sovereignty of the United States. Lastly, economic and political merger of the nations in a binational union. And in the nuptial agreement, a commitment to share the wealth and power.

Stated bluntly, the Aztlan Strategy entails the end of the United States as a sovereign, self-sufficient, independent republic, the passing away of the American nation. They are coming to conquer us.

Mexican-American, But Mexican First

On July 16, 2002, the Web site of the Mexican government stated that Juan Hernandez, a U.S. citizen born in Fort Worth of a Mexican father and American mother, had been "commissioned to bring a strong, and clear message from the President [Fox] to Mexicans abroad—Mexico is one nation of 123 million—100 million who live in Mexico and 23 million who live in the United States—and most importantly to say that although far, they are not alone."[21]

Earlier, on August 23, 2001, Hernandez had declared in El Paso, "we are a united nation . . . 100 million within the borders [of Mexico] and 23 million who live in the United States."[22] The Mexican regime considers all persons of Mexican blood to be part of the nation and is resolved to retain or regain their loyalty, even if they were born American citizens and have sworn allegiance to the United States. In their campaign to subvert the loyalty of Mexican-Americans, Fox & friends have allies among our own multiculturalists. When Fox met with George Bush in 2001, Hernandez was at his side. His assignment: Organize and mobilize Mexican-Americans. As Stanley Renshon, perhaps America's foremost expert on dual loyalties and dual allegiances, writes, "What is he [Hernandez] mobilizing them to do? In an interview with Ted Koppel, he made it quite clear: He wants Mexican Americans in the United States to think 'Mexico First. . . . I want the third generation, the seventh generation, I want them all to think Mexico First.' "[23]

Columnist Bruce Fein notes that Hernandez, who headed the Office for Mexicans Abroad from 2000 to 2002, told the *Denver Post* that Mexican immigrants "are going to keep one foot in Mexico" and "are not going to assimilate in the sense of dissolving into not being Mexican."[24]

Hernandez's assignment was to ensure that Mexican-Americans and Mexican immigrants who take an oath of allegiance to the United States do not let loyalty to America supersede their higher loyalty. Adds Bruce Fein, "Mexican officials have candidly acknowledged that offering Americans of Mexican ancestry Mexican citizenship aims to weaken their attachment to the United States."[25] As columnist Georgie Anne Geyer wrote in April 2006, when hundreds of thousands of Mexicans marched under Mexican flags to force Congress to grant them amnesty and citizenship, what is

happening with illegals in America—the riots, the refusal to become American while demanding all the rights of committed citizens, the desperate hanging on to "Mexicanness"—is not accidental. It is the result of careful and cynical plans on the part of the Mexican government to develop its own constituency inside American society—and to keep it forever Mexican.

The closest comparison to what Mexico is about today in the United States, writes Geyer, is the German-American *Bund* of the 1930s.[26]

America as Safety Net

Another reason Mexico must retain an open border is regime survival. America must continue to accept the millions of Mexico's poor and jobless lest these *Misérables,* full of resentment at a series of failed regimes, foment a new Mexican revolution. Fox's answer to insurrections of the rural poor in places like Chiapas is: Send them north and let Bush and the Gringos take care of them.

By pushing her poor into the United States, Mexico relieves herself of the burden of providing for their welfare and receives a bonanza of billions in the remittances Mexican workers in the States send back to support their destitute families. The figure has been estimated at $16 billion a year, the second highest source, after oil, of Mexico's hard currency.[27]

America has become the safety valve for an exploding population of 106 million that Mexico is unable to employ or provide for. Fox's national security adviser, Adolfo Zinser, conceded that Mexico's "economic policy is dependent on unlimited emigration to the United States."[28] If Mexico's misgoverned people cannot escape, they will rebel. Mexico uses America as a dumping ground for her discontented millions.

The "onetime Communist supporter" and Yanqui-baiting academic Jorge Castañeda, Fox's first foreign minister, warned years ago in the *Atlantic Monthly*: Any American "effort to cut back immigration from the south by sealing the border . . . will make social peace in the barrios and pueblos of Mexico untenable. . . . Some Americans dislike immigration, but there is very little they can do about it!"[29] If the U.S. border is sealed and the invasion is halted, Mexico City stares revolution in the face.

Unfolding of the Aztlan Plot

Thus, not only has President Fox's regime failed to help secure the border, it is abetting the invasion. To Fox, Mexicans who cross into the United States illegally are "heroes."[30] His government has prepared brochures on how they can evade the Border Patrol, where they can go to pick up documents, how they can sign up for welfare. In January 2006, Mexico's National Human Rights Commission (HRC) was caught preparing 70,000 maps for border crossers. "The only thing we are trying to do is warn them of the risks they face and where to get water, so they don't die," protested Mauricio Farah of the HRC.[31] A year earlier, Mexico had distributed a "32-page manual in comic book format for easy comprehension, titled *The Guide for the Mexican Migrant,* with tips on how to cross the border and then evade detection."[32] When even the Bush White House expressed outrage, the Fox regime stopped issuing the maps.

Mexico interferes with impunity and without protest in U.S. internal affairs. Mexican consuls campaigned against Propositions 187 and 227 in California. The latter restricted bilingual education in state public schools. Mexican agents fought Proposition 200 in Arizona, that requires proof of citizenship before becoming eligible for welfare. Mexican consuls routinely issue "matricula consular" cards to illegals. As Mexicans here legally have passports, visas, or green cards, there is only one purpose for the "matriculas": assure the permanence of the invasion. Some 4.7 million cards have been issued since 2000.[33]

Mexican lobbyists work state capitals to have driver's licenses issued to illegal aliens and illegals made eligible for "in-state" tuition rates at state colleges. In school appearances and public speeches, Mexican consuls urge loyalty to Mexico first and the preservation of Mexican culture. Wherever they encounter U.S. citizens of Mexican ancestry, Mexican consuls preach against assimilation and Americanization. And they are succeeding.

Not only does California recognize Cinco de Mayo, which celebrates a small Mexican victory over French troops when 600,000 Americans were dying in our Civil War, but the Golden State has made March 31, the birthday of the Latino leader of the state's farm workers, Cesar Chavez, a holiday. Texas, Arizona, and New Mexico have done the same. In San Jose, a statue of Thomas Fallon, the Union officer who captured the city in the Mexican War, was set aside as a statue of the Aztec serpent god Quetzacoatl, who is to return and rule, went up in Cesar Chavez Plaza. Governor Davis allocated $400,000 for another statue of Quetzacoatl in Los Angeles.[34]

La Reconquista is not to be accomplished by force of arms, as was the U.S. annexation of the Southwest and California in 1848. It is to be carried out by a nonviolent invasion and cultural transformation of that huge slice of America into a Mexamerican borderland, where the dominant culture is Hispanic and Anglos will feel alienated and begin to emigrate, as, indeed, they already have—back over the mountains their fathers and grandfathers crossed generations ago. Each year now, 250,000 native-born Californians pack up and leave forever in what demographer William Frey calls the "flight from diversity."[35] Meanwhile, since 2000, a million new illegal aliens, almost all Mexicans, have arrived to make Los Angeles home.

"California is going to be a Hispanic state," said Mario Obledo, the cofounder of MALDEF, "and anyone who doesn't like it should leave. They should go back to Europe."[36] In 1998, Obledo was awarded the Medal of Freedom by President Bill Clinton.

Immigrants of a Different Kind

Given the history of U.S.-Mexican relations, there are profound differences in attitudes between the immigrants who came from Europe, carrying a burning desire to be part of the American people, and today's immigrants, mostly illegal and mostly from Mexico. With one-sixth of all people of Mexican ancestry here and half a million more entering every year, Americans must understand these crucial differences.

First, the number coming from Mexico is larger than from any other country in history. In the 1990s, people of Mexican ancestry here grew by 7 million, or 50 percent, to 21 million. That 7 million exceeded the number that any nation on earth previously sent to America over four centuries. It does not include the 6 million Hispanics who refused to give census takers their nation of origin. By midcentury, an estimated 102 million Hispanics will be in the United States, more than half of them of Mexican ancestry.

Though Mexican immigrants have begun spreading out across the country, the greatest concentration remains in the Southwest, a region that Mexicans have been taught and believe is theirs by right. In Texas and California, Hispanics already make up 34 percent of the population and a higher percentage of public school enrollment. In New Mexico, 43 percent of the people are of Hispanic descent.

In Clark County, home of Las Vegas, the fastest-growing big city in America, Hispanics who numbered 85,000 in 1990 exceeded 375,000 by 2004. Of far greater significance, writes *Las Vegas Sun* columnist Hal Rothman, there are nearly 100,000 Hispanic kids in county schools, 35 percent of the total, and Spanish-surnamed kids are a majority of the new students entering each year. Rothman issued this warning to his city and country:

> In the recent chaos in France and Australia, we have seen how societies that fail to integrate minority populations pay. . . .
>
> The United States remains the best example of a polyglot nation; simply put, we bring all kinds of people under the tent better than anybody on Earth. . . . The problem is we're not doing it in Latino Las Vegas. . . . Latinos are the future. Their population has grown so quickly that the town, like the nation, is only beginning to recognize its significance, much less come to grips with it.
>
> That oblivious attitude does not change reality; after Miami and Los Angeles, Las Vegas will become the third American city to overwhelmingly speak Spanish.[37]

To assure assimilation, the Founding Fathers wanted to prevent the concentration of immigrants in port cities and spread them out among the people. In a letter to John Adams, President Washington deplored the situation in which newcomers would remain isolated in immigrant enclaves and cling to their old ways:

> . . . the policy . . . of its [immigration] taking place in a body (I mean settling them in a body) may be much questioned; for, by so doing, they retain the Language, habits and principles (good or bad) which they bring with them. Whereas by an intermixture with our people, they, or their descendants, get assimilated to our customs, measures and laws: in a word soon become one people.[38]

Before the rise of multiculturalism, America's leaders insisted that immigrants learn our language and way of life. Madison wanted to exclude any "persons unlikely to 'incorporate [themselves] in our society.' "[39]

But many Mexicans are not assimilating, they are self-segregating, forming their own towns within our cities, maintaining their language and identifying with one another, not America.

Not only do Mexicans come from a different culture, they are, 85 percent of them, mestizo or Amerindian. History teaches that separate races take even longer to integrate. Our 60 million citizens of German descent are fully assimilated, but millions of African, Latin American, and Caribbean descent are not. For some peoples, assimilation is a process of generations. For others, it has not yet occurred. And Latin elites intend that it shall not. Instead, America is to be changed. As the novelist and Nobel laureate Gabriel García Márquez puts it: "The great power of Latin America is its culture. We don't spend a dime trying to penetrate culturally; yet, we're changing the United States. . . . We're changing the language, the food, the music, the way of being. We're changing you into a Latin country."[40]

At least 6 million Mexicans are here illegally. They broke the law to get in. They break it every day to stay here. This wholesale trampling on U.S. law and the constant lies illegals must tell to stay here and to stay employed engender a contempt for the law and the moral authority of the United States.

Unlike the immigrants of a century ago, who bade farewell to their native lands forever when they boarded the ships, for Mexicans the mother country is only hours away. Millions have no desire to become Americans or to learn English. Why should they? Mexico is their home. They have come here to work and, rather than assimilate, create Little Mexicos in U.S. cities, as Cuban refugees have created Little Havana in Miami. Only there are ten to twenty times as many people of Mexican descent here as Cubans. With its Spanish-language radio and TV programs, newspapers, movies, and magazines, the Mexican diaspora has created a separate culture and is becoming a separate nation within a nation—inside the United States. And that is how Zedillo and Fox see Mexican-Americans—as Mexicans first.

Samuel P. Huntington, author of *The Clash of Civilizations,* calls migration "the central issue of our time." He separates immigrants into "converts," who come to convert to our way of life, and "sojourners," who come to work a few years and return home. "New immigrants," he writes, "are neither converts nor sojourners. They go back and forth between California and Mexico, maintaining dual identities and encouraging family members to join them."[41] About the 1 to 2 million aliens arrested each year breaching the U.S. border, Huntington warns:

> If over one million Mexican soldiers crossed the border Americans would treat it as a major threat to their national security and react accordingly. The invasion of over one million Mexican civilians, as [President] Fox seems to recommend, would be a comparable threat to American societal security, and Americans should react against it with vigor.

But American leaders have not reacted "with vigor." They have reacted with indolence and torpor. Huntington concludes: "Mexican immigration is a unique, disturbing and looming challenge to our cultural integrity, our national identity, and potentially to our future as a country."[42]

Finally, the waves of Mexicans are coming to an America that is not the confident country of Theodore Roosevelt. Racial consciousness is rising. A belief in group rights and ethnic entitlements has taken root. Our cultural and intellectual elites do not celebrate the melting pot. They regard the forging of foreigners into Americans— where they give up their national and cultural identity to assume ours—as a form of cultural genocide.

The New Class—the elites that emerged triumphant from the cultural revolution of the 1960s—celebrates diversity and preaches a multiculturalism in which immigrants are encouraged to preserve their national identities and cultures and to reject ours. This conforms perfectly to the agenda of the Hispanic militants. For racial chauvinism is rife in the barrios, and every ethnic enclave is urged to maintain its unique and separate identity.

Several years ago, Glenn Garvin of *Reason* magazine wrote that "the integrationist impulse of the 1960s is dead. Liberal chic in the 1990s is segregation, dressed up as identity-group politics."[43] If Coolidge today declared, "America must remain American," he would be charged with a hate crime.

By plotting, aiding, and abetting the invasion of the United States for Mexican ends, the Fox regime is engaged in a hostile act similar to Castro's incitement of the *Mariel* "boat lift" that brought 125,000 Cubans to Florida, with several thousand psychotics and vicious criminals seeded among them.

And there is malevolence in what Mexico is doing, for Mexico harbors an animus against this country dating to the wars of 1835–48. Mexican militants and revanchists believe that Texas, the Southwest, and "Alta California" belong to them, that *we* are the intruders, *we* are the usurpers. One day soon we may wake up to find our bemused tolerance was the fatal blunder of an unserious people.

Uncle Sam is taking a hellish risk importing a vast diaspora from a neighbor nation so different from our own. If it proves an historic blunder, our children will live in a Balkanized country that will not be the America we knew. "If assimilation fails," writes Huntington, "the United States will become a cleft country with all the potentials for internal strife and disunion that entails."[44] It is already happening. Why are we taking this risk with something so precious and irreplaceable as our country?

9

What Is a Nation?

America is more than an idea, it is a nation.[1]
—JOHN O'SULLIVAN, 1993

We're becoming the first universal nation.[2]
—BEN WATTENBERG, 2001

All countries are basically social arrangements. . . . No matter
how permanent and even sacred they may seem . . .
they are all artificial and temporary.[3]
—STROBE TALBOTT, 1992

In an address to the Young Men's Lyceum of Springfield, Illinois, on January 27, 1838, the twenty-eight-year-old lawyer, newly arrived in town, spoke on "The Perpetuation of Our Political Institutions." Early in his address, Abe Lincoln asked and answered a rhetorical question:

At what point then is the approach of danger to be expected? I answer, if it ever reach us, it must spring up amongst us. It cannot come from abroad. If destruction be our lot, we must ourselves be its author and finisher. As a nation of freemen, we must live through all time, or die by suicide.[4]

Lincoln saw ahead a quarter of a century—to civil war.

The question that must be asked a century and a half after Lincoln's death is the one that troubled his generation: Are we on the path to national suicide?

To Americans who cannot recall the Cold War, the question may seem frivolous. But to many who have lived through a half century of radical change, it is not. For the America of yesterday has vanished and the America of tomorrow holds promise of becoming a land our parents would not recognize. Considering the epochal changes that have taken place in our country, the centrifugal forces pulling us apart, the political and economic powers working toward an end to national sovereignty and independence, it is impossible to be sanguine about the permanence of the nation. But what is a nation? What is America? Who *are* we?

An Economy Is Not a Country

In Catholic doctrine, death occurs when the soul departs the body, after which the body begins to decompose. So it is with nations.

Patriotism is the soul of a nation. It is what keeps a nation alive. When patriotism dies, when a nation loses the love and loyalty of its people, the nation dies and begins to decompose.

Patriotism is not nation-worship, such as we saw in Europe in the 1930s. It is not that spirit of nationalism that must denigrate or dominate other nations. It is a passionate attachment to one's own country—its land, its people, its past, its heroes, literature, language, traditions, culture, and customs. It is what enables a people to endure crushing oppression, as the Poles did for fifty years of Bolshevik and Nazi rule. "Intellectuals tend to forget," wrote Regis Debray, "that nations hibernate, but empires grow old. The American nation will outlast the Atlantic Empire as the Russian nation will outlast the Soviet Empire."[5]

This is the traditionalist view of a nation. It is how General de Gaulle saw France. "According to the Gaullist vision," writes the conservative scholar Roger Scruton, "a nation is defined not by institutions or borders but by language, religion, and high culture: in times of turmoil and conquest it is those spiritual things that must be protected and affirmed."[6]

In his 1967 visit to Canada, de Gaulle ignited a storm by declaring from the balcony of Montreal's City Hall, "Vive le Québec libre!"—the defiant cry of the Québécois, who yet dream of secession and nationhood. Quebec remains a province of Canada, but the nation, Quebec, lives in the hearts of millions of French-Canadians.

A century ago, the French historian and philosopher Ernest Renan described a nation:

> A nation is a living soul, a spiritual principle. Two things, which in truth are but one, constitute this soul, this spiritual principle. One is in the past, the other in the present. One is the common possession of a rich heritage of memories; the other is the actual consent, the desire to live together, the will to preserve worthily the undivided inheritance which has been handed down.... The nation, like the individual, is the outcome of a long past of efforts, and sacrifices, and devotions.... To have common glories in the past, a common will in the present; to have done great things together, to will to do the like again—such are the essential conditions for the making of a people.[7]

This community called a nation is much more than a "division of labor" or a "market" that may encompass the nation. Added Renan:

> Community of interests is assuredly a powerful bond between men. But ... can interests suffice to make a nation? I do not believe it. Community of interests makes commercial treaties.

There is a sentimental side to nationality; it is at once body and soul; a *Zollverein* is not a fatherland.[8]

"A *Zollverein* is not a fatherland." An economic union like the European Union is not a nation. An economy is not a country. An economic system should strengthen the bonds of national union, but the nation is of a higher order than the construct of any economist. A nation is organic; a nation is alive; a nation has a beating heart. A constitution does not create a nation. A nation writes a constitution that is the birth certificate of the nation already born in the hearts of its people. So it was with the American nation.

For a nation to endure, its people must form a moral and a social community and share higher values than economic interests. At the time of the Civil War, that moral community, that social union, had ceased to exist. In the South, there was no longer the will to stay together, but a fierce will to separate, to divorce, to live apart. Slavery and the tariff were but the battleground quarrels behind which was a burning Southern desire to be free of all the North had come to represent.

The 133rd Psalm speaks of an embryonic nation: "Behold, how good and how pleasant it is for brethren to dwell together in unity!" The word occurs even earlier in the Old Testament. Genesis 10:32, after listing the descendants of Noah, relates: "These are the families of the sons of Noah, after their generations, in their nations; and by these were the nations divided in the earth after the flood."

In Genesis 12, God makes His promise to Abram, "I will make of thee a great nation," and gives him a new name, Abraham, the "father of many nations." God promises to make a great nation of his son Ishmael. Arabs trace the origin of their peoples to Ishmael. God told Rebekah two nations were struggling in her womb: Esau and Jacob.

" 'Nation'—as suggested by its Latin root *nascere*, to be born—intrinsically implies a link by blood," wrote Peter Brimelow in the *Na-*

tional Review in 1992. "A nation in a real sense is an extended family. The merging process through which all nations pass is not merely cultural, but to a considerable extent biological through intermarriage."[9]

Brimelow describes a nation as an "ethno-cultural community—an interlacing of ethnicity and culture," that "speaks one language." He cites the late senator from New York.

> In his recent book, *Pandaemonium,* Senator Daniel Patrick Moynihan even used this rigorous definition, in an effort to capture both culture and ethnicity: a nation is a group of people who *believe* they are ancestrally related. It is the largest grouping that shares that belief. (Moynihan's italics)

To be a nation, a people must *believe* they are a nation, and that they share a common ancestry, history, and destiny. Whatever ethnic group to which we may belong, we Americans must see ourselves as of a unique and common nationality—in order to remain a nation.

In *From Under the Rubble,* Solzhenitzyn quotes the Russian Christian dissident Vadim Borosov on nations as creations of God Himself.

> In Christ's time there were many peoples already existing on earth, occupying various territories, speaking various languages, and warring with one another. Was their appearance merely a historical accident? The words of the Bible about the "nations thou has made" answer this question in the negative; the existence of peoples was part of the plan of creation, forming part of God's design for the world.[10]

Solzhenitzyn believed in the Providential origin of nations and, in his Nobel prize address, spoke of their indispensability to mankind's existence and essential worth: "The disappearance of nations would impoverish us no less than if all men had become alike with one personality, one face. Nations are the wealth of mankind. . . ."

Is America a "Creedal Nation"?

There is a rival view, advanced by neoconservatives and liberals. It is that America is a different kind of nation. Unlike Ireland, Italy, or Israel, the United States is not held together by the bonds of history and memory, tradition and custom, language and literature, birth and faith, blood and soil. Rather, America is a creedal nation, united by a common commitment of all her citizens to a set of ideas and ideals.

"Americans of all national origins, classes, religions, creeds and colors, have something in common . . . a political creed," wrote Gunnar Myrdal in 1944.[11] During the battle over Proposition 187 in 1994, when 59 percent of the California electorate voted to cut off welfare to illegal aliens, Jack Kemp and Bill Bennett, in opposing 187, accepted Myrdal's idea, declaring, "The American national identity is based on a creed, on a set of principles and ideas."[12]

Cokie Roberts of NPR and ABC agreed: "We have nothing binding us together as a nation—no common ethnicity, history, religion, or even language—except the Constitution and the institutions it created."[13]

Irving Kristol embraced the Bennett-Kemp view when he strikingly compared the United States to the former USSR: "[L]arge nations, whose identity is ideological, like the Soviet Union of yesterday and the United States of today, have ideological interests in addition to more material concerns."[14] To Kristol, America is first and foremost an "ideological" nation.

Allan Bloom, author of *The Closing of the American Mind,* also subscribed to the view that "America was the implementation of a rational plan for 'freedom and equality.'" As Claes G. Ryn comments in his essay, "Cultural Unity and Diversity":

"This is a regime founded by philosophers and their students," wrote Bloom. "America is nothing but a great stage" on which theories have been acted out. "There are almost no accidents." American order and freedom were thus spun out of a few enlightened minds. Abstract ideas, not historically formed personalities, built the United States. In Bloom's interpretation, the Framers were on much the same wavelength as Rousseau and the French revolutionaries. They had a plan for an egalitarian and majoritarian order, which the American people adopted.[15]

Ryn calls this the "civics approach to social order." Social order "is supposed to result when all are taught the same allegedly universal democratic ideas."[16] Bloom wrote: "Class, race, religion, national origin or culture all disappear or become dim when bathed in the light of natural rights, which give men common interests and make them truly brothers."[17] To Bloom, it is our common ideological beliefs that make us brothers.

FDR seemed to agree, asserting that "Americanism is a matter of the mind and heart. Americanism is not, and never was, a matter of race and ancestry. A good American is one who is loyal to this country and to our creed of liberty and democracy."[18] To be one nation, said Bill Clinton, all we need do is define ourselves by "our primary allegiance to the values that America stands for and values we really live by."[19]

Samuel Huntington, too, seems to consider America a creedal and ideological nation. He wrote in 1981 that

It is possible to speak of a body of political ideas that constitutes "Americanism," in a sense in which one can never speak of "Britishism," "Germanism," or "Japaneseism." Americanism in this sense is comparable to other ideologies and religions. . . . To reject the central ideas of that doctrine is to be un-American. . . . This identification of national with political Creed or values makes the United States virtually unique.[20]

Arthur M. Schlesinger, Jr., is among the most articulate champions of the idea of America as a nation united by a shared belief in the ideas found in the Declaration of Independence, the Constitution, and the Gettysburg Address:

The American Creed envisages a nation composed of individuals making their own choices and accountable to themselves, not a nation based on inviolable ethnic communities. . . . For our values are not matters of whim and happenstance. History has given them to us. They are anchored in our national experience, in our great national documents, in our national heroes, in our folkways, our traditions, and standards. . . . [Our values] work for us; and, for that reason, we live and die by them.[21]

In his first inaugural, George W. Bush endorsed the creedal nation concept: "America has never been united by blood or birth or soil. We are bound by ideals that move us beyond our backgrounds, lift us above our interests, and teach us what it means to be citizens."[22]

To this idea of America as a creedal nation bound together not "by blood or birth or soil" but by "ideals" that must be taught and learned, there is a corollary that has driven immigration policy for forty years. It is that people of any culture, country, creed, or continent, once they arrive on our shores, can be assimilated with equal ease, depending only upon whether they assent to the tenets of our national creed: equality and democracy.

Demonstrably, this is false. Human beings are not blank slates. Nor can they be easily separated from the abiding attachments of the tribe, race, nation, culture, community whence they came. Any man or any woman, of any color or creed, can be a good American. We know that from our history. But when it comes to the ability to assimilate into a nation like the United States, all nationalities, creeds, and cultures are not equal. To say that they are is ideology speaking, not judgment born of experience.

"During my life, I have seen Frenchmen, Italians, Russians, and so on," wrote the great conservative Joseph de Maistre, "but I must say, as for man, I have never come across him anywhere; if he exists, he is completely unknown to me." De Maistre's point, notes Sam Francis, "was that 'tribal behavior' is what makes human beings human. Take it away from 'man' or 'humankind' and what you get is not 'pure man' or 'liberated man' but dehumanization. . . ."[23]

Americans are an identifiable people. When traveling abroad, they are recognizable by their speech and mannerisms, not because they have been interrogated on their beliefs in democracy and free markets.

While Kemp and Bennett were saying that America was about ideas, the voters of California were saying that no matter what ideas these illegal aliens brought with them, they were not Americans, they were not part of our nation, they did not belong here, they were not entitled to the benefits of American citizens, and they ought to go back where they came from.

FDR declared that "Americanism is not, and never was, a matter of race and ancestry." Yet he was himself an enthusiast of the complete exclusion of Japanese immigrants in 1924, and readily agreed, as president, to incarcerate 110,000 Japanese, 75,000 of them fellow citizens, because he did not trust Japanese-Americans in a war with Japan. FDR's actions in wartime exposed the fraudulence of his peacetime pieties.

When Bill Clinton says that "our primary allegiance is to the values that America stands for and values we really live by," he challenges Stephen Decatur's "Our country! . . . may she always be in the right; but our country, right or wrong."

When President Bush declared in his first inaugural, "America has never been united by blood or birth or soil," he not only ignored history, he denied much of what it has meant to be an American.

At the birth of the nation we were 80 percent of British origin. In the most famous depiction of Americans as a new, unique, and separate people, John Jay, a coauthor of the *Federalist Papers,* wrote in *Federalist No. 2:*

> Providence has been pleased to give this one connected country to one united people—a people descended from the same ancestors, speaking the same language, professing the same religion, attached to the same principles of government, very similar in their manners and customs, and who, by their joint counsels, arms, and efforts, fighting side by side throughout a long and bloody war, have nobly established their general liberty and independence.

"This country and this people seem to have been made for each other," Jay continues, calling his countrymen "a band of brethren."

Thus, before the Constitution was ratified, John Jay considered Americans "one united people," "one connected country," and "brethren," of common blood. What holds this "one united people" together? Says Jay: language, faith, culture, and memory.

Moreover, Americans are as deeply rooted in the soil of the land of their birth as any other people. How can the president, so rightly proud of his father's service to his country, and of his own Texas roots, deny the claims of blood and soil? As the song goes, "This land is my land/This land is your land/From the redwood forest/To the New York island." Song and music, story and myth do more to make a people than ideology or political creed.

In his farewell address, President Reagan declared: "If we forget what we did, we won't know who we are. I'm warning of the eradication of the American memory that could result, ultimately, in an erosion of the American spirit."[24] To Reagan, it was critical that parents introduce their children to America's history and heroes. He cherished the anecdotes and stories of those heroes and deployed them constantly in speeches to make his points and embed himself in the great tradition, which is what made him so beloved of so many common folk. "Nations survive only if they unite around common emblems of nationhood," wrote Emile Durkheim.[25]

In refutation of Bush's contention that to be an American is not a matter of "blood or birth or soil," Francis replied:

As for being an American, of course, it's a matter of blood and birth. If it were merely the watery abstractions the president invokes, the nation would be meaningless. In so far as those ideas do inform our nationhood, they are meaningless apart from the particularities of place, race, and culture that give them meaning.[26]

"Language, culture and history bind a nation together and distinguish nations from each other," writes conservative commentator Selwyn Duke. "We share a continent with Mexico, but we are not one nation with them, chiefly if not solely because of those three factors."[27]

Each nation's culture, be it that of France, England, or America, gives the nation its particular and unique character. In introducing a set of essays on *Immigration and the American Identity*, Tom Fleming, editor of *Chronicles*, notes:

> Culture . . . means the cultivation of a certain kind of character.
>
> Cultural institutions . . . are the agents that make us who and what we are. Like Tennyson's Ulysses, you and I can say, "I am part of all that I have met": the books we read, the music we listen to, the pictures we look at, the prayers we say. A culture is the sum of all these things and many more, including table manners and styles of dress. As an American poet put it, "The way you wear your hat, the way you drink your tea. . . ."[28]

The title of Schlesinger's *Disuniting of America* implies his deep concern that the centrifugal forces pulling America apart have begun to overwhelm the ideas and ideals that he believes hold us together.

To traditional conservatives, this "creedal nation" exists in the minds of men of words. It is an intellectual construct, to which men can render neither love nor loyalty. For two centuries, men have died for America. Who would lay down his life for the UN, the EU, or a "North American Union"?

When Japan attacked Pearl Harbor, college students stood beside sharecroppers' sons to enlist. These men were not volunteering to defend abstract ideas. For democracy was not attacked. Equality was not attacked. America was attacked. They were enlisting to fight Japanese for what they had done to our country and countrymen. Many had likely never read Jefferson, Hamilton, or Madison, and some would die never having read them. Yet, whether they had been taught or not, or learned or had not, the ideals and principles of which President Bush spoke in his first inaugural, they were patriots united by nationality. They were Americans, and they fought, bled, and died as Americans, no matter what they believed.

Every true nation is the creation of a unique people, separate from all others. Indeed, if America is an ideological nation grounded no deeper than in the sandy soil of abstract ideas, she will not survive the storms of this century any more than the Soviet Union survived the storms of the last. When the regime, party, army, and police that held that ideological nation together lost the will to keep it together, the USSR broke down along the fault lines of nationality, faith, and culture. The true nations—Estonia, Lithuania, Latvia, Ukraine, Russia—emerged from the rubble. A true nation is held together not by any political creed but by patriotism.

Stalin understood this. In the great crisis of his empire, Hitler's invasion, Stalin did not call on his subjects to save communism or defend the Soviet Constitution. He called on Russia's sons to defend the Rodina, Mother Russia, against the Germanic hordes, and suspended his suppression of the Orthodox Church so its bishops and priests could bless "The Great Patriotic War." Communist to the core, Stalin yet knew that men do not die for secular creeds like Marxism or Leninism, but for the "ashes of their fathers and the temples of their gods." Hitler and Mussolini succeeded as long as they did because they grounded their Nazi and Fascist ideologies in the deeper soil of nationality and culture.

France considers herself a creedal nation, whose unifying beliefs date to the Enlightenment and Revolution. But when the Revolution tore France to pieces, what held her together through the Napoleonic wars, Sédan, the loss of Alsace, and Verdun, as she divided ever more deeply over ideology and faith, was nationality and culture. Whether monarchical, republican, imperial, or democratic, the French nation and people endure. And if the French cease to be the dominant tribe, adherence to Enlightenment ideas will not save France.

Should America lose her ethnic-cultural core and become a nation of nations, America will not survive. For nowhere on this earth can one find a multicultural, multiethnic, multilingual nation that is not at risk. Democracy is not enough. Equality is not enough. Free markets are not enough—to hold a people together. Without patriotism, a love of country and countrymen not for what they believe or profess but for who they are, "Things fall apart; the centre cannot hold."

"Nationalism remains, after two centuries, the most vital political emotion in the world," concedes Schlesinger, "far more vital than social ideologies such as communism or fascism or even democracy." And inside the nation, "nationalism takes the form of ethnicity and tribalism."[29]

Before the Creed Came the Nation

America is more, much more, than a "proposition nation." As Samuel Huntington himself has written:

> America is a founded society created by seventeenth- and eighteenth-century settlers, almost all of whom came from the British Isles. . . . They initially defined America in terms of race, ethnicity, culture, and most importantly religion. Then in the eighteenth century they also had to define America ideologically to justify their independence from their home-countrymen.[30]

The ideology was created by colonial elites to justify the breaking of blood ties with their British brethren. But before the ideology came the country. Before her greatest documents were written, America existed in the hearts of her people. The Constitution did not create the nation; the nation adopted the Constitution. Many of the fathers did indeed believe in universal principles and rights, but all were loyal to a particular nation and to kinfolk with whom they shared ties of blood, soil, and memory.

George Washington had once sought to become an officer in the British army. But by the end of the French and Indian War, he had begun to see the British not as kinsmen but as overlords. In heart and soul, well before the Second Continental Congress, Washington was an American.

After the Boston Tea Party in 1773, Patrick Henry declared to the First Continental Congress in Philadelphia's Carpenters' Hall, "The distinctions between Virginians, Pennsylvanians, and New Yorkers and New Englanders are no more. I am not a Virginian, but an *American*." That was two years before Jefferson wrote the first draft of the Declaration of Independence. Before the guns fired at Lexington, Henry declared, "The next gale that sweeps the north will bring to our ears the clash of resounding arms! Our *brethren* are already in the field!"[31]

"Our *brethren*." The nation was forged in the fire of rebellion and war, not from a document, memorable as it was, signed in Philadelphia one year after the rebellion had begun and thousands had perished.

The Declaration stated what was already known: The Americans had become a people. In his first draft, Jefferson had written of "our British brethren," who have failed to honor "the ties of our common kindred" and proven themselves "deaf to the voice of . . . consanguinity." These are matters of blood and kinship. The Native Americans shared our continent but were not our kinsmen. To Jefferson and the signers of '76, they were those "merciless Indian Savages, whose known rule of warfare, is an undistinguished destruction, of all Ages, Sexes & Conditions."[32]

Jefferson charged George III with the crime of having sent out to attack Americans mercenaries who were not "of our common blood." The blood ties had been dishonored. These "unfeeling brethren" were brothers no longer. The Declaration of Independence provided the words to a decision the heart had already made.

"What then is the American, this new man?" was the famous question of the French émigré Henri St. John de Crèvecoeur. To which he gave his classic answer:

> *He* is an American, who leaving behind all his ancient prejudices and manners, receives new ones from the new mode of life he has embraced, the new government he obeys, and the new rank he holds. The American is a new man, who acts upon new principles. . . . *Here individuals of all nations are melted into a new race of men.*[33]

To Crèvecoeur, we Americans were "a new race of men."

To preserve this "new race of men," Washington, in a 1792 letter to John Adams, urged that immigrants not be allowed to congregate, but be spread out among the people.

> [T]he policy . . . of [immigration] taking place in a body (I mean settling them in a body) may be much questioned; for, by so doing, they retain the language, habits and principles (good or bad) which they bring with them. Whereas by an intermixture with our people, they or their descendants get assimilated to our customs and laws: in a word soon become one people.[34]

The Father of our country believed that, before they could become Americans, immigrants must embrace our language, customs, and habits, as well as our principles.

For Hamilton, America's success depended on the "preservation of a national spirit and national character" that immigrants must come to share with our native-born. The safety of the republic rested on "love of country" and the "exemption of citizens from foreign bias and prejudice." Assimilation, he wrote, would enable "aliens to get rid of foreign and acquire American attachment. . . ." In Hamilton's republic, there was no room for dual loyalty.

For both Washington and Hamilton, immigrants must cease to be who they were and become who we are. Madison urged excluding immigrants who were unlikely to "incorporate . . . into our society."[35]

Interviewed by a German baron thinking of immigrating to America, John Quincy Adams set down the conditions for newcomers: "*They must cast off the European skin, never to resume it.* They must look forward to their posterity rather than backward to their ancestors. . . ."[36] They must cease to be Englishmen, Dutchmen, Germans, and Irish—and become Americans, a new nationality.

Lincoln, in his cry from the heart to his countrymen in his first inaugural, not to take the path of civil war, appealed to the deeper bonds that existed between patriot-sons whose fathers had fought side by side:

> I am loath to close. We are not enemies, but friends. We must not be enemies. Though passion may have strained, it must not break our bonds of affection. The mystic chords of memory, stretching from every battlefield, and patriot grave, to every living heart and hearthstone, all over this broad land, will yet swell the chorus of the Union, when again touched, as surely they will be, by the better angels of our nature.[37]

Lincoln's ultimate appeal, then, is not to principles of democracy, but to "bonds of affection" and "The mystic chords of memory."

Theodore Roosevelt echoed Adams's conviction that all immigrants must cast off their old identities and loyalties. He thundered again and again against "hyphenated-Americanism."

Woodrow Wilson, speaking to naturalized citizens in Philadelphia in 1915, echoed his great rival: "You cannot become thorough Americans if you think of yourselves in groups. America does not consist of groups. A man who thinks of himself as belonging to a particular national group in America has not yet become an American. . . ."[38]

Both Wilson and T.R. saw Americans as separate in far more than their principles of government. "Either a man is an American and nothing else, or he is not an American at all," said T.R.[39]

Israel Zangwill, an English writer of German-Jewish origin, inserted this idea—that the American is a new man—into his 1908 play, *The Melting-Pot.* In the words of the lead character David Quixano, a Russian-Jewish composer, "America is G-d's Crucible, the Great Melting-Pot where all the races of Europe are melting and re-forming!"[40]

Zangwill was saying that Europeans were being reforged, as in a fiery furnace, into an entirely new people: the American people. This is the traditionalist view: that Americans—whatever or wherever our ancestral roots—are a people separate and apart from all others of the earth, with far more in common than political beliefs. We are of a unique country, with its own unique history, heritage, heroes, language, literature, law, mores, traditions, customs. It is this America that is imperiled by the mass migration of tens of millions and perhaps hundreds of millions this century from countries whose peoples have never before been assimilated. And if the organic America of the traditionalists dies, the "creedal nation" of Kemp, Kristol, Bennett, and Bush will not survive.

Stanley Renshon, author of *The 50 percent American,* is emphatic that the American Creed is insufficient to unite us as a people or save us as a nation.

The traditional answer to this question is this: The American Creed will unite us. Theorists on both the left and the right generally agree that a belief in justice and democracy, also known as the Creed, will be our salvation. I think this view is profoundly mistaken. People are not united primarily by abstractions operating at the stratospheric level—not unless they are connected to something that carries a deeper emotional power. The critical issue facing this country is not a matter of abstract values, as laudable as they might be, but of attachment.[41]

The heart has reasons that the mind knows not.

What is that indispensable bond of attachment, if not the American Creed? Again, in a word, it is patriotism, love of country:

The glue that holds this country together is a much maligned, wholly misunderstood psychological force: patriotism. Far from being the "last resort of scoundrels" . . . it is the indispensable foundation of our attachments to each other and the institutions that form our national community. It is critically important that we understand what patriotism really is, and the role it plays in American public life. We cannot ask much of immigrants if we do not understand it ourselves.[42]

Is the Real Nation Dying?

And one does not come to a love of country through studying texts—even great texts penned by Jefferson, Madison, or Lincoln on the train to Gettysburg. Many of the boys and men who marched into the Union guns at Gettysburg, and who fired those guns, could neither read nor write.

By Jay's definition, can anyone say today that we Americans are "one united people"? We are no longer descended from the same ancestors. The European core of the country—almost 90 percent of all

Americans as late as 1965—has fallen well below 70 percent and will be less than half the nation by 2050.

We no longer speak the same language, nor do we insist, as our fathers did, that immigrants learn English. Of the 9 million living in Los Angeles County, 5 million do not speak English at home. Schoolchildren in Chicago are taught in one hundred languages. The fastest growing radio and TV stations in America broadcast in Spanish.

Nor do Americans any longer profess the same faith. We are no longer *Protestant, Catholic, and Jew,* as sociologist Will Herberg described us in 1955. We are Protestant, Catholic, Jew, Orthodox, Mormon, Muslim, Hindu, Buddhist, Taoist, Shintoist, Santeria, New Age, voodoo, agnostic, atheist, humanist, Rastafarian, and Wiccan.

We never fought "side by side throughout a long and bloody war." The Greatest Generation did, and, in nostalgic recall of those days of hope and glory, we celebrate their victories again and again. But the Greatest Generation is passing on, and if the rest of us recall "a long and bloody war," it was Korea, Vietnam, or Iraq, and not for long did we remain "side by side." For a time the Cold War united us. But that, too, is over. And, as Rabbit Angstrom lamented, "Without the Cold War, what's the point of being an American?"

We are yet "attached to the same principles of government." But this is not enough to hold a nation together. The South was attached to the same principles of government. But that did not prevent the South from fighting four bloody years to be free of a Union headed by Abraham Lincoln.

Robert E. Lee spurned an offer to lead the Union army in putting down secession. When the kinsmen of his native state took up arms against a Union he had served all his life, he led them in battle. Neither the oath he had taken nor the ideals of the Constitution and Declaration could keep Lee loyal to a Union he believed had no right to invade his native state.

If Lee, son of Washington's friend and comrade in arms, "Light-Horse Harry" Lee, could ride across the Long Bridge to Virginia to take up arms against the United States, is it not naive to believe that scores of millions of aliens without roots here will put America ahead of the homelands they left behind? How many Americans, forced to work in Mexico, would become loyal Mexicans in a decade rather than remain Americans in exile? Why do we think that Mexicans are any less attached to the land of their birth?

Nor do Americans treasure the history or revere the heroes as we once did. What many still see as a glorious past, others see as shameful history. Columbus, Washington, Jefferson, Jackson, Lincoln, and Lee, heroes of the old America, are all under attack. To many, the discovery of America by the explorers from Columbus to Captain John Smith, and the winning of the West by pioneers, soldiers, and cowboys are no longer seen as heroic events but as matters of which Western man should be ashamed.

Those who believe that the ideas of the Declaration of Independence, the Constitution, and the Gettysburg Address—liberty, equality, democracy—constitute an "American Creed" that holds us together as a nation are ignoring or rewriting history. For even the most famous words in those documents, "All men are created equal," do not mean the same thing to all Americans. They never did.

Were Our Fathers Un-American?

As we have seen, Samuel Huntington writes that "To reject the central ideas of that doctrine [our political Creed] is to be un-American." Two of the central ideas of Huntington's political creed are democracy and equality. How do the Founding Fathers measure up?

Jefferson was a slaveholder unto death who wrote, late in life, of an "aristocracy of virtue and talent, which nature has wisely provided for the direction of the interests of society. . . ."[43] Madison, the author of the Constitution, headed, until his death, the American Colonization Society, "in the belief that its plan to return slaves to Africa represented the most sensible way out of that long-festering crisis."[44] At Madison's death, leadership passed to Henry Clay, who was eulogized in 1852 by Abraham Lincoln. Lincoln celebrated his hero's lifelong association with the American Colonization Society, proudly quoting Clay's 1827 address to that society: "There is a moral fitness in the idea of returning to Africa her children, whose ancestors have been torn from her by the ruthless hand of fraud and violence. Transplanted in a foreign land, they will carry back to their native soil the rich fruits of religion, civilization, law and liberty."[45]

Praising Clay's vision, Lincoln declared: "May it indeed be realized!"

Slavery was a great moral evil and we condemn it. The unequal treatment of our fellow Americans of African descent for a century after Appomattox was a grave injustice and historic wrong. Nonetheless, we cannot deny that the greatest of our forefathers did these things and said these things and approved these things. The point of the recitation is this: If a belief in equality is the *sine qua non* of being an American in our "creedal nation," then the authors of the Declaration of Independence, the Constitution, and the Gettysburg Address do not qualify as Americans.

What of a belief in democracy being an indispensable part of the "American Creed" that makes us a nation? Did the Founding Fathers hold so lofty a view of democracy?

"Democracy . . . wastes, exhausts, and murders itself. There is never a democracy that did not commit suicide," wrote Adams.[46] "A democracy [is] the only pure republic, but impracticable beyond the limits of a town," added Jefferson.[47]

Madison was more negative. Writing in *Federalist No. 10,* he declared, "democracies have ever been spectacles of turbulence and contention: have ever been incompatible with personal security or the rights of property; and have in general been as short in their lives as they have been violent in their deaths."[48] Said Hamilton: "The ancient democracies, in which the people themselves deliberated, never possessed one feature of good government. Their very nature was tyranny."[49]

So, again, if a commitment to democracy is an indispensable element of the American Creed that unites the nation, the Founding Fathers seem not to qualify as 100 percent American. Their ideas on equality and one-man, one-vote democracy seem to mark them down, in Professor Huntington's book, as decidedly "un-American."

As for the Constitution, it no longer unites us, if ever it did. Indeed, it divides us bitterly. We see that division manifest with each nomination to the Supreme Court. Why does not the organic document of American union unite us? Because we Americans disagree on what it says and means—about homosexuality, abortion, racial quotas, affirmative action, burning Old Glory, prayer in schools, posting the Ten Commandments in the public square, the death penalty, and pornography, among other issues.

Celebrants of the creedal nation seem not to understand that it is the violent disputes over what our creedal documents mean that is the *casus belli* of the culture war tearing us apart.

Creed or Culture

Here we approach the heart of the matter.

Whether America is a nation like all others, or a different kind of nation, is more than an academic question. For who wins the argument determines America's destiny. As Huntington points out, "National interest derives from national identity. We have to know who we are before we can know what our interests are."[50]

The scheme to redefine America's identity as other than what America has always been, is an historic fraud, concocted by ideologues to divert the nation away from a traditional foreign policy into crusades to remake the world in a democratist mould. They have forged America's birth certificate—to claim custody of the child.

"Who controls the present controls the past. Who controls the past controls the future," wrote Orwell. Inventing a new past for America as a creedal nation—the kind of nation our forefathers would have rebelled against—neoconservatives hope to control the future, a future they see as fulfilling America's mission: to democratize mankind. Americans are being indoctrinated in a fabricated creed that teaches they are being untrue to themselves and faithless to their fathers unless they go abroad in search of monsters to destroy.

As Claes Ryn writes in his essay, "Leo Strauss and History: The Philosopher as Conspirator,"

> The America [the Straussians] champion is not the actual, historically distinctive America with its deep roots in Christian and English civilization but a country of their own theoretical invention, which owes its greatness to what are alleged to be its ahistorical, rational founding principles. The America of neoconservatism breaks sharply with the America of history.[51]

Whether America is a traditional nation or an ideological nation is critical to the immigration debate.

For if America is a "propositional nation," a creedal nation, then who comes to America and whence they come does not matter. Indeed, the more who come and assent to the American "proposition," the stronger and better nation we become. That way lies the remaking of America into the first universal nation of Ben Wattenberg's dream and Teddy Roosevelt's nightmare, when he warned against our becoming a "tangle of squabbling minorities" and no longer a nation at all.

Before Americans ever adopted a creed, Americans were a people and America was a nation. Those who equate the creed with the nation are contradicted by the history they distort. They rewrite that history, like Winston in the Ministry of Truth, to convert America into something she never was: an imperial democracy imposing her ideology on a resisting world, to the ruin of the republic she was meant to be. And they will turn America into something she cannot survive becoming: a multicultural, multiethnic, multilingual Tower of Babel.

Who Are We?

To know what our national interests are, and what we should send our sons and daughters to die to defend, we must know who we are.

If we are a creedal nation, united by a commitment to democracy, equality, and liberty, with a mandate and mission to impose those ideas and ideals on mankind, we shall have a foreign policy like that of George W. Bush. But if we are a traditional nation, our national interests will be traditional: the defense of our land and the preservation of the lives and liberty of our people. And we will regard as enemies those who imperil what we hold most dear.

How we define who we are defines our interests, and how we define our interests tells us *whom* we must fight—and whom we need not fight.

Language, faith, culture, and history—and, yes, birth, blood, and soil—produce a people, not an ideology. After the ideologies and creeds that seized Germany, Italy, and Russia by the throat in the twentieth century—Nazism, Fascism, Communism—were all expunged, Germans remained German, Italians remained Italian, and Russians remained Russian. After three decades of Maoist madness,

the Chinese remain Chinese. Had America succumbed to dictatorship in the Cold War, we would still be Americans, recognizable by
far more than the political beliefs we profess.

"Historically," Huntington writes, "American identity has had
two primary components: culture and creed. . . . If multiculturalism
prevails and if the consensus on liberal democracy disintegrates, the
United States could join the Soviet Union on the ash heap of history."[52]

Democracy is not enough. If the culture dies, the country dies.

10

The Return of Tribalism

All is race; there is no other truth.
—BENJAMIN DISRAELI, *Tancred* (1847)

The hostility of one tribe for another is among the
most instinctive human reactions.[1]
—ARTHUR M. SCHLESINGER, JR., *The Disuniting of America* (1991)

Most of us agree that the notion of "race" is a
human creation, with no basis in genetics or biology.[2]
—ANDREW HACKER, *New York Review of Books,* 2003

In 1994, Sam Francis, the syndicated columnist and editorial writer for *The Washington Times,* speaking at a conference on ethnicity and culture, volunteered this thought:

"The civilization that we as whites created in Europe and America could not have developed apart from the genetic endowments of the creating people, nor is there any reason to believe that the civilization can be successfully transmitted by a different people."[3]

Had Francis said this of Chinese civilization and the Chinese people, it would have gone unnoted. But he was suggesting Western civilization was superior and that only Europeans could have created it. If Western peoples perish, as they are doing today, Francis was implying, we must expect our civilization to die with us. No one would deny that when the Carthaginians perished, Carthaginian civilization and culture perished. But by claiming the achievements of the West for Europeans, Francis had passed beyond the bounds of tolerance. He was summarily fired.

In an essay published after his death, Francis wrote of the restrictions imposed upon any discussion of race in America:

> In the Victorian era, the Great Taboo was sex. Today . . . the Great Taboo is race. The Victorians virtually denied that sex existed. Today, race is said to be "merely a social construct," a product of the imagination, and of none too healthy imaginations at that, rather than a reality of nature. The Victorians severely punished people who talked about sex, made jokes about sex, or wrote too openly and frankly about sex. Today, journalists, disc jockeys, leading sports figures, public officials, distinguished academics, and major political leaders who violate the racial taboos of our age are fired from their newspapers, networks, or radio stations, forced to resign their positions, condemned by their own colleagues, and subjected to "investigations" of their "backgrounds" and their "links" to other individuals and groups that have also violated the race taboo.[4]

"Jimmy The Greek" [Snyder] of CBS Sports, John Rocker of the Atlanta Braves, Al Campanis of the Los Angeles Dodgers, Agriculture Secretary Earl Butz, Senate Majority Leader Trent Lott, authors of *The Bell Curve* Richard Herrnstein and Charles Murray, can all testify to the truth of what Francis wrote. Rush Limbaugh had to resign from ESPN's *Sunday NFL Countdown* for suggesting that some sportswriters were cutting slack for Philadelphia Eagles' quarterback Donovan McNabb because McNabb was black.

But to submit to the Great Taboo is like not telling one's doctor of a recurring pain that could kill you. All over the world, issues of race, religion, and ethnicity are tearing nations apart. The last decade and a half has borne out the 1991 prediction of Arthur Schlesinger: "Ethnic and racial conflict, it now seems evident, will soon replace the conflict of ideologies as the explosive issue of our time."[5]

Centrifugal Forces

During the twentieth century, the terrible wars of empire and ideology often obscured the deeper and never-ending wars of tribe and culture.

People Forget. When the Sudeten Germans departed Czechoslovakia in 1938, preferring German Nazis to democratic Czechs as countrymen and rulers after Munich, the Slovaks seceded, six months later, and Hungarians and Poles in the disintegrating state welcomed military intervention by their kinsmen. Blood ties proved stronger than democracy. Reunited after World War II, Czechs and Slovaks separated again when free of Soviet domination. For centuries, they had lived side by side in the Hapsburg Empire, but could not live together in a democracy. It appears a truism: multicultural, multiethnic, multilingual states are held together either by an authoritarian regime or a dominant ethnocultural core, or their breakup is inevitable.

In 1991, the Soviet Union shattered into fifteen nations along the fault lines of race, religion, and ethnicity. Uzbekistan, Kyrgyzstan, Tajikistan, Turkmenistan, and Kazakhstan were Asian as well as Muslim. Latvia, Lithuania, and Estonia rejected not only Communist rule but Russian rule. Russians in Latvia, descendants of those transferred there by Stalin over sixty years ago, are still regarded as intruders. The Caucasus seems about to subdivide into statelets like Chechnya, Dagestan, Abkhazia, and North and South Ossetia, based on ethnicity.

Ukraine, divided into a Russian east, an Orthodox center, and a Catholic west, faces a threat of secession of the Crimea, which Khrushchev in 1954 ceded to Ukraine when it was part of the Soviet Union. The dominant Russian-speaking people of the Crimea charge that a "repressive government in the capital, Kiev, is bent on imposing an [alien] nationalistic identity" upon them. Adds Steven Lee Myers in the *New York Times,* "stark ethnic and cultural differences . . . continue to haunt Ukraine. . . ."[6]

After Marshal Tito died, Yugoslavia, heir to the Kingdom of Serbs, Croats, and Slovenes that came out of the Paris Peace Conference of 1919, collapsed and disintegrated. Slovenes, who had been part of the Austro-Hungarian Empire, broke free of Belgrade, followed by Croatians, who were of a different Christian faith than Serbs and had memories of mutual savagery in World War II. Macedonia departed and Montenegro has now seceded. In Bosnia and Kosovo, Serbs violently resisted rule by Muslims or Albanians. These peoples have lived together on the same peninsula since time immemorial and in the same nation for seventy years. Yet the viciousness of the Balkan wars of the 1990s was the worst Europe had seen since the Hungarian Revolution, if not the Hitler-Stalin war.

Rather than fading away, issues of nationality long considered dead are resurfacing. Scottish nationalists wish to be free of England after three centuries, as the Irish broke free in 1921. The English are replacing the Union Jack with the red St. George's Cross that was the national flag before union with Scotland and Wales. Corsicans want out of France. Walloons and Flemish yet call for dissolving Belgium. The Northern Alliance has no more given up on separation from Italy than the Québécois have given up the dream of "Québec libre!"

In March 2006, the Basque ETA, whose terror bombings took the lives of eight hundred over four decades, declared a permanent cease-fire. Juan Jose Ibarretxe, president of the Basque region, in announcing the news, said: "It is time for the Basque people to be allowed to decide their own future in peace and freedom." Ibarretxe's dream: a Basque nation. "Many others among Spain's 17 regions, particularly Catalonia," notes the *Times* report, "are also keenly interested in loosening ties with the central government . . ."[7]

In Alberta and Saskatchewan, independence parties have sprung up and some in British Columbia favor secession. In June 2006, in the U.S. Senate, the Native Hawaiian Government Reorganization Act, providing for a race-based government with tribal sovereignty not unlike that enjoyed by the Apache, Sioux, and Navajo, garnered fifty-six votes.

The Israeli historian Martin van Creveld, chronicler of the fall of the nation-state, writes of the forces tearing at the seams of the Third World: "[T]here has hardly been any newly independent country in Asia or Africa that did not undergo some kind of coup, revolution, or violent internecine conflict between opposing ethnic or religious groups."[8]

Of India, which the UN population division projects will become the world's most populous nation, Van Creveld writes: "It has witnessed and is still witnessing ethnic and religious disturbances in such places as Bengal, the Punjab, and Kashmir; some of these are so massive that, had they taken place in a country with fewer than 900,000,000 inhabitants, they would have merited the name of civil war."[9] In our time, India and Pakistan, Pakistan and Bangladesh, Malaysia and Singapore, Ethiopia and Eritrea have split apart.

In the winter of 2006, Iraq seemed on the brink of religious war between Sunni and Shiite and breakup of the nation. In late spring, Turkish-speaking Azeris in northwest Iran rioted over a cartoon insulting to their people. Four were killed and 70 injured. The newspaper was closed and the cartoonist and editor jailed, but that failed to satisfy the Azeris, who demanded that their children henceforth be taught in their own language and that TV channels be provided that would broadcast in Turkish Azeri.

Nigeria, the most populous nation in Africa, came close to sundering during the Ibo war of Biafran secession in the late sixties. Sudan, the largest nation in Africa, is ethnically and religiously two countries: a Muslim north persecutes and represses a Christian south. In Brazil, the predominantly white southern states of Rio Grande do Sul, Santa Catarina, and Paraná have considered a divorce from the racially mixed north.[10]

Evidence is piling up that Van Creveld's pessimistic analysis of the end of an epoch may be correct:

The State, which since the Treaty of Westphalia (1648) has been the most important . . . of modern institutions, is dying. Wherever we look, existing states are either combining into larger communities or falling apart; wherever we look, organizations that are not states are taking their place.[11]

Roots

Disraeli called race "the key to history." But by race, he meant what we call ethnicity or nationality, or what Churchill meant in speaking of the British as "our island race." The terrorism that is a curse of modernity proceeds out of this sense of ethnic or national identity, as well as across religious divides, in Sri Lanka, Kashmir, Sudan, Nigeria, Iraq, Gaza, the West Bank.

As Stalin transferred Russians into Latvia, Beijing seeks to swamp the Tibetan, Uighur, and Mongol majorities in its borderlands and inundate their culture by moving in millions of Han Chinese. What Mexico is doing to the American Southwest has, from time immemorial, been the way one tribe has slowly conquered and colonized the land of another.

With China, race and history matter deeply. The Academy Award–winning film *Memoirs of a Geisha* was banned there in 2006 because Beijing was insulted that Chinese actresses had played the role of Japanese geishas.[12]

Robert Mugabe is today stealing the land of white farmers who remained in Zimbabwe after Rhodesia came to an end. Yesterday, his Shona tribesmen engaged in a massacre of the Matabele, whose Joshua Nkomo had as great a claim as he to being the Mandela of his country. The genocide in Rwanda and Burundi was not ideological but tribal—Tutsi and Hutu share a long and bloody history.

A surge of ethnic chauvinism is sweeping across Latin America. In Bolivia, Evo Morales, an Aymara Indian, swept to victory in 2005 on the votes of indigenous peoples. The *New York Times* described his preinaugural:

On Saturday, in a ceremony attended by tens of thousands of Aymara and Quechua Indians at this archaeological site some 14,000 feet above sea level, Mr. Morales donned the replica of a 1,000-year-old tunic similar to those once used by Tiwanaku's wise men, was purified in an ancient ritual and accepted the symbolic leadership of the myriad indigenous groups of the Andes.

"We are not alone," Mr. Morales told the crowd.

"The world is with us. We are in a time of triumph. . . ."[13]

At his inaugural, Morales, noting that 62 percent of Bolivia's people were Indians like himself, declared: "Five hundred years of . . . popular resistance by indigenous peoples has not been in vain. We are here, and we say we have achieved power to end the injustice, the inequality and oppression that we have lived under."[14]

Five hundred years takes us back to the arrival of Europeans in the Americas. This idea of *reconquista*—reconquest by indigenous people of lands lost to European invaders, occupiers, and colonizers—propels populist rebellions from the Andes to Alta California.

In the June 4, 2006, runoff between ex-president Alan Garcia and radical Ollanta Humala, Isaac Humala, patriarch of the clan and leader of the Peruvian Nationalist Movement, injected race into the campaign. In its final hours, he declared that "copper people," descendants of the Incas, have a right to rule superior to that of Peruvians whose ancestors came from Europe. "We are racists," Isaac Humala proclaimed. "We advocate saving the copper race from extinction, disintegration and degeneration. Everyone is a racist because nationalism is something that is in the blood, just like it is with the Japanese in Japan and the Germans in Germany."[15]

During the Proposition 187 battle in California, a brochure of the Chicano Mexicano Mexica Empowerment Committee declared that whites were the illegals, and their ancestors were guilty of genocide against the original and true owners of the land:

> The hidden past (23 million of our people killed by Europeans) and the future of our people are our main concern. The vast majority (over 90 percent of our people) are of Original Inhabitant (Indigenous) origin. We are descendants of the original inhabitants of this land and the rightful owners of the Southwest and Mexico.[16]

Yeh Ling-Ling of the Diversity Alliance for a Sustainable America notes in the *Journal of Social, Political and Economic Studies* that radical Chicano intellectuals are calling for racial resistance to any integration with or assimilation into America:

> [A]ccording to its editor, Elizabeth Martinez, the purpose of *Five Hundred Years of Chicano History,* a book used in over

300 schools throughout the West, is to "celebrate our resistance to being colonized and absorbed by the racist empire-builders." . . . For Rodolfo Acuna, author of *Occupied America: The Chicano's Struggle Toward Liberation*, probably the most widely assigned text in U.S. Chicano Studies programs, the Anglo-America invasion of Mexico was as "vicious as that of Hitler's invasion of Poland and other Central European nations. . . ."[17]

The African-American scholar Shelby Steele appears to endorse the Martinez-Acuna verdict on the Europeans' history in North America:

No group in recent history has more aggressively seized power in the name of its racial superiority than Western whites. This race illustrated for all time—through colonialism, slavery, white racism, Nazism—the extraordinary evil that follows when great power is joined to an atavistic sense of superiority and destiny. This is why today's whites the world over, cannot openly have a racial identity.

Because of the unforgivable sins of "Western whites," Steele instructs us, "Racial identity is simply forbidden to whites in America. . . . Black children today are hammered with the idea of racial identity and pride, yet racial pride in whites constitutes a grave evil. Say 'I'm white and I'm proud,' and you are a Nazi."

But if black children are being "hammered with the idea of racial identity and pride," the "color-blind society" of Dr. King's dream is dead. And how are white Americans to achieve redemption for the sins of their fathers? Steele does not leave us hanging. Whites must deal with their history through the acceptance and embrace of guilt: "White guilt—the need to win enough moral authority around race to prove that one is not a racist—is the price whites today pay for this history. Political correctness is a language that enables whites to show by wildly exaggerated courtesy that they are not racist; diversity does this for institutions."[18]

Yet, since Americans of European descent—unlike Germans—are not into sackcloth-and-ashes, but take immense pride in their ancestors' achievements and bridle at reverse discrimination, it is hard to see a happy future of peace and reconciliation if many folks are thinking like Shelby Steele.

"Lest We Forget"

History, too, remains a cause of conflict between nations. When Japanese leaders visit the Yasukuni shrine to the 2 million dead in World War II, where fourteen A-Class war criminals including Tojo are buried, China and South Korea profess outrage, though the war ended sixty years ago.

Israelis remember 1948 as the year of resurrection and birth of the nation. Palestinians recall it as the year of the "Catastrophe," when terror and war drove their people out of their ancestral land and turned them into exiles and refugees with no home of their own. Americans look upon Mexicans as neighbors. Mexicans look on the United States as the nation that stole half of their country when they were young and weak.

The conservative scholar Robert Nisbet believed that the twentieth-century revolutions against Western imperial powers were racial revolutions. Marxism "has on the whole endeavored to persuade blacks and other races historically under white domination that they fall into the more general category of the proletariat," Nisbet wrote; but the "single fact . . . that stands out" is

that racial revolution as an aspiration is becoming increasingly separate from other philosophies or strategies of revolution. . . .

The distinguishing feature of twentieth-century revolutionary behavior and thought has proved to be . . . precisely its
racial character. The signal revolts of the past half-century, the
major insurrections and mass liberations have been precisely
those buoyed up by appeal to race and color. The greatest single
twentieth-century revolutionary movement has been that of the
blacks revolting against not capitalists primarily, but *whites*—in
Africa and, to a modified degree, in the United States and other
Western countries. And ethnic revolt—whether black, Orien-
tal, Chicano, or whatever—has commonly carried with it hostility to all manifestations of Western-white culture, not merely
those identifiable as capitalist.[19]

Professor Nisbet has more than a small point. Mao, Castro, Ben
Bella, Ho Chi Minh, and "Comrade Bob" Mugabe imposed Marxist
rule on taking power, but their revolutions were propelled by resent-
ments rooted in race and nationality.

In the first week of September 2001, in Durban, South Africa, a
UN World Conference Against Racism, Racial Discrimination,
Xenophobia and Related Intolerance was held. It quickly degener-
ated into an anti-white, anti-Western, anti-Israel jamboree. At the
end a demand was made on the United States for reparations for the
transatlantic slave trade. Islamic nations that perpetuated slavery
into the modern era, long after the Christian West had brought the
evil to an end, were exempted from the reparations demands.

The seething racial resentment in the Third World against the
West—decades after independence and trillions in foreign aid—
should cause second thoughts about opening our borders to mass
immigration from that world. Not everyone coming here brings in
his or her heart the passionate attachment to America we attribute to
the peoples of Ellis Island.

Are We Immune?

In America, the issues of race and history, language and culture have resurfaced to divide us, as the integrationist ideal of the 1960s has given way to identity politics. The idea that men should be judged not by the color of their skin but by the content of their character has been superseded by a regime of affirmative action, quotas, entitlements, and contract set-asides grounded in race, ethnicity, and gender. Even the Republican Party, last bastion of the meritocracy, has bent the knee to the new dispensation.

Ethnic diversity in the student body and workplace has replaced ability, experience, and excellence as the indispensable feature. Al Gore may have captured the new America with his famous malapropism, when he translated our national slogan, *"E pluribus unum,"* as "Out of one, many." On college campuses, demands for separate dorms, dining halls, fraternities, sororities, and graduations for African-Americans, Asians, and Hispanics are being met. Segregation is acceptable, so long as one is an Hispanic, African-American, or Asian insisting upon it. As Shelby Steele noted, "Racial identity is simply forbidden to whites."

Those who believed in the civil rights decade that we would move "beyond race" have been proven wrong. Tragically, we seem to focus more on what divides us by ancestry, rather than what unites us as Americans. In schools, it is common to see black children who do their homework and perform well in class abused for "acting white." In colleges and universities, there are "speech codes" built around the issues of ethnicity and race, violations of which call forth public anathemas, followed by confession, ritual apology, and repentance. In the larger society, we have "hate crimes" where an assault, or even an insult that is seen as rooted in racial animosity, brings a more severe or added sentence.

When Hurricane Katrina struck in August 2005 and the Seventeenth Street levee broke, low-lying areas of New Orleans where African-Americans lived were flooded. Instantly, word went out that President Bush had delayed the rescue effect because only black folks were suffering at the Superdome and convention center. White America dismissed the slander. Black America believed it.

Back in 1990, a *New York Times* poll found that

Sixty percent of black respondents thought it true or possibly true that the government was making drugs available in black neighborhoods in order to harm black people. Twenty-nine percent thought it true or probably true that the AIDS virus was invented by racist conspirators to kill blacks.[20]

Every four years, our racial divide manifests itself anew as African-Americans—incited by charges that Republicans look with indifference on the burning of black churches, or that George W. Bush did not care about the dragging death of a retarded black man in Texas—vote 90 percent or higher for the Democratic candidate. After Katrina, Bush's support among blacks in one poll sank to 2 percent.

In 1960, 18 million black Americans, 10 percent of the nation, were not fully integrated into society, but they had been assimilated into our culture. They worshipped the same God, spoke the same language, had endured the same depression and war, watched the same TV shows on the same four channels, laughed at the same comedians, went to the same movies, ate the same foods, read the same newspapers, and went to schools where, even when segregated, we learned the same history and literature and shared the same holidays: Christmas, New Year's, Washington's Birthday, Easter, Memorial Day, Fourth of July, Labor Day, Columbus Day. Segregation existed, but black folks were as American as apple pie, having lived in this land longer than almost every other group save the Native Americans. We were of two races, but of one nationality: Americans.

That cultural unity, that sense that we were one people, is now gone. The term "Negro" was replaced by "black" to emphasize the racial difference, and has been replaced in turn by "African-American" to emphasize that we are not only of separate races but come from different continents. One recalls the words of Theodore Roosevelt to the Knights of Columbus, a heavily Irish, Italian, and German-American assembly in 1915:

> There is no room in this country for hyphenated American-ism . . . a hyphenated American is not an American at all. . . .
>
> The men who do not become Americans and nothing else are hyphenated Americans; and there ought to be no room for them in this country. . . . He has no place here; and the sooner he returns to the land to which he feels his real heart-allegiance, the better it will be for every good American. There is no such thing as a hyphenated American who is a good American. The only man who is a good American is the man who is an American and nothing else.[21]

Were Roosevelt to make such remarks today before an assembly of Hispanic- or African-Americans, he would be shouted down and hounded out of politics for a hate crime.

In the 1960s, black leaders from basketball great Lew Alcindor to boxing legend Cassius Clay, to poet Leroi Jones, to radicals like H. Rap Brown and Stokely Carmichael, began to adopt African and Is-lamic names to stress the degrees of separation from an American Christian mainstream.

The Black-Brown War

But it is in the crime statistics that one sees most starkly the levels of racial animosity in society. In its latest analysis of the Justice Department crime statistics, *The Color of Crime: Race, Crime and Justice in America,* the New Century Foundation lists the following findings:

Asian-Americans are the most law-abiding group, with a crime rate a fourth that of white Americans. Hispanics have a crime rate three times as high as white Americans, while black crime rates are seven times those of white Americans, and "black imprisonment rates are 33 times higher than the Asian imprisonment rate."[22] More jarring are the statistics on interracial crime. The most common interracial crime is black-on-white. "Blacks are an estimated 39 times more likely to commit a violent crime against a white than vice versa, and 136 times more likely to commit robbery."[23]

These statistics are so jolting they almost never appear in the press.

There is other disturbing news in the Department of Justice figures. Young Asian males are nine times as likely as white youths to belong to a gang, and Hispanic youths are nineteen times more likely.[24] A disproportionate share of Hispanic young and poor are thus assimilating into a misogynistic, rebellious youth subculture of drugs, gangs, crime, contempt for formal education, and hostility to police. Writes the Manhattan Institute's Heather Mac Donald:

In many immigrant communities, assimilation into gangs seems to be outstripping assimilation into civic culture. Toddlers are learning to flash gang signals and hate the police, reports the *Los Angeles Times*. In New York City, "every high school has its Mexican gang, and most 12–14 year olds have already joined," claims Ernesto Vega, an 18-year-old illegal alien.[25]

In February 2006, Los Angeles County jails were seized by a week of rioting as Hispanics and blacks brought their gang wars into the cell blocks. The Mexican Mafia had ordered reprisals for an alleged attack on Latino gang members outside. When Latino inmates, in a two-tiered dormitory at the Pitchess Detention Center, rained furniture down on black inmates, killing one, the Los Angeles Sheriff's office suspended all privileges and locked down all cell blocks in a jail system that is the nation's largest, with 21,000 inmates, 90 percent of them African-American and Hispanic.

John Pomfret of *The Washington Post* described what was behind the surging violence in the jails of L.A.:

A series of deadly racial attacks in the jails of this sprawling metropolis has cast a spotlight on long-simmering but little discussed tensions between a shrinking black presence and an ascendant Latino one in California.

In almost every area of public life—schools, politics, hospitals, housing and the workplace—African-Americans and Hispanics are engaged in an edgy competition, according to interviews with teachers, students, politicians, researchers, government officials, civil rights lawyers, street cops and businesspeople.[26]

Sheriff Lee Baca said the jail fights were part of an "ongoing gun battle" between black and Latino gangs.[27] The historian Roger McGrath, who grew up in L.A. County, writes that the violence in the jails mirrors what is happening on the streets:

There have been racial brawls between Latino and black students that have closed down several Los Angeles high schools ... during the last few years, and on the streets Hispanic gang members have been killing black gang members at record rates. In predominately black South Central Los Angeles and in Compton, Latinos are taking control through both numbers—illegal immigration has added a million Hispanics to L.A. County just since 2000—and violence.[28]

"Crips and Bloods Together!"—the slogan painted on walls in South Central—has new meaning: Gang wars among blacks must end. Crips and Bloods must unite to fight Hispanics. Says Earl Ofari Hutchinson, who hosts the weekly Los Angeles Urban Policy Roundtable, a discussion group that addresses the rising conflict between blacks and Latinos: "What you are seeing in the jails is symptomatic of a much deeper malaise. . . . Blacks and Latinos have been clashing in schools, on the streets, in the workplace, in hospitals. . . . I don't necessarily mean physically clash, but struggling over turf as neighborhoods change and become predominantly Latino."[29]

Adds McGrath, "On the inside, be it a jail or a prison, everything eventually comes down to race. It is tribal, and the warfare is savage."[30]

Academics who hold, with Andrew Hacker, that the notion of "race" is "a human creation, with no basis in genetics or biology," or "a meaningless concept," should probably not raise the issue in South Central. There, the hallowed hope of the 1950s and 1960s that America would become a color-blind society is moldering in the grave.

As it is their neighborhoods that are most affected and their jobs that are most threatened, African-Americans overwhelmingly support tougher border enforcement and reduced immigration. But in California the battle appears lost. Citing Nicolas C. Vaca, author of *The Presumed Alliance: The Unspoken Conflict Between Latinos and Blacks and What It Means for America,* Pomfret notes that while the Latino share of the population of California shot from 19 percent in 1980 to 34 percent today, the African-American share fell from 7.7 percent to 6.7 percent. There are fewer than 2.5 million

African-Americans in all of California, but 12 million Hispanics, and the number is soaring due to immigration—legal and illegal—and higher birth rates. In Los Angeles, Hispanics are now the accused in 73 percent of all hate crimes against blacks, and blacks are the accused in 80 percent of hate crimes against Hispanics. With L.A. County home to no fewer than 1,000 gangs, as one civil rights lawyer put it, "the underclass is at war."[31]

A teacher at one of the county's premier schools, the Los Angeles Center for Enriched Studies, says black kids now skip school on May 5, because they have been warned if they come on Cinco de Mayo, they will be shot. Channa Cook, an African-American teacher, told Pomfret, "When I arrived at class [on Cinco de Mayo] all the black kids had stayed home."[32]

Query: If the calls of race, religion, and ethnicity are being heeded by the Third World poor, above the claims of fellow citizenship, is it not an invitation to national suicide to bring tens of millions more into the United States in the prayerful hope they will assimilate as did the immigrants of old?

Is cowardice silencing our leaders in the face of what may prove a mortal peril to our unity and national cohesion? The French poet Charles Péguy once observed, "It will never be known what acts of cowardice have been motivated by the fear of looking insufficiently progressive."[33]

In Our Diversity Is Our Strength?

America differs from most nations in her receptivity to immigrants. We have believed the American family is strengthened by the adoption of sons and daughters. But while there have been periods of relatively high immigration—the Irish in the famine years 1845–49, the "Great Wave" from Southern and Eastern Europe in 1890–1920—there have also been periods of low or no immigration. From 1924 to

1965, America decided she needed generations to absorb, assimilate, and Americanize the millions who had come from European countries whence few Americans had ever come before.

This was natural and normal, and it succeeded. But what is happening now is not natural or normal. Without the support of the American people, indeed, against their opposition, the regime has embraced an ideology that teaches, without any evidence, that it does not matter how many millions come, what countries or cultures they come from, what creeds they may profess, or what language they may speak. All immigration is good; the more the better. For the more diverse we become, racially, ethnically, culturally, religiously, the better people we become. As for the America of 1960, which was 89 percent of European stock, the further away we get from that time, the better people we are. As for those who seek to stem the tide to preserve the country they knew and loved, they are merely bigots.

Open-borders enthusiasts say it does not matter how many come or where they come from. All can be assimilated, all can be Americanized. For, after all, what is America but an idea, a proposition, an ideological nation? As we all believe in freedom, equality, human dignity, and democracy, that is all it takes to become an American.

This ideology is the antithesis of conservatism, for it is rooted in a belief in the plasticity and malleability of human beings. It teaches that history and race, religion and culture do not matter, that roots mean nothing. Though this is gospel among our New Class elite, it is rejected by Middle America. The people sense something is dangerously wrong when millions who do not share our nationality, speak our language, or have any loyalty to our country are crossing our borders illegally and entering our land.

Jesse Jackson and Mayor Ray Nagin both protested when they saw illegal aliens taking rebuilding jobs in New Orleans from black folks who had lived there. And when 90,000 people in Los Angeles

Coliseum, in a game between the United States and Mexico, tear down the American flag, disrupt our national anthem, hurl cups of beer and insults on the U.S. team leaving the field, we ignore the pull of ethnicity at our peril.

Arthur Schlesinger, Jr., whose *Disuniting of America* Tom Tancredo cites as awakening him to the issue, describes this new "cult of ethnicity":

> The new ethnic gospel rejects the unifying vision of individuals from all nations melted into a new race. Its underlying philosophy is that America is not a nation of individuals at all but a nation of groups, that ethnicity is the defining experience for most Americans, that ethnic ties are permanent and indelible, and that division into ethnic communities establishes the basic structure of American society and the basic meaning of American history.[34]

To refute the gospel of ethnicity we need a new patriotism, a sense of belonging, not to the people whence our ancestors came, but to the people we have become and who we are: Americans. Writing at the time of the moratorium declared on immigration in 1924 in order to assimilate the Ellis Island generation, the great American thinker Irving Babbitt issued a warning against the inherent dangers of multiculturalism: "We are assured . . . that the highly heterogeneous elements that enter into our population will, like the various instruments in an orchestra, merely result in a richer harmony; they will, one may reply, provided that, like an orchestra, they be properly led. Otherwise, the outcome may be an unexampled cacophony."[35]

The Ellis Island generation was "properly led," and we became the one nation and people we knew in the Eisenhower era. But the triumph of the counterculture in its long march through the institutions has made us seem less like the harmonious orchestra of 1960 than the fractionated "cacophony" of Babbitt's warning.

The "No-Whites-Need-Apply" Caucus

In the spring of 2002, a three-day conference was held—no press invited—in Leesburg, Virginia. Attendance was restricted—by ethnicity and race. This was not a secret conclave of the White Citizens Council, but a joint meeting of the Black, the Hispanic, and the Asian Pacific caucuses of the House of Representatives of the United States. The invitation list seemed to have been made up with but one stipulation: No whites need apply.

As described in a front-page story in the *New York Times*, the goal of the "tri-caucus retreat" was to "create an atmosphere of understanding among groups that have often felt pitted against one another for resources and recognition."[36] But as the caucuses claimed to represent only those of African, Asian, and Hispanic descent, it is not unfair to ask: What were they uniting for, and whom were they uniting against?

The closer one read Lynette Clemetson's story, the more it appeared the Leesburg summit was not about aiding the poor and powerless against the rich and powerful, but about how people of color can unite to extract power and resources from white America.

Attendees pointed to their common front on the $175 billion farm bill. The Black Caucus had demanded an expansion of the food stamp program and the Hispanic Caucus demanded restoration of food stamps for immigrants. They found common ground. Another "shining example" of collaboration had been in Texas, where Hispanics and blacks joined forces to nominate Hispanic Tony Sanchez for governor and African-American Ron Kirk for the Senate.

But all the talk of racial and ethnic solidarity of peoples of color raises a question. If it is acceptable for blacks and Hispanics and Asians to plot to take power from white Americans, why is it a violation of civil rights for whites to collude to increase their representation in legislatures at the expense of minorities?

It is a law of Newtonian physics that for every action, there is an equal and opposite reaction. The same holds true for politics. If it has become acceptable for people of color to join forces against the white majority, a shrinking white majority will some day begin to identify itself by race as well, rather than by party or philosophy, to defend what it has. And, indeed, it is already happening. Let us hope this is not the destiny toward which we are drifting.

But all was not harmony at Leesburg. That January, Latino businessmen had left the National Minority Auto Dealers Association to form a National Hispanic Auto Dealers Association. Can one imagine the reaction to a European-American Auto Dealers Association?

The Spirit of Leesburg revealed itself in the entertainment:

Audience members sat rapt as Sarah Jones, a socially conscious writer and actress . . . slipped in and out of accents to portray characters from a Mexican-American labor organizer to a new immigrant from Haiti who scolded listeners: " 'God bless America, but not because of you. Remember, your ancestors came here, too.' "[37]

Nor was this the end of the fun, says Ms. Clemetson: "Beau Sea, a Chinese-American slam poet from Oklahoma, raised eyebrows with his confrontational number: 'The Asians are coming.' "

> We are everywhere
> We are programming your Websites
> Making your executives look smart
> And getting into your schools—for free
> And you know what?
> It's only gonna get bigger.[38]

From what went down at Leesburg—recall this was a meeting of members of the U.S. House of Representatives and staff—it is clear that the old ideas of integration and assimilation are yielding to the claims of ethnic entitlement. And as "Anglos" are already a minority in California, New Mexico, and Texas, they might start asking what kind of America it is going to be when they are a shrinking minority in the nation.

For Americans to believe that, unlike the rest of the world, we are immune to, exempt from, or unaffected by the powerful undercurrents of race, ethnicity, and culture that are pulling nations apart may prove a fatal delusion. Time to recall the insight of James Baldwin: "Not everything that is faced can be changed, but nothing can be changed until it is faced."[39]

11

Eurabia

[T]o see, and not to speak, would be the great betrayal.[1]
—ENOCH POWELL, 1968

All of Europe marches to its death.[2]
—JEAN RASPAIL, 2005

Europe is steadily committing suicide.[3]
—BRUCE BAWER, *While Europe Slept* (2006)

It was April 1968, only days after Dr. King had been assassinated in Memphis and riots had erupted in a hundred American cities. Fires, visible from the embassies, had blazed in the nation's capital where mile-long stretches of Seventh and Fourteenth streets had been looted, gutted, and burned. At this moment in that critical year, there arose to raise the alarm on the explosive issue of immigration and race a British hero of the war and scholar of the classics, the Tory shadow minister of state for defence, Enoch Powell.

"The supreme function of statesmanship," Powell began his address to the West Midlands Conservatives, "is to provide against preventable evils . . . the discussion of future grave but, with effort now, avoidable evils is the most unpopular and at the same time the most necessary occupation for the politician."

"Only resolute and urgent action," Powell continued, could avert the "horror" unfolding on the far side of the Atlantic: "[W]hether there will be the public will to demand that action, I do not know. All I know is that to see, and not to speak, would be the great betrayal."

As Powell spoke, the immigrant flow into Great Britain from the Commonwealth nations of Africa, Asia, and the Caribbean was 50,000 a year, a trickle compared to the 1.2 million legal and illegal aliens who have been entering the United States every year for a generation.

Powell warned that if stern action were not taken to stem the tide and encourage remigration out of Britain, by 2000, 5 to 7 million people of color would be there. "It is like watching a nation busily engaged in heaping up its own funeral pyre," Powell thundered, then spoke the words that ended his illustrious career and would serve as his epitaph:

"As I look ahead, I am filled with foreboding; like the Roman, I seem to see 'the River Tiber foaming with much blood.' "[4]

Powell was instantly gone from the shadow cabinet, dropped by Edward Heath for what that future prime minister called a speech "racialist in tone, and liable to exacerbate racial tensions."[5] British elites cut Powell dead. His working-class supporters could not save him. Yet he endured as one of the most popular figures in Britain. But in 1974, when Heath's government fell and the Tories were looking for a new leader, Powell was not in Parliament, which, under party rules, disqualified him from leading the Tories in opposition. The mantle fell to Margaret Thatcher. A career that might have closed with Powell as prime minister was finished, though he retained a great following until his death in 1998. He is famous (or infamous) today for nothing so much as the "Rivers of Blood" speech.

Powell once said that, had he to do it over again, he would have quoted the line in Latin to emphasize he was not predicting a bloodbath, only evoking the Sibyll's prophecy in Virgil's *Aeneid*: *"Et Thybrim multo spumantem sanguine cerno."*

It is said every great truth begins in blasphemy. Was Enoch Powell a racial incendiary? Or had he spoken an intolerable truth about what mass immigration from alien cultures must mean for his beloved country?

History suggests Powell spoke truth to power. By the turn of the century, racial riots were breaking out in the north of England in the old industrial towns of Burnley, Bradford, Oldham, and Leeds. By the end of 2004, 13 percent of British Muslims answered in a *Guardian* poll that they favored more terrorist attacks on the United States. One in ten admitted to "being willing to commit terrorist acts," and one in three to being willing to protect Muslim terrorists.[6] In July 2005 came the London atrocity in which Muslims, born, raised, and educated in England, massacred fifty-two Britons and wounded seven hundred on subways and a bus with suicide bombs. On the eve of the rioting in the Arab and Muslim suburbs of Paris in the fall of 2005, there were nights of street fighting between Asian- and African-Caribbean gangs in England's second city, Birmingham.

"Britain is now a deeply divided land where suspicion, intolerance and aggression cast their shadow over urban areas," writes Leo McKinstry, a biographer of Lord Rosebery and contributor to the *Spectator,* the *Sunday Telegraph,* and the *Daily Mail.* In an essay entitled "Dis-United Kingdom" in *The Weekly Standard,* McKinstry identifies multiculturalism as the cause of Britain's social crisis:

This sorry situation has been created by a deliberate act of public policy. For the last three decades, in response to waves of mass immigration, the civic institutions of Britain have eagerly implemented the ideology of multiculturalism. Instead of promoting a cohesive British identity, they have encouraged immigrant communities to cling to the customs, traditions, and language of their countries of origin. The emphasis is on upholding ethnic and cultural differences rather than achieving assimilation.

"Racial segregation is woven into the fabric of British public services," notes McKinstry.[7] One in eight children in Britain has a first language other than English. "Londonistan" is now the most linguistically diverse city in the world, with three hundred languages spoken by pupils in public schools, ranging from Punjabi and Nigerian Yoruba to Polish and Tamil.

In October 2005, *The Independent* reported on the arrest of eight members of a "people-trafficking gang" that had, at £3,000 to £5,000 per person, smuggled an estimated 100,000 Turks, mainly Kurds, into Britain. There most had melded into the growing Turkish community in North London, been provided with phony papers, gone to work in menial jobs, and, with the little cash they earned, sent for their families to join them.[8]

"The Camp of the Saints"

Five years after Powell's "Rivers of Blood" speech, the French writer Jean Raspail stunned Europe with his allegory *Le Camp des Saints*, its title taken from the Book of Revelation:

The thousand years is expired. Those are what departs the nations which are at the four corners of the Earth and which are equal in number to the sand of the sea. They will go forth in expedition across the surface of the Earth, they will surround the camp of the saints and the beloved city.[9]

Raspail describes a "Last Chance Armada" of the diseased and destitute from the hellholes of Calcutta, who embark aboard a vast fleet of leaky and decrepit ships and steer around the Cape of Good

Hope to Europe—to be taken in or die. As the armada enters the Mediterranean and reaches the Riviera, the French government, awash in humanitarianism and paralyzed by pity, refuses to repel the invaders and invites them in. Around the world, the wretched of the earth watch the televisions, and wait. When the Last Chance Armada triumphs, they emerge in an orgy of looting, rape, and pillage to overrun the fat rich lands of the West, "the Camp of the Saints."

The novel was a smashing success. Though many reviewers were repelled, others compared the provocative work to Camus's *The Plague* and Swift's *Gulliver's Travels*:

> Publishers' Weekly declared the book to be "remarkable . . . riveting." The *Wall Street Journal*'s Edmund Fuller said, "sensational." Linell Smith in the *Baltimore Sun* said, "no reader will remain unaffected by the questions it raises." The *Library Journal* said, "This book will succeed in shocking and challenging the complacent contemporary mind." . . . *The San Francisco Chronicle* called Raspail's tale "audacious and imaginative fiction."[10]

"One of the most chilling books of this generation," said James J. Kilpatrick. "Our children and grandchildren may soon discover that Jean Raspail wrote not fiction, but fact." Wrote *National Review*'s Jeff Hart, "Dismissed by some as mere fantasy, Raspail's nightmare vision of a Third World invasion of the Western world has become today's reality."[11]

Sam Francis ranked Raspail's work with Huxley's *Brave New World* and Orwell's *1984* as "one of the great dark prophecies of the last century . . . a somber but oracular account of the impact of mass Third World immigration on Europe and the West and the flaccid Western non-reaction to it."[12] The Western ruling class read the prophetic work and dismissed it as fantasy. And as America succumbed to the cultural regime of political correctness, Raspail's novel was moved onto the Index of Forbidden Books.

In 2004, the novelist surfaced in *Le Figaro* to accuse France's political elite of treason. "La Patrie Trahie par la République," the title of Raspail's 2004 essay, translates as "The Fatherland Betrayed by the Republic." By "the Republic," Raspail meant not just the Fifth Republic of Mitterand and Chirac, but France's ideology of inclusiveness rooted in the Revolution's ideology of *liberté, égalité, fraternité*. French law forbids any census of the racial, ethnic, or religious identity of citizens. Alluding to the waves of immigrants from Africa, the Middle East, the Caribbean, and Asia, Raspail grimly asserted: "The deed is done."

> Because I am convinced that the fate of France is sealed, because "My house is their house" (Mitterand) inside [a] "Europe whose roots are as much Muslim as Christian" (Chirac), because the situation is moving irreversibly toward the final swing in 2050 which will see French stock amounting to only half the population of the country, the remainder comprising Africans, Moors and Asians of all sorts from the inexhaustible reserve of the Third World, predominantly Islamic, understood to be fundamentalist Jihadists, this dance is only the beginning.[13]

"France is . . . a country of common blood," Raspail thundered, but "the Republic, which is only one shape of government, is synonymous for them with ideology, ideology with a capital 'I,' the major ideology." It seems that "they betray the first for the second."[14]

By inviting in millions of people from alien cultures and civilizations who may become French citizens but can never be truly French, Raspail is saying, the state has committed treason against the nation. The elites have betrayed the France of blood and soil, history and heritage, by sacrificing her on the altar of ideology. Not only the elites of France but the elites of all Europe are guilty of treason. With a demographic tidal wave rolling over the Continent, Raspail uttered his cri de coeur: "All of Europe marches to its death."[15]

Raspail writes with contempt of the "almost sepulchral silence of the media, governments and community institutions on the demographic crash of the European Union," and recalls the threat of Algerian president Houari Boumedienne in 1974, a year after *Camp of the Saints* appeared:

No amount of atomic bombs will be able to dam up the tidal wave comprising human beings in their millions which one day will leave the southernmost and poor part of the world, to swamp the relatively open spaces of the wealthy northern hemisphere, in search of survival.[16]

The New France

Three weeks after September 11, 2001, in a public relations gesture to showcase the integration of immigrants, the first soccer game between France and Algeria since the Algerian war was held at the Stade de France in the Paris suburb of Saint-Denis. With twelve minutes left and France ahead 4–1, Algerian youth, who had booed France's national anthem and thrown objects at two French ministers, rioted, threw bottles at police, and stormed the field.[17] Rather than highlight the melding of immigrants into the life of France, the game revealed that in France there reside two peoples. Both may be citizens, both may, like Zacarias Moussaoui, carry French passports. But their hearts do not belong to the same country.

"Where are the *beurs* going?" asked the cover story of *Le Nouvel Observateur*, using the slang for Arabs. The question was placed above photos of second- and third-generation immigrant youth invading the soccer field.[18]

During the fall of 2005, Raspail seemed a prophet. In the heavily Arab and African suburbs of Paris, riots erupted; they spread rapidly to Rouen, Lille, Marseille, Toulouse, Dijon, Bordeaux, Strasbourg, Cannes, Nice, and three hundred other cities, continuing for weeks. Ten thousand cars and buses were torched, two hundred public buildings firebombed. Hundreds of schools, offices, churches, and shopping malls were vandalized. One man was beaten to death. A French woman was doused with gasoline and set ablaze. More than two hundred police were injured and more than four thousand were arrested. Not until the twelfth night of the insurrection did President Chirac declare a state of emergency.

The criminals were the children and grandchildren of subjects once ruled by the French Empire. Severed from the countries and cultures of their parents, these deracinated youth may hold French citizenship, but they have never been assimilated into the French people.

The French government estimates its Muslim population at 4–5 million. Yet, "Most social scientists believe this number is too low, speaking of as many as eight million Muslims in France...."[19] Millions of the Muslims are no more French than Americans living in Paris. They are *in* France but not *of* France. Outside society, they seek out community and comradeship at mosques where imams preach that the West is not their home, but a civilization alien to their values and hostile to Islam.

Like America's urban riots of the 1960s that the Kerner Commission blamed on "white racism," the Paris riots were blamed on France's failure to bring African and Arab immigrants into the national mainstream.

"The reality is that we have allowed urban ghettos to develop in which French people . . . do not feel in any way part of French society," said Nicolas Sarkozy, the interior minister with an eye on the presidency who had vowed to "hose down" the *banlieus* to cleanse the "scum."[20] Economic and social solutions advanced to ease the crisis ranged from granting voting rights to noncitizens to affirmative action in hiring. To understand why this will not end France's crisis, consider how the United States succeeded, and failed, in resolving its own racial crisis.

Black Americans were not fully integrated into society in the 1950s, but they had been marinated in a common culture. Whether our ancestors had come from Europe or Africa, we had shared this land and lived together for centuries. We had no other loyalty or allegiance. We spoke the English language and embraced a Christian faith. Though of two races, we were of one nationality: We were all Americans. And America in the 1950s had a history of assimilating peoples.

But no modern European nation has ever assimilated a huge cohort of immigrants, let alone tens of millions of Muslims. Not one. And unlike African-Americans, the Islamic people pouring into Europe—there are 20 million in the European Union alone—are strangers. Millions do not wish to give up their Arab and Islamic identities and cultures and become Europeans. They wish to remain Algerian, Moroccan, Tunisian, Turk—and Muslim. Most adhere to a faith historically hostile to Christianity that is growing in militancy and recoils from a secularized, sex-saturated European culture. In the threatened war of civilizations, this vast Muslim cohort is a potential fifth column in the heart of a post–Christian Europe.

Writing six months after the riots, *National Review*'s David Pryce-Jones reported that while French authorities were fighting terrorism with conviction, they

seem impotent in the face of a level of disaffection among Arab and Muslim immigrants approaching permanent lawlessness.

In one of the Stalinist-style suburbs, Adel Boumedienne, of Moroccan origin, caught and beheaded his neighbor, a Jewish disc jockey, and gloated to his own mother, "I killed my Jew, I will go to paradise." Elsewhere a Muslim gang kidnaped Ilan Halimi, a Jewish salesman of cellphones. They called his family to read the Koran to them in such a way he could be heard in the background screaming under torture. After three weeks of this, they set fire to him and he died.[21]

The Muslim gang that kidnapped and tortured Halimi to death was known as *les Barbares*—the Barbarians. "There has to be reform," Pryce-Jones warns, "or it may be 1789 all over again."[22]

Across France, there is growing despair about the future. "Even the world of haute couture is reflecting the gloom," wrote a Paris correspondent of *The Washington Post*; "the Paris fashion runways this season featured Muslim-inspired head wraps and hemlines and tunics splattered with simulated blood in what some *fashionistas* dubbed carnage couture."[23]

Did France Rule an Evil Empire?

In December 2005, just weeks after the riots, France was torn again over issues of nationality and history. In February of that year, a law had been enacted mandating that French schools teach a positive view of France's empire, how it had introduced its colonies to France's language, culture, and science. The new law stipulated that "school programs recognize in particular the positive character of the French overseas presence, notably in North Africa."[24]

Textbooks were to teach about the "national contribution" of the *pieds noirs*, the French settlers, and the Arab and Berber *harkis* who fought alongside the Foreign Legion to keep Algeria French. Many Frenchmen believe that the colonists and the Algerians who fought beside them were as honorable and heroic as the British do the Loy-alists who fought for king and country in the American Revolution.

Christian Vanneste, sponsor of the measure in the French Parlia-ment, told *The Washington Post*: "I wanted to pay homage to all the troops from our overseas territories who fought so valiantly for France during World War II and to pay tribute to the one million Frenchmen and 150,000 repatriates who had to leave Algeria in 1962."[25]

The law was the product of a conservative government, and protests exploded all across the left. This new history, roared So-cialists, Trotskyists, Communists, immigrant spokesmen, and lead-ers of the ex-colonies, ignored or slighted France's role in the perpetuation of slavery and France's torture and massacre of indige-nous peoples, especially in the war of Algerian independence from 1954 to 1962.

Jean-Marc Ayrault, leader of the main Socialist opposition party, mockingly told colleagues the law sought to recall "the good old times of the colonial troops, when France came to convert the na-tions to enlightened civilization. This means passing over in silence the acts of violence, the abuses, the oppression with which this pe-riod is riddled."[26]

So furious was the reaction it derailed a friendship treaty with Al-geria, whose parliament called the new law on French history a "grave precedent." Algerian president Abdelaziz Bouteflika said the law showed a "mental blindness," and accused France of crimes akin to those of Hitler and Stalin.[27]

The French "have no choice but to recognize that they tor-tured, killed, exterminated from 1830 to 1962," [Bouteflika] said at a rally. They "wanted to annihilate the Algerian iden-tity," so that "we were neither Berbers nor Arabs nor Mus-lims. We had neither culture nor language nor history."[28]

Reeling from the onslaught, Prime Minister Dominique de Villepin declared in the National Assembly and on national television that France has "no official history." President Chirac denounced the law as a "screw-up," adopting a Pilate-like "What-is-truth?" stance, declaring, "the recording of our collective memory can only be a task for historians."[29]

So enraged were the leaders of Guadalupe and Martinique, Caribbean islands that remain part of France, that Sarkozy had to cancel trips. Should Sarkozy come, they warned, they would snub him. But riding a wave of popularity for the tough stand he had taken during the Paris riots, Sarkozy was unfazed: "This permanent repentance, which means we have to apologize for France's history, borders on absurdity."[30]

One French newspaper happily poured gasoline on the flames. As the Associated Press described it,

The newspaper *Libération* last week published drawings from "France Overseas," an illustrated colonial atlas of 1931 that showed "before" and "after" drawings—one a sketch of Africans cooking and eating another human being, the second a schoolhouse on a well-manicured street with a French flag flying overhead.[31]

While incendiary and provocative, these drawings raised profound questions that a morally conflicted and confused West has never confronted. Was "Africa" in Conrad's title *Heart of Darkness* when French, British, Germans, Belgians, and Portuguese arrived in the nineteenth century? Were not the lives of the vast majority of African peoples improved by the Europeans, who came to Africa secure in a belief in the superiority of Christianity and the civilization and culture it had created?

Colonial rule was marked by such evils as chattel slavery and the exploitation of African labor in the mines of the Congo and South Africa. But was not the arrival of the West of immense benefit to the colonized peoples? Can Western civilization not claim credit for having advanced all of mankind morally, politically, culturally between 1492 and 1960? Was not Western civilization vastly superior to the indigenous civilizations it encountered and crushed, from the Aztecs and Incas in the Americas to the Muslim, Hindu, Buddhist, Taoist civilizations from Africa to the Far East? Has not Western Man more to be proud of than ashamed of?

But if Western imperialism was not uniquely exploitative, evil, savage, and shameful, why should the West be made to do eternal penance and pay eternal reparations? Or do we accept the Sontag verdict: "The white race is the cancer of human history"?

Most prefer to avoid such questions. But they are not going away. For they are at the heart of the clash of civilizations now underway.

"Historians Upset as France Burnishes Its Colonial Past," ran one headline during the blazing controversy. In it we see the heart of the conflict. Are Algeria, Morocco, Tunisia, Syria, Lebanon, Vietnam, Cambodia, Laos, and the Francophone countries of the African subcontinent better off having belonged to the French Empire? Or would these peoples have been better off had the French never come?

There is truth in both renditions of French history. Western rule was not always benign and, in cases like the Belgian Congo, it was brutal and disgraceful. Yet there is no denying that the Americas of the Aztec, Inca, Iroquois, and Apache, the tribalist Africa of the nineteenth century, the India of suttee, benefited from generations and even centuries of Western rule. After all, it was not the indigenous peoples but the West that ended slavery and introduced the ideas and ideals of God-given human rights and rule of, by, and for the people.

But the ultimate issue here is not what foreigners or immigrants think of the history of France. The issue is what the French think, and whether the children of France shall be taught that their nation's history is glorious or sordid. Leaders of France should decide this, no one else. If immigrants object, let them go home to their own countries and study their own history as their own historians teach it. For if French children are taught to believe France's past is one long catalogue of crimes and their forbears were little better than Nazis, they will not love France, and France will die. For love of country—patriotism—is the soul of a country; and when the soul departs, the body dies.

Like the Paris riots, the struggle over French history raises grave questions for Europe. How does the presence of 20 million Muslims who come from nations where men believe their grandfathers were exploited and persecuted by Europeans advance the unity and security of Europe? How is Europe made stronger by such "diversity"?

Yet, while the question is being debated, or ignored, Muslim numbers grow. Not only is their birth rate higher than that of the European native-born, no European nation save Muslim Albania has a birth rate (2.1 children per woman) that will enable it to survive many more generations. Europe is aging, shrinking, and dying. To keep the economies of Europe growing and taxes coming in to fund the promised health care and pensions for the surging numbers of retired and elderly, Europe will need scores of millions of new workers. And Europe can only find them in the Third World, for Western peoples are everywhere dying out.

From 1492 to 1914, Europeans went forth to conquer, colonize, and command the peoples of this earth. Then, between 1914 and 1945, Europe's imperial powers indulged themselves in two of the bloodiest wars in all history, on their own continent. Comes now the closing chapter: the colonization of the mother countries by the children of the subject peoples that Europe once ruled. "France's present . . . is our future," writes *National Review*'s John Derbyshire. "Western—let us be blunt about it: White European civilization—is on its way out."[32]

On New Year's Day, 2006, France got another glimpse of her future. On a train trip from Nice to Lyon, "A gang of more than 20 youths—thought to be North African immigrants—terrorized hundreds of train passengers in a rampage of violence, robbery and sexual assault . . . [a] five-hour long 'criminal frenzy' in which passengers were robbed and beaten and women were cornered and sexually molested."[33]

Diversity does have its drawbacks.

By spring 2006, the National Front was making a comeback. Jean-Marie Le Pen had surged to 21 percent approval, against 29 percent for embattled Prime Minister de Villepin. A third of those responding to the French poll agreed the National Front was in tune with "the concerns of French people." "Le Pen foretold it!" has become a slogan to which many in France are now nodding agreement.[34]

Return of the Moor

In the year of Columbus, 1492, Isabella and Ferdinand completed *La Reconquista,* driving the Moors out of Granada and Spain after eight hundred years. But the second Islamic invasion of Iberia has now begun.

Morocco is the port of embarkation for aliens from Arab and African nations whose destination is Spain. Three million have made it, bringing the immigrant share of Spain's population up to 8.4 percent, one of the highest for any European country, a country whose birth rate is among the lowest on earth.[35] But the Spanish have begun to rage against the immigrant tide and the tolerant policies that permit it. Understandably, for in the Madrid train bombings of March 11, 2004, which killed 190 and wounded 1,800, the ringleader who committed suicide was a Tunisian, and eleven of the fifteen men charged with terrorism were Moroccans. Spanish authorities identified the Moroccan Islamic Combatant Group as the focus of their investigation.[36]

When hundreds of Africans stormed the Spanish enclaves of Ceuta and Melilla on the North African coast in September and October 2005, and Prime Minister Jose Luis Zapatero amnestied 600,000 illegal aliens, his approval rating plummeted and the percentage of Spanish who consider immigration the nation's number one problem shot from 31 percent to 54 percent.[37]

Holland and Germany weighed in with denunciations of the "call effect" of Zapatero's amnesty on Africans and Arabs who use Morocco as the stepping-off point to Spain, and Spain as the port of entry into Europe.

Melilla is a Spanish town of 60,000 on the North African coast, with a six-mile border with Morocco. It is protected by high fences topped with razor wire and policed by the Spanish Legion and Moroccan civil guard. The Africans attack the security forces with rocks, and are met with rubber bullets, bayonets, and shotguns. Daniel Pipes describes two incidents in the late summer of 2005:

In mid-September, the Africans began assaulting the frontier en masse. Deploying crude ladders made of branches, they used their weight to bring the fences down in places. As one of them put it, "We go in a group and all jump at once. We know that some will get through, that others will be injured and others may die, but we have to get through, whatever the cost."

The tactic works. When over 1,000 persons tried to enter Melilla at a single go in September, an estimated 300 succeeded. In early October, 650 persons ran for the fence and 350 are said to have made it.[38]

A dozen Africans were killed in the September episode. Morocco then arrested 3,000 of those attempting to breach the fences, flying 1,000 back to their native countries and transferring 1,000 more to the desert south, far from the Spanish enclaves.[39] Pipes describes the dilemma Europe faces:

> Giant smuggling rings and human waves cascading over forti-
> fied positions represent the starkest manifestations of pro-
> found and growing dilemmas: how islands of peace and plenty
> survive in an ocean of war and deprivation, how a diminishing
> European population retains its historic culture, and how
> states from Turkey to Mali to Mexico solve their problems
> rather than export them.[40]

With the Ceuta-Melilla route closed by Morocco and Spain, by late winter 2006, the Africans had found a more dangerous route to Spain and Europe. A thousand West Africans washed up on the Canary Islands, 300 miles from Mauritania. They were put into over-crowded detention camps. Leslie Crawford of the *Financial Times* writes:

> Many migrants were rescued after their flimsy vessels cap-
> sized or sank in the perilous, 300-mile journey from
> Mauritania—the latest launch pad for Africans attempting to
> reach Europe. Spanish officials estimate that some 15,000 West
> Africans are waiting to attempt the crossing, after Morocco
> and Algeria closed the northern migration routes to the
> Mediterranean last year.[41]

Said Manuel Pombo, Spanish ambassador-at-large for humanitar-ian issues, "You put a barrier to the flow of immigrants through the straits [of Gibraltar] and they are going to go to Mauritania and try to get through almost 300 miles of sea in a very, very terrible voyage into the Canary Islands."[42] Not even the risk of death, which these immigrants have freely accepted, is going to stop them from coming—coming to Europe.

Holland—Awakened by Assassins

In May 2002, Pim Fortuyn, a flamboyant homosexual and right-wing populist campaigning for prime minister on an anti-immigration platform—he had called Islam a "backward" religion and demanded that Holland's borders be closed—was shot six times in the head, neck, and chest in the Dutch city of Hilversum. Europe was jolted.

In 2005 came another stunning assassination.

Theo van Gogh, forty-seven, the great-great-grand-nephew of the Dutch master, was by all accounts a repulsive, foul-mouthed character.[43] "In writings and speeches he made crude jokes about Jews and riled Muslims with scatological insults," describing one Muslim leader as the "prophet's pimp," wrote the *Wall Street Journal.*

In August 2004, "the Michael Moore of Holland" aired on Dutch TV a ten-minute English-language film entitled *Submission.* The movie, noted the BBC, "caused an uproar."

The outcry centered on the stories of four Muslim women who were beaten, raped and forced into marriage, and were asking for Allah's help. It becomes apparent that their chadors and gowns are transparent and their half-naked bodies are visible through their dress. On their bodies are written Koranic verses describing the permitted physical punishments for women who "misbehave."

Submission was to be the first of three installments. It proved to be the last directed by Van Gogh. *Slate*'s Ronald Rovers describes how the Dutch filmmaker met his end:

> On the morning of Nov. 2 in a busy street in east Amsterdam, a 26-year-old Dutch Moroccan named Mohammed Bouyeri pulled out a gun and shot . . . Theo van Gogh, who was riding a bike to his office. Van Gogh hit the ground and stumbled across the street to a nearby building. He didn't make it. As the Moroccan strode toward him, Van Gogh shouted, "We can still talk about it! Don't do it! Don't do it!"
>
> But the Moroccan didn't stop. He shot him again, slit Van Gogh's throat and stuck a letter to his chest with a knife. He was slaughtered like an animal, witnesses said. "Cut like a tire," said one.

Bouyeri's letter fulminated against "infidels" and warned: "Hair-raising screams will be squeezed from the lungs of the non-believers." It closed with a Dutch incantation written in the style of Islamic verse: "I know for sure that you, O America, are going to meet with disaster. I know for sure that you, O Europe, are going to meet with disaster. I know for sure that you, O Netherlands, are going to meet with disaster."

Holland was shaken. Bouyeri had been born and educated in that most permissive of countries, where drugs are done openly and sex is on public sale. When police went to arrest Bouyeri's friends, they put up a fight. Mosques were torched, churches burned in reprisals. Dutch leaders who denounced Islamic fanatics were threatened with ritual slaughter and beheadings. Dutch police now believe that, among her million Muslims, Holland has a sizable nest of home-grown terrorists. The great port city of Rotterdam is 40 percent

Muslim.[44] By 2010, Amsterdam and The Hague will have Muslim majorities.[45] Where the Germans came and left, the Muslims are in Holland to stay.

Passing of the Multicultural Moment

Welcome to Eurabia.

Twenty million Muslims reside there and are the fastest growing minority on the smallest continent where the native-born are failing to reproduce themselves. Europe is facing the crisis of post-Christian civilization. Through birth control, abortion, and sterilization, the suicide potions of modernity, its population is aging, shrinking, and dying, as its need for workers to sustain its generous health and pensions programs and take care of its retired and elderly forces European governments to bring in millions of Muslims. Many of the children of these Muslim immigrants are becoming a lost generation, an unrooted generation that is turning to militant Islam to find identity, community, and a cause for which to live, and die. Writes *Slate*, "The Dutch filmmaker believed that insulting people was his right as a free citizen. The Muslim fanatic who slaughtered him didn't agree."[46]

A year to the day after Van Gogh's murder, Francis Fukuyama wrote in a *Wall Street Journal* essay, "A Year of Living Dangerously": "There is good reason for thinking . . . that a critical source of contemporary radical Islamism lies not in the Middle East, but in Western Europe. In addition to Bouyeri and the London bombers, the March 11 Madrid bombers and the ringleaders of the September 11 attacks such as Muhammad Atta were radicalized in Europe."[47]

Behind the radicalism of these Arabs is a failure to assimilate them. Their passports may read British, Dutch, French, German, Spanish; their hearts speak of another residence. "The identity problem is particularly severe" among Muslim youth, notes Fukuyama.

"They grow up outside the traditional culture of their parents, but unlike most newcomers to the United States, few feel truly accepted by the surrounding society."[48]

How does Europe deal with a militant faith making converts by the millions that preaches that to do God's will is to punish unto death insulters of that faith, be it a Van Gogh or a Rushdie?

By March 2006, Fukuyama, a creedal-nation multiculturalist and critic of this writer's *Death of the West* and Tony Blankley's *The West's Last Chance,* about the rising threat from radical Islamism, was conceding that Europe was now listening to us:

> the deeper source of Europe's failure to integrate Muslim immigrants . . . is not really trendy multiculturalist ideas embraced by the left, but precisely Buchanan's blood-and-soil understanding of identity. . . .
>
> The alarmist prognosis in these books has been taken much more seriously in Europe in the last few months as a result of Islamist violence. . . . Old-style multiculturalism is now seen as a failure in Holland and is being seriously questioned in Britain. There is a huge backlash brewing among the ordinary citizens in Europe, who last year voted in France and Holland against the new European constitution at least in part because they thought it affirmed Turkish membership in the EU.[49]

Behind Fukuyama's despair is the visceral and violent reaction across Europe and the Middle East to the blasphemous cartoons of the Prophet published in a Danish newspaper, then reprinted by many of Europe's major newspapers on their front pages. For weeks, the cartoon war raged, driving deeper the wedge between Muslims and Europeans.

"The cartoon controversy," writes Fukuyama, "while beginning with a commendable European desire to assert basic liberal values, may constitute a Rubicon that will be very hard to re-cross."[50] But if the West believes insulting and provoking a billion Muslims by mocking the most revered figure in their faith is an assertion of "basic liberal values," then Europe had best prepare for the clash of civilizations. For it is coming.

Radicalization of the German Turks

Around 1960, the first of what is now a community of 2.6 million Turks began arriving in Germany as "guest workers"—*Gastarbeiter*—to take the menial jobs Germans were leaving behind as their industrial economy was booming to become the third largest on earth. Half a century later, many Germans believe their parents made a terrible and tragic mistake.

In Kreuzberg, a neighborhood of Berlin known as "Little Istanbul," a "cultural tug of war is plain to see," writes Robert Collier of the *San Francisco Chronicle.* With Islamic fundamentalism rising, Turkish women are returning to their native dress, wearing head scarves and long cloaks.

"People are beginning to get back to nationalism, to Islam, to the worst combination of both," says Safter Cinar, a secularist and spokesman for the Turkish Union of Berlin. "Young people especially are becoming radical. Many of them are deciding, 'Okay, if they want us to be foreigners, we will act like foreigners. We don't like German society.' "[51]

Unassimilated, alienated from German culture, second- and third-generation Turks are embracing militant Islam. "There is a new wall rising in the city of Berlin," noted the German writer Peter Schneider in *The New York Times Magazine* in December 2005. Schneider dates a national awareness of the new wall to the days after the 9/11 massacres.

Parallel to the declarations of "unconditional solidarity" with Americans by the German majority, rallies of another sort were taking place in Neukolln and Kreuzberg. Bottle rockets were set off from building courtyards; a poor man's fireworks, sporadic, sparse and joyful; two rockets here, three rockets there. Still, altogether, hundreds of rockets were shooting skyward in celebration of the attack, just as most Berliners were searching for words to express their horror.[52]

Seyran Ates, a lawyer of Turkish descent and author of a book on forced marriages and the "honor killings" of Turkish women, believes the Muslim young are moving away from identification with Germany and the West. The subway and bus bombings in London by British-born Muslim youth, she says, "were in the eyes of many Muslims a successful slap in the face of the Western community. The next perpetrators will be children of the third and fourth immigrant generation, who—under the eyes of well-meaning politicians—will be brought up from birth to hate Western society."[53]

The two Germanies on opposite sides of the new wall are separated by economics as well as ethnicity and culture. Unemployment is 12 percent in Germany; among Turks it is 25 percent. Among Turks in Berlin it is 42 percent, with 50 percent of Muslim youth in the city unable to find work.[54]

"About 30 percent of Turkish students drop out of high school and another 40 percent graduate in the *Hauptschule,* or vocational program, which trains them for industrial jobs that are becoming increasingly rare," writes Collier. Yet still they come to Germany, although, according to ex-interior minister Otto Schily, "seventy percent of the newcomers land on welfare the day of their arrival."[55]

Alienation, idleness, and boredom have ever been the combustible elements of revolution. "In the modern day, chronic joblessness, especially among youth . . . produces its baneful results," wrote Robert Nisbet, and first among them is "the mindless violence of youth on the streets. . . . Boredom is almost certainly the secret canker in utopias, as Schopenhauer warned."[56] *The Economist* called the Paris riots "the angry rebellion of a beardless, Nike-wearing teenage underclass."[57]

In 2005, Berlin was transfixed by the "honor" killing of a young Turkish woman who left her husband to live a Western lifestyle, and the televised trial of her accused murderers—her three brothers, who kept photos of their dead sister on the walls of their jail cells. When Turkish students defended the honor killing, Germans were shaken. What was happening? Answered German-Turkish author Necla Kelek, "The guest workers turned into Turks, and the Turks turned into Muslims."[58]

Exactly. In 2001, the Islamic Federation of Berlin succeeded after a decades-long campaign in having Islam taught in the Berlin public schools, and the cultural change has been rapid ever since. Writes Schneider:

> Since the introduction of Islamic religious instruction, the number of girls that come to school in head scarves has grown by leaps and bounds, and school offices are inundated with petitions to excuse girls from swimming and sports as well as class outings.
>
> There are no reliable figures showing how many Muslims living in Germany regularly attend a mosque; the estimates vary between 40 and 50 percent.[59]

If those estimates of mosque attendance are close to accurate, the 20 million Muslims of Europe are the most devout believers on the Continent. One cannot think of a nation where Christian attendance at Sunday mass or weekly services approaches 40 to 50 percent.

These are percentages one finds in thriving Evangelical churches in our own Bible Belt.

Secular Turks blame Germany's crisis on "liberal multiculturalism" and German guilt over Hitler's crimes against minorities and Jews. This guilt, embedded in the national consciousness, causes Germans to recoil from demanding that immigrants speak their language and embrace their culture. Rather than be accused of intolerance, Germans capitulate to Turkish and Muslim demands, no matter the cost in national cohesion.

"Before I can get to the Islamic patriarchs," says Ates, "I first have to work my way through these mountains of German guilt." Where Britain and France have begun to expel the radical imams, Germany refuses. One Berlin councilwoman, writes Schneider,

> points to the Imam Reza Mosque . . . whose home page— until a recent revision—praised the attacks of Sept. 11, designated women as second-class human beings and referred to gays and lesbians as animals. "And that kind of thing," [the councilwoman] said, "is still defended by the left in the name of religious freedom."[60]

As second- and third-generation Turks identify as Muslim Turks rather than Germans, a backlash is developing. Chancellor Angela Merkel won office on an anti-immigration stand and, along with 74 percent of Germans, opposes Turkey's entry into the European Union, as do 70 percent of French people and 80 percent of all Austrians.[61]

Again, understandably so. For under the EU charter, Turkey's 70 million Muslims would be free to travel from Bulgaria to the British Isles to settle and work in twenty-five countries. Turkey would become the land bridge for the Islamic invasion of what is left of the cradle of Christianity. The great project begun by Darius and

Xerxes, who built the bridges of boats across the Hellespont to invade Europe from Asia, would be completed.

A measure of the deepening estrangement of Germans and Turks is the success of *Valley of the Wolves,* the most expensive film ever made in Turkey, where the gala premiere was attended by the wife of the prime minister. The movie depicts American GIs humiliating Turkish soldiers and slaughtering innocents and a Jewish doctor harvesting organs from Iraqi prisoners, à la Josef Mengele, to sell in the West. The Bavarian governor Edmund Stoiber, a former national leader of Germany's ruling party, called *Valley of the Wolves* a "racist and anti-Western hate film."[62] That did not prevent 130,000 people, mostly young Arab and Turkish males, from seeing the film in its first five days of general release. A Reuters reporter describes the audience reaction in a Berlin theater:

> They clapped furiously when the Turkish hero of the film was shown blowing up a building occupied by the U.S. military commander in northern Iraq.
>
> In the closing sequence, the hero is shown plunging a dagger into the heart of a U.S. commander called Sam. The audience responded by standing up and chanting, "Allah is great!"[63]

Aging Mother Russia

No nation provides a more graphic example of what the future holds than Russia. The Soviet Union was three times the size of the United States, with tens of millions more people; but in 1991, the USSR lost a third of its territory and half of its population as it dissolved into fifteen nations, half a dozen of them Muslim. Russia yet remains the largest nation, with twice the territory of the United States, but its population is less than half that of the United States and is annually shrinking. And Russia is home to between 14 and 23 million Muslims, most of them concentrated in the south but with a million living in Moscow.

The presence of these Muslims has fomented a nationalist backlash and birthed a new party, Rodina, or the Motherland Party, the nation's second largest after President Vladimir Putin's United Russian Party. In November 2005, two weeks before the Moscow City Council elections, Rodina ran an ad featuring a blond Russian woman walking in Moscow, "surrounded by dark-skinned immigrants from ex-Soviet republics. It ends with the slogan, 'Let's clean the city of rubbish.' "[64]

The ad was denounced as racist and a court purged Rodina from the ballot. But a Rodina spokesman noted that the court acted only after polls had shown the party moving into second place.

For ten centuries, Christians and Muslims have lived together in Russia. But with Russian nationalism and Islamic fundamentalism on the rise, tensions are growing. And with the Soviet Empire and the Soviet Union now history, there is no ideology, no empire, no Cold War conflict to hold these peoples together. As ethnic Russians seek community with their own kinsmen and identity in an Orthodox faith, Muslims hear the call of Islam and Islamism. Ethnic and religious clashes across Russia and bloodshed in the Caucasus are the consequence.

Just as Chinese leaders invoke nationalism and racial solidarity to hold their country together and keep its people loyal, Putin plays the patriot card and cracks down on ethnic rebellion and Islamic irredentism. Yet it seems inevitable that the Caucasus will long be a scene of religious and revolutionary violence, disuniting Mother Russia. And as one looks at Russia's anemic birth rate, dying population, the growing militancy of her Muslim minority, and the encroachment into Siberia by Chinese, one cannot but believe Russia will be a radically reduced nation by 2050.

"Despite calamitous social problems," notes the conservative British editor Derek Turner, "Russia still clings grimly onto relics of the Soviet Empire in the Caucasus and central Asia—as the people of Beslan were reminded horribly a couple of months ago. The 2002 census figures are mired in controversy, but there are an estimated 176 peoples and nationalities living within Russia. Of the 146 million population [as of 2002], 81.5 percent is regarded as Russian. . . ."[65]

In a December 2005 study, *Dying Too Young,* the World Bank described the demographic "devastation" of a Russia whose population had fallen by 7 percent in fifteen years and is now down to 143 million.[66] According to the UN population survey of 2005, between now and 2050, 52 million Russians and Ukrainians—more than one in four—will vanish from the earth. The Slavic race is dying out. And, lest we forget, Russia guards the eastern frontier of Western civilization. Donne's words come to mind:

No man is an island, entire of itself; every man is a piece of the continent, a part of the main. If a clod be washed away by the sea, Europe is the less, as well as if a promontory were, as well as if a manor of thy friend's or of thine own were: any man's death diminishes me, because I am involved in mankind; and therefore never send to know for whom the bells tolls; it tolls for thee.[67]

Ave Atque Vale, Europe

By the 1990s, parties had sprung up all over Europe to demand an end to the immigration that was changing the face of the Continent: the National Front of Jean-Marie Le Pen; the British National Party; Austria's Freedom Party; the Flemish Vlaams Bloc of Belgium and Francophone Front National in the Walloon region; Pim Fortuyn List in Holland; the National Alliance in Italy; the Danish People's

Party; the Swiss People's Party; Norway's Party of Progress; Sweden's Democrats; and the Rodina Party in Russia. Some boast a charismatic leader. All have in common populism, nationalism, and opposition to further immigration—and pariah status in the eyes of their national establishments.

Yet, just as the platform of the U.S. Socialist Party of six-time presidential candidate Norman Thomas was plagiarized by New Deal Democrats, major parties of Europe are cribbing stands on immigration and the EU long advocated by the populist parties.

But it appears to be too late for Europe.

In researching for *Death of the West* in 2001, I discovered that not one European nation, save Muslim Albania and perhaps Iceland, had a birth rate, 2.1 children per woman, that could prevent it from dying. In every country, the median age was rising; in half, the native-born population had ceased to grow or begun to die. The 2005 UN population projections reconfirm my research for *The Death of the West*.[68]

By 2050, it is now estimated, the 7 million people living in Estonia, Latvia, and Lithuania will have fallen to 5.3 million. Slovakia will lose 15 percent of its population of 5.4 million. With one of the lowest birth rates in the world—1.1. child per woman—Ukraine will see its population of 46.5 million sliced to 26 million. Of the 143 million Russians alive, 32 million, a fourth, will vanish. The massacres and starvations of Lenin and Stalin are said to have caused 30 million deaths. Europe is suffering a population collapse unseen since the Black Death of the fourteenth century. "In essence," writes columnist James Bemis, "Europe is suffering a 'White Death.'"[69]

Southern Europe is expected to lose 10 million by 2050, with Italy leading the way as its population plummets from 58 to 50 million. As no "Christian" nation has a birth rate at replacement levels, the reason Western and Southern Europe will not shrink more dramatically is that the dying Europeans will be replaced by Africans, Asians, Arabs, and Muslims.

Given the generous pensions and health care benefits the welfare states of Europe provide to their peoples—whose average age will be fifty by 2050, with a third having reached sixty-five, and 10 percent over eighty—the only way they can be sustained is by a massive influx of new workers, who will pay the taxes and take care of the elderly in their retirement centers, nursing homes, hospitals, and hospices.

Where will the workers come from to do the servile and service labor Europeans will no longer do? The answer is at hand. The populations of the nations of West Africa will double, from 264 million to 586 million by 2050, while those of the nations of North Africa will increase by over 50 percent.

Nation	Pop. 2005 (millions)	Pop. 2050 (millions)
Morocco	31.5	46.3
Algeria	32.9	49.5
Tunisia	10.1	12.9
Libya	5.9	9.6
Egypt	74.0	125.9
Sudan	36.2	66.7
Totals:	190.4	310.9

Islamization of Europe is an unavoidable consequence, indeed, an inevitability, once Europe ceases to reproduce itself. The descendants of the men who went out from Europe to conquer and Christianize the world are leaving fewer and fewer heirs. The culture of death triumphs—and the poor but fecund Muslims, expelled centuries ago, return to inherit the estate.

"Now it is beginning to dawn on Europeans," writes Tony Blankley, "that the combination of a shrinking ethnic European population combined with an expanding and culturally assertive Muslim population might lead to the fall of Europe's Western Civilization within a century."[70]

"The Anglosphere"

Two other continent-sized nations besides America belong to what has come to be called "the Anglosphere": Canada and Australia. Both, in the 1960s, threw out as discriminatory and racist an immigration policy that had kept their nations European. They threw open their doors, and invited the world in. And the world came.

The experiment seems to be more troubled in Australia, where one-fourth of the population is foreign-born and most immigrants now come from Third World nations.

On the heels of the Paris riots came the battle of Cronulla Beach. Some five thousand whites, wrapping themselves in Australian flags and chanting racist slogans, went on a drunken tear, chasing and beating Arab youth for an Arab gang assault on two lifeguards. One Aussie youth had painted on his back: "We grew here, you flew here."[71] In reprisal for Cronulla Beach, Arab youths rode in convoys into the suburbs of Sydney, smashing cars and assaulting whites.

Behind the violence was seething anger at Lebanese toughs who Aussies claim make a practice of gang-raping girls they regard as "white sluts."[72] The same charge, writes columnist Mark Steyn, is made against Muslim youth in France: "From opposite ends of the planet there are nevertheless many similarities: non-Muslim women are hectored and insulted both on the streets of Clois-sous-Bois and Brighton-le-Sands. The only difference is that in Oz, the 'white youths' decided to have a go back."[73] Learning of the systematic assaults on these young women, *Figaro*'s Marie-Estelle Pech investigated. *Financial Times* columnist Chris Caldwell reported her results.

Pech's interview subjects told her that a girl who wears a dress, or other well-fitting Western clothing is "asking for it." She often gets it, too. The most alarming stories in Pech's investigation concerned *tournantes,* or gang-bangs. Girls who, for whatever reason, lack a father or brother to defend them get loaned out by their boyfriends to fellow gang members.[74]

This suggests the Aussie rage at the Lebanese Muslims of Sydney is not without warrant. And just as Americans remember the twin towers, Aussies remember the Bali bombing of 2002, where Muslim terrorists targeted a bar favored by vacationing Australians, killing eighty-eight. They reacted as we would to a massacre of college kids on spring break in Cancun.

Prime Minister John Howard denied the violence revealed widespread racism. "I'm not going to put a general tag [of] racism on the Australian community."[75] Labor Party leader Kim Beazley, insisting that multiculturalism was alive and well, dismissed both the white rampage and Arab response: "This is simply criminal behavior; that's all there is to it."[76]

Perhaps. But as in Europe, immigration is moving up the charts as a political issue in Australia, returning to the prominence it held when Pauline Hansen's One Nation, riding the backlash against open immigration, was a national sensation.

Decades ago, as the Australians were rejecting their traditional "White Australia" immigration policy, Canada was doing the same. Many Canadians consider their new policy a moral and social success. At the time of Stephen Harper's elevation to prime minister in early

2006, the philosopher John Ralston Saul celebrated open-borders Canada as

> on the cutting edge, the most experimental country in the world on immigration and citizenship. . . .
>
> We accidentally came up with the post-modern idea of a nation-state, with no dominant group or no dominant ideas. . . . The idea is that you could have a nation of minorities, that there would be no idea of a majority—in fact, the idea of a majority would be catastrophic.[77]

In June 2006, Saul's "experimental country" awakened to the news that seventeen Muslim men had been arrested in a plot to storm Parliament, take hostages, behead Prime Minister Harper—and seize media outlets to demand the release of Taliban POWs. If NATO failed to respond, Canada's political leaders would be beheaded.

Multiculturalism, it seems, does have its disadvantages.

And was Canada really so "catastrophic" a country when almost all Canadians were of European ancestry? Wasn't that the Canada to which the world wanted to come?

About the new immigration policies the four Anglosphere nations have adopted, opening them up to tens of millions from the Third World, it needs to be said: all were imposed from above by ruling elites. None came of popular demand. All are resented by huge minorities or, as in the United States, huge majorities of the people. Which raises several questions. Who should decide what Western nations will look like at midcentury? Are ethnicity and religion valid considerations in deciding who shall come—and who shall not?

12

"A Nation of Immigrants"?

Give me your tired, your poor,
Your huddled masses yearning to breathe free.
—**EMMA LAZARUS,** "The New Colossus," 1883

Wide open and unguarded stand our gates,
And through them passes a wild motley throng.[1]
—**THOMAS BAILEY ALDRICH,** "Unguarded Gates," 1895

The most emotional and powerful argument for open borders and unrestricted immigration runs thus:

America is a nation of immigrants! Immigration is our proudest tradition. To send "undocumented workers" back is to betray our highest ideals and turn our backs on the best of our history and heritage. It is to sin against our past. Do you not recall the words of Emma Lazarus?

> *Give me your tired, your poor,*
> *Your huddled masses yearning to breathe free,*
> *The wretched refuse of your teeming shore.*
> *Send these, the homeless, tempest-tossed to me,*
> *I lift my lamp beside the golden door!*

It is among our most beautiful myths. It appeals to the heart. And there is truth to it. Many of us can trace bloodlines back to ancestors who came over in the seventeenth, eighteenth, nineteenth, or twentieth centuries. But save for the 36 million here now, we are not "a nation of immigrants."

Rarely have immigrants constituted 10 percent of our number. Since the Revolution, the vast majority of Americans were born here and take pride not only in their roots but in what sets us apart and defines us as a people separate from all others. We are not just some microcosm of mankind.

John F. Kennedy, in his celebratory book *A Nation of Immigrants,* wrote that in the 350-year history of the United States from Jamestown to Eisenhower, 42 million people had migrated to America, almost all from Europe.[2] By 1958, almost all had been assimilated.

What is different about today's immigration?

First, it is a tsunami unlike any wave ever seen in the history of the world. We have almost as many foreigners here today as came in the first 350 years of our history. Second, most of those coming are breaking in. They have no right to be here. When President George Bush reported in 2006 that 6 million people had been caught breaking into the United States in the last five years—more intruders than we had soldiers in Europe in 1945—we are not talking Ellis Island. We are talking about an invasion.

Third, almost all immigrants today, legal and illegal, come from countries and cultures whose peoples have never before been assimilated into a First World nation. Fourth, the melting pot is cracked and broken, and our elites believe it should be smashed as a relic of cultural repression. They do not want immigrants reforged into Americans. They want the United States to accommodate itself to immigrants, to become a stew of all the languages, creeds, and cultures of the world, a country that looks less like the America we grew up in than the UN General Assembly.

Fifth, among those coming now, many bring with them no love

of America or any desire to be one of us. Most come to work; some bring hostility in their hearts. And the president of the United States now wants to allow companies to go abroad to find workers to do jobs American can't take at the wages these companies offer. We are to have *Gastarbeiter* like the Turks of Germany. The republic is to be sacrificed to Kipling's "Gods of the Market . . . and their smooth-tongued wizards."

As the *New Republic* writes, these "guest workers" are to be

slotted into a caste, with no real hope of ever rising above it. Indeed, Bush's guest-worker program would codify a large group of people in the United States as second-class citizens [who] . . . would never be viewed . . . as equals. Instead, they would be seen as transient figures here only to make a buck. They would not be immigrants or future Americans. They would merely be janitors, construction workers and house-workers.

America would be divided between citizens and the *proles* of Orwell's *1984*. Far from "humane" and "compassionate," the *New Republic* notes, the Bush plan is "un-American."[3]

What we have today is not immigration as we knew and cherished it, but the perversion of a proud tradition, to convert America into something she never was and our forefathers were determined she never become.

The "Mother of Exiles" Myth

As a symbol of the friendship between the two republics born of revolutions against absolutism, France in 1883 decided to give the United States an immense statue by Frédéric-Auguste Bartholdi, named by him *Liberty Enlightening the World*.

As Otis Graham, author of *Unguarded Gates,* relates, the statue was assembled, placed on a pedestal on Bedloe Island in October 1886, and dedicated with President Grover Cleveland in attendance.

The poem by Emma Lazarus, who had been horrified by the Russian pogroms after the 1881 assassination of the czar liberator, Alexander II, was written as part of a campaign to raise funds for the pedestal while the statue was being built. "The New Colossus" was read along with other poems at the opening of the Bedloe Island exhibition in 1883. But poem and poetess were soon forgotten, as Emma Lazarus died within a year of the dedication of the statue of Lady Liberty.

In 1903, a friend of Lazarus gained permission to place a bronze plaque containing her poem inside the pedestal. But a far more famous literary figure, Thomas Bailey Aldrich—a friend to Whittier, Hawthorne, Lowell, and Mark Twain—had already published a collection of poems, of which the most famous was "Unguarded Gates."

Aldrich was a white nationalist who traced his lineage to colonial times. As he wrote to a friend in 1892, his anger at having been robbed by an immigrant had inspired the "misanthropic poem . . . in which I mildly protest against America becoming a cesspool of Europe." Aldrich's 1895 poem was raw and racist. Its theme is captured in four lines:

> *Wide open and unguarded stand our gates,*
> *And through them passes a wild motley throng. . . .*
> *O Liberty, white Goddess! Is it well*
> *To leave thy gates unguarded?*[4]

Charles F. Samuels, Aldrich's biographer, refused to consider the poem "Unguarded Gates," commenting, "the less one says of it the better." Yet what is important is that, in that time, Aldrich's view of immigration as introducing "Accents of menace alien to our air" was as widely or even more widely shared as that of Emma Lazarus. For Aldrich's circle of friends represented America's literary elite. Fame did not come to Lazarus until decades later.

As Graham notes in *Unguarded Gates,*

The arrival of millions of immigrants whose first view of America included that statue in the harbor generated among them a certain mythology of welcome and asylum around the upheld torch—the Lazarus interpretation of the monument— but to most Americans, the statue was a local curiosity, or a proud acknowledgement that liberty did indeed enlighten the world.

This would begin to change in the 1930s, as journalists and history textbook writers began to link the statue not with liberty but with immigration.[5]

In a 1936 birthday celebration of the island, FDR made the first direct link between the Statue of Liberty and immigration. Since then, the national media and Park Service interpreters have completed Lady Liberty's transformation into "Mother of Exiles," a "beacon guiding the world's huddled masses to a place of eternal asylum."[6]

The descendants of Great Wave immigrants now claim the Statue of Liberty as their own. But when FDR made the first link of the statue with immigration, America was taking in fewer immigrants than she had in a hundred years. We were living under the Immigration Act of 1924, which severely restricted immigration to people primarily from the northwest of Europe and secondarily from Southern and Eastern Europe. No others need apply.

In his famous play *The Melting-Pot,* Israel Zangwill had specified that it was the "races of Europe" who were to be smelted in America. Among his litany of peoples to be reforged and re-formed, Zangwill made no mention of any Africans, Asians, or Latin Americans:

> Here you stand, good folk, think I, when I see them at Ellis Island, here you stand in your fifty groups, with your fifty languages and histories, and your fifty blood hatreds and rivalries. But you won't be long like that, brothers, for these are the fires of God you've come to—these are the fires of God. A fig for your feuds and vendettas! Germans and Frenchmen, Irishmen and Englishmen, Jews and Russians—into the Crucible with you all! God is making the American.[7]

In Zangwill's play, the Almighty was given only European ore out of which to mold Americans. That is consistent with American history until 1965, if not with the American myth. And, no, Franklin Roosevelt never began an address to the Daughters of the American Revolution with the bold and booming salutation: "Fellow immigrants!"

What President Roosevelt said was: "Remember, remember always, that all of us, and you and I especially, are descended from immigrants and revolutionists."[8] As FDR had just told the ladies he had ancestors on the *Mayflower*, and as the ladies were proud "daughters" of American "revolutionists," this was scarcely a defiant act of identification with the "huddled masses" or "wretched refuse" of Ellis Island.

What, then, is the true history of immigration in America?

Who Are Our Fathers?

If one excludes the Indians, and the Spanish who arrived in Florida and New Mexico in the sixteenth century, England's Lost Colony, and Quebec, the first permanent settlements in North America were Jamestown in 1607 and Plymouth in 1620. These settlers were English, and they would give the nation its language, law, form of government, and traditions of freedom.

As James Edwards, the immigration scholar at the Hudson Institute, notes, even in colonial times laws were passed to keep out undesirables. Among these were "social misfits, convicts, and men . . . driven by desperation to take a chance in the wilds of America," as well as Quakers, Catholics, disease-carriers, and separatists. And especially Catholics, for in the Old World religious conflicts had resulted in "papist" victories that meant the persecution of their Protestant brethren. "In the eyes of America's predominantly Protestant community, it hardly seemed prudent to have established a society for religious dissenters from the Old World Establishment only to allow a hostile takeover by potential persecutors. Hence, Virginia in 1643 provided for the deportation of Catholic priests within five days of arrival."[9]

Edwards adds that the recoil against Catholics in America "was further intensified by the imperial wars of the eighteenth century, during which Catholic powers and their Indian allies decimated frontier settlements, and by the efforts of Spaniards in Florida to incite slaves to rebel or run away from their masters in Carolina and Georgia."[10]

At the time of the Revolution, there were 2.5 million people living in the thirteen colonies, mostly English, Scottish, and Scotch-Irish, with 100,000 emigrants from Germany and a smattering of Dutch, Huguenots, and Jews. In 1775, His Majesty's government halted all immigration to the colonies. "Between a third and a half of fighting men of the Revolutionary Army were of Scottish and Scotch-Irish descent. Many of those at Valley Forge were German."[11] (This may explain General Washington's famous admonition, "Put none but Americans on guard tonight!")

Of the fifty-six signers of the Declaration of Independence, forty-eight were American-born, eight were British-born, and one was a Catholic, Charles Carroll of Maryland.[12]

From our first days as a united nation, there was anxiety over who was coming. In 1793, French envoy Citizen Genet arrived to agitate America to join France's war on England, alarming President Washington. In 1798, Congress passed the Alien Act, which authorized the expulsion of foreigners "dangerous to the peace and safety of the United States." The residence requirement for naturalization was extended from five to fourteen years.[13]

For sixty years after the Revolution, an era known as the Great Lull, immigration was tiny by today's standards. All importation of slaves had been halted in 1808. During the 1820s, 150,000 immigrants came—an average of 15,000 a year. Not until the 1840s did immigration become a burning issue. For two hundred years before that, New England had experienced almost zero immigration. But crop failures in Germany and Holland in 1846, the potato famine in Ireland from 1845 to 1849, the revolutions of 1848 across Europe, and the repression that followed, sent 1.7 million people—most of them Irish—streaming to our shores.[14]

The shock was tremendous. Immigrants inundated cities like Boston, New York—and Chicago, where they outnumbered the native-born. As many of the immigrants were Catholics coming to a Protestant America, a backlash developed. The Order of the Star-Spangled Banner was founded around 1850. Its political arm was the American Party, whose members, on being asked what they knew of it, were told to reply, "I know nothing about it." Known as the "Know-Nothing Party," they have entered history as anti-Catholic and nativist bigots. And there was anti-Catholic prejudice and violence in those years.

But what must be understood is that America in 1850 was a nation born of revolution that deeply empathized with the European revolutions of 1848. The Holy Father in Rome, the traditionalist Pius IX, had backed the Catholic monarchs who crushed those revolutions. The Catholic Church and the Vatican States were seen as the quintessence of reactionary rule. As JFK noted, even Ralph Waldo Emerson wrote to Thomas Carlyle of "the wild Irish element . . . led by Romanish priests, who sympathize, of course, with despotism."[15]

Moreover, like today's underclass, the Irish had terrible problems with alcohol, violence, crime, and family breakup. There was a reason police vans came to be called "Paddy wagons." In the Mexican War, some Irish soldiers deserted the Union army, created a San Patricio Battalion, and defected to Mexico to fight alongside fellow Catholics against Protestant America.

The savage ethnic clash between Irish Catholic immigrants and the native-born American descendants of the British Protestants who had built the country was captured in *The Gangs of New York*, which ends with the crushing of Irish-dominated antidraft riots by Union forces in 1863.

After the Civil War, Irish-American "Fenians" made repeated raids into Canada to provoke a war with the British Empire to bring about the liberation of the kinfolk they left behind in Ireland.

Although the "Know-Nothings" are held up to contempt in our history books, they were not all evil men. As Peter Brimelow has written, they "*never actually proposed restricting immigration. They simply urged the country, in the words of Know-Nothing Governor of Massachusetts Henry J. Gardner, to 'nationalize before we naturalize' any new immigrants."*[16]

In 1854, they elected six governors and seventy-five congressmen; and in 1856, they got almost 25 percent of the national vote for their presidential candidate, ex-President Millard Fillmore.[17] By then the Irish had stopped coming and the Know-Nothings, most of them antislavery abolitionists, moved to the Republican Party and helped elect its first president, Abraham Lincoln. Not only could the Know-Nothings boast of being led by an ex-president, the commander of the Union army and future president, Ulysses S. Grant, had been one of them.[18]

During the Civil War, Irish and German immigrants, some right off the boat, were put into uniform and sent into battle, where many died never coming to know the land "where the streets are paved with gold."

In 1882, Congress passed the first restrictive immigration law: the Chinese Exclusion Act. It was renewed in 1892 and 1902. Native Chinese were denied U.S. citizenship and many returned home. With their strange language, customs, and dress, Chinese were considered unassimilable and were resented as they were willing to work for "coolie wages." The ban on Chinese would not be repealed until Chiang Kai-shek became a U.S. ally during World War II.

In that 1882 law, the government also "undertook to exclude certain classes of undesirables, such as lunatics, convicts, idiots and persons likely to become public charges. In 1891, certain health standards were added as well as a provision excluding polygamists."[19]

After the assassination of President McKinley by anarchist Leon Czolgosz, the United States in 1903 raised a bar against anyone who advocated the violent overthrow of the government of the United States.

In 1897, Congress imposed a literacy test on immigrants, but it was vetoed by President Cleveland. Taft and Wilson vetoed similar bills; but in 1917, with war tension rising, Congress overrode Wilson's second veto. By now, wrote JFK, "Those who were opposed to all immigration and all 'foreigners' were joined by those who believed sincerely, and with some basis in fact, that America's capacity to absorb immigration was limited."[20]

Kennedy's stance is understandable, for in 1958, he was courting liberals and intellectuals in a bid for the presidency. And the political forbears of those liberals were progressives who had joined Negro leaders like Booker T. Washington and W. E. B. DuBois and union leaders like Sam Gompers in seeking to halt the waves of immigrant labor that were depressing wages and taking jobs from our native-born, both black and white.

"Cast Down Your Bucket Where You Are"

On September 18, 1895, Booker T. Washington, picking up where Frederick Douglass had left off, delivered an address to the Atlanta Cotton States and International Exposition. The founder of Tuskegee Institute opened with a story:

> A ship lost at sea for many days suddenly sighted a friendly vessel. From the mast of the unfortunate vessel was seen a signal, "Water, water; we die of thirst!" The answer from the friendly vessel at once came back, "Cast down your bucket where you are." A second time the signal, "Water, water; send us water!" ran up from the distressed vessel, and was answered, "Cast down your bucket where you are." And a third and a fourth signal for water was answered, "Cast down your bucket where you are." The captain of the distressed vessel at last heeding the injunction, cast down his bucket, and it came up full of fresh sparkling water from the mouth of the Amazon river.

Booker T. Washington's point? He was pleading with industrialists searching for workers in their rising new factories: Look to my people first! "Cast down your bucket where you are."

> Cast it down among the eight millions of negroes whose habits you know, whose fidelity and love you have tested in

days when to have proved treacherous meant the ruin of your firesides. Cast down your bucket among these people who have, without strikes and labor wars, tilled your fields, cleared your forests, builded [sic] your railroads and cities, and brought forth treasures from the bowels of the earth and helped make possible this magnificent representation of the progress of the South. Casting down your bucket . . . you will find that they will buy your surplus land, make blossom the waste places in your fields, and run your factories.[21]

Do not wait, said Washington, for "those of foreign birth and strange tongue and habits."[22] Take my people first!

America did not listen. Millions of jobs in burgeoning industries went to immigrants who poured into the United States between 1890 and 1920. These men and women enriched our country. But they also moved ahead of and shouldered aside black men and women whose families had been here for generations and even centuries. Not until after immigration had been dramatically cut in the Coolidge era, and World War II created an all-consuming demand for industrial workers, were black Americans brought by the hundreds of thousands north to the manufacturing cities of America. And when they were, a black middle class was created upon which the civil rights movement was built. When immigration stopped, Black America advanced, as Frederick Douglass, Booker T. Washington, and A. Philip Randolph said it would.

National Origins Quotas

Immigration had been halted during the European war of 1914–18; in its aftermath, several incidents sparked national outrage and demands that the U.S. government take a hard look at who was coming. In 1919, an anarchist bomb was detonated in the front yard of the Georgetown home of Attorney General A. Mitchell Palmer. In 1920, another huge bomb was exploded in a pushcart at the corner of Wall and Broad in the financial district of Manhattan, killing thirty-one people and wounding hundreds more. The slaughter was comparable to the London subway bombings of 2005.

Thus began the Red Scare and the Palmer Raids, led by twenty-nine-year-old federal agent John Edgar Hoover, in which thousands were arrested and hundreds deported—some, like famed anarchist Emma Goldman, back to what was now the Workers' Paradise of Lenin, Trotsky, and a rising J. V. Stalin. Yet still the immigrants arrived in such numbers that "by February 1921, Ellis Island was so jammed that boats were redirected to Boston."[23]

With America demanding a halt to mass immigration and the Ku Klux Klan making converts in the millions, there came the first of the laws that would set policy until 1965 and cut immigration to the lowest levels in a century.

As the Census of 1890 had declared the frontier closed, the restrictive immigration laws of the Harding-Coolidge era would declare that America, whose population had more than tripled in sixty years—from 33 million at Fort Sumter to 110 million in 1920—needed time to assimilate millions who had come in the Great Wave. The need for a time-out was apparent. Organized crime and violence and the social problems caused by crowding millions of destitute and poor immigrants into tenements in America's great cities propelled progressives to join with conservatives in calling for tighter restrictions on who came, and how many.

The Quota Law of 1921 rolled back immigration to 357,000 a year. Annual quotas were established based on a nationality's share of the U.S. population in 1910. In 1924, the act was revised, rolling back immigration even further, to 160,000 a year. Annual quotas were reset at 2 percent of the number of foreign-born of any nationality here in the 1890 Census. This meant that English, Scotch-Irish, Irish, and Germans would be most of those coming. In 1929, immigration was cut to 157,000, and the quotas were again reset, based on the national origins of the population in the 1920 Census.

What Harding, Coolidge, and the U.S. Congress were saying with these laws was: First, immigration must be reduced so the melting pot can do its work and meld into Americans the 15 million Southern and Eastern Europeans who came in the previous forty years. Second, immigration must not alter the ethnic composition of the country. Ideally, the human cargo of every immigrant ship should look like America.

One of the Wilsonian progressives most supportive of the exclusion of Asians from the immigrant ships was the Democratic candidate for vice president in 1920, Franklin D. Roosevelt. "Californians have properly objected" to Japanese immigrants, wrote FDR, "on the sound basic ground that ... the mingling of Asiatic blood with European or American blood produces, in nine cases out of ten, the most unfortunate results."[24]

To civil rights leader A. Philip Randolph, then a Socialist, the Harding-Coolidge quotas did not go nearly far enough:

we favor reducing [immigration] to nothing ... shutting out the Germans ... Italians ... Hindus ... Chinese ... and even the Negroes from the West Indies. The country is suffering from immigration indigestion ... excessive immigration is against the masses of all races and nationalities in the country.[25]

While the Republican proponents of quotas were savagely attacked for racism, and had in Harding and Coolidge inarticulate champions, the *New York Times* rose to their defense:

It is both natural and wise that the American race wishes to preserve its unity and does not wish to see its present blend greatly changed [because it] prefers immigrants who will be easily absorbed and . . . it strenuously objects to the formation of alien colonies here [and not because it] adheres to silly notions of "superior" and "inferior" races.[26]

Though advocates of national origin quotas did not emphasize race, opponents attacked them as practitioners of "Nordic supremacy." Perhaps the most effective rebuttal came from Congressman William Vaile of Colorado. "Let me emphasize here," declared Vaile,

that the restrictionists of Congress do not claim that the "Nordic" race, or even the Anglo-Saxon race, is the best race in the world. Let us concede, in all fairness, that the Czech is a more sturdy laborer, with a very low percentage of crime and insanity, that the Jew is the best businessman in the world, and that the Italian has a spiritual grasp and an artistic sense which have greatly enriched the world . . . [and] which the Nordic rarely attains. It well behooves them to be humble.

What we do claim is that the Northern European, and particularly the Anglo-Saxon made this country . . . yes, the others helped. . . . They came to this country because it was already made as an Anglo-Saxon commonwealth. They added to it, they often enriched, but they did not make it, and they have not yet greatly changed it.

We are determined that they shall not.

It is a good country. It suits us. And what we assert is that we are not going to surrender it to somebody else or allow other people, no matter what their merits, to make it something different. If there is any changing to be done, we will do it ourselves.[27]

There was a rationale and a logic to the immigration laws that America enacted from the 1920s to the 1950s, writes *Social Contract* editor Wayne Lutton. "[W]e intended to be what we had always been: a European nation."[28]

But, after the horrors of Hitler's Reich were exposed, elite opinion changed. As Professor Mae M. Ngai of the University of Chicago writes, "After World War II, many liberals believed that the national origins quotas were an illiberal and racist anachronism: as the Harvard historian Oscar Handlin described the quotas in 1953, they were the 'unlovely residue of outworn prejudices.' "[29]

In 1958, JFK echoed Handlin, calling the national origins quota system an "anachronism . . . without basis in either logic or reason." The examples Kennedy used were that Poles, Greeks, Italians, Hungarians, and Balts could not use the unfilled quotas of Germans and Brits. But nowhere did JFK complain that no quota had been set aside for Africa, though one-tenth of the nation traced its roots there. "*A Nation of Immigrants* did not discuss Latino or Asian immigration at all, save for a brief paragraph on Chinese exclusion, which said it was 'shameful.' "[30]

Not until the updated version of JFK's book came out in 1964, with an introduction by Robert F. Kennedy, were two paragraphs added on Asian and Mexican immigrants, along with several photographs.[31]

John Kennedy's book was targeted at voters who had come, or whose parents had come from Europe. Kennedy's collaborator was the Anti-Defamation League of B'nai B'rith, which copyrighted the 1964 edition of *A Nation of Immigrants*.

As a result of the 1924 act, immigration fell sharply. By the 1930s, it was down to 50,000 a year. During World War II, it was halted, though 400,000 Displaced Persons were brought to the United States following the war.

In 1952 came the National Immigration and Nationality Act, or as it came to be known for its sponsors, the McCarran-Walter Act. As JFK writes, under this law, the racial bar against the naturalization of Japanese, Koreans, and other East Asians was removed, and a minimum annual quota of one hundred was provided for each of those countries. But the national origins quota system was retained, angering Harry Truman, whose veto had been overridden by both Houses of Congress: "The idea behind the discriminatory policy was, to put it boldly, that Americans with English or Irish names were better people and better citizens than Americans with Italian or Greek or Polish names. . . . Such a concept is utterly unworthy of our traditions and our ideals."[32]

With Truman as with Kennedy, the focus seems always to be on opening the door slightly to more immigrants from Eastern and Southern Europe, not on throwing the door wide open to millions from Asia, Africa, the Middle East, and Latin America. While denouncing McCarran-Walter, Kennedy and Truman both seemed to have their own preferences as to the national origins of who should come. Neither was for open borders. And back in 1954, Ike, with little protest, had ordered all illegal aliens deported from the United States in "Operation Wetback."

What caused Eisenhower to act was a flood of illegal aliens from Mexico after World War II that rose from a few thousand a year to a million by 1954. In July 1954, the Immigration and Naturalization Service, under General Joseph May Swing, began to round up illegal aliens and deport them by land and sea to the interior of Mexico. These Mexicans had been working the farms and fields of Texas and the Southwest at half the wages of Americans. Ranchers and growers were charged with exploiting the workers. But U.S. citizens were angered by the rising crime rates, the prevalence of disease among the illegals, and the undercutting of wages of U.S. farm workers. Although the INS claim of 1.4 million deported seems a wild exaggeration, Operation Wetback was an undeniable success. Scores of thousands were deported, many more returned home voluntarily, and by the late Eisenhower years, the inflow of illegal aliens had fallen 90 percent.[33]

In 1956, the ex-head of the State Department Visa Office, Robert C. Alexander, writing in *American Legion Magazine,* pointedly demanded to know exactly what opponents of the national origins quota were seeking: "When they glibly advocate action which would result in a change in the ethnological composition of our people . . . perhaps they should tell us what is wrong with our national origins?"[34]

This was a time, recall, when 156,700 per year was the quota limit, and JFK did not seem to object: "There is . . . a legitimate argument for some limitation upon immigration." Indeed, Kennedy insisted that reformers and restrictionists were not all that far apart:

A superficial analysis of the heated arguments over immigration policy . . . might give the impression that there was an irreconcilable conflict, as if one side wanted to go back to the policy of our founding fathers of unrestricted immigration, and the other side wanted to stop all further immigration. In fact, there are only a few basic differences between the most liberal bill offered in recent years, sponsored by former Senator Herbert H. Lehman, and the supporters of the status quo. The present law admits 156,700 quota immigrants annually. The Lehman bill . . . would admit 250,000.

If this were the range of disagreement today, America's immigration crisis could be solved. Senator Lehman's figure, 250,000, in what JFK called the "most liberal bill offered in recent years," would be within the range of acceptability for restrictionists today. And Kennedy reassured Americans that his proposal "does not seek to make over the face of America."[35]

Indeed, in his litany of famous immigrants who have contributed mightily to America, JFK does not mention a single African or Asian, or any woman at all. All are males and all were from Europe, except one West Indian: Alexander Hamilton. And JFK assures the nation, "Immigrants would still be given tests for health, intelligence, morality and security."[36]

"These changes," Kennedy concludes, "will have little effect on the number of immigrants [156,700] admitted annually."[37]

Today, people are denounced as racists for promoting ideas identical to JFK's. The reason? The true and hidden agenda of the open-borders lobby *is* exactly that: "To make over the face of America." To realize it, they will call their opponents names that more aptly apply to themselves.

The Immigration Act of 1965

History will record that the Immigration Act of 1965 did more to change America than the Civil Rights Act of 1964, which simply imposed on the South antidiscrimination laws other states had already adopted. But the Immigration Act of 1965 was stealth law, its results the very opposite of what its champion had promised. As Robert F. Kennedy wrote in his introduction to *A Nation of Immigrants,* "The number of people who wish to come here today is much smaller than it was in the nineteenth century."[38] Senator Edward Kennedy, the chairman of the subcommittee that conducted the hearing on the immigration bill, pledged:

[O]ur cities will not be flooded with a million immigrants annually. Under the proposed bill, the present level of immigration remains substantially the same. . . . Secondly, the ethnic mix of this country will not be upset. . . . Contrary to the charges in some quarters, S. 500 will not inundate America with immigrants from any other country or area, or the most populated and economically deprived nations of Africa and Asia. . . . [39]

Only haters would make such assertions, thundered Kennedy. "The charges I have mentioned are highly emotional, irrational, and with little foundation in fact. They are out of line with the obligations of responsible citizenship. They breed hate of our heritage."[40]

Teddy Kennedy was assuring a nation that, in a Harris Poll in 1965, had stated by a majority of two to one that it did not want to ease the immigration laws. What happened? As Dean Steven Gillon of the Honors College at Oklahoma University told a 2006 gathering of the American Immigration Control Foundation:

The U.S. added at least 40 million immigrants after 1965. Before 1965, 95 percent of the new immigrants had come from Europe. After 1965, 95 percent came from the Third World. The 1965 act has transformed American society and had consequences exactly the opposite of what we were promised.[41]

The 1965 Celler-Hart bill was the greatest bait-and-switch in history. Americans were promised one result, and got the opposite result that they had been promised would not happen. They were misled. They were deceived. They were swindled. They were told immigration levels would remain roughly the same and the ethnic composition of their country would not change. What they got was a Third World invasion that is converting America into another country.

The effect of the 1965 act was to remove national origins quotas from Europeans and give them to the Third World, then to throw open America's doors to mass immigration from Asia, Africa, and Latin America. In the last four decades, tens of millions have poured in. When, a generation ago, illegal aliens began to arrive at a rate of 500,000 a year, the U.S. government threw up its hands, abdicating its constitutional duty to defend the states from invasion.

Nor was it conservatives alone who were alarmed at the risks we were taking. In a 1987 interview with the *Christian Science Monitor,* CBS commentator Eric Sevareid said that one of the "truly major issues" with which America must deal was "the vast tidal wave of human beings" coming from the Third World. "There is a fragmentation going on in this country," Sevareid warned. "At what point does cultural, racial diversity become a kind of social anarchy? How do you get national cohesion this way?"[42]

Theodore White, who lived to see the early consequences of the 1965 Immigration Act, called it "noble, revolutionary—and probably the most thoughtless of the many acts of the Great Society." In his memoirs, LBJ does not even mention the Immigration Act of 1965.[43]

Edward Kennedy's adversary in the immigration bill fight was Senator Sam Ervin of North Carolina, who would achieve fame as chairman of the committee that investigated the Watergate scandal. Ervin openly defended the national origins quotas of McCarran-Walter: "The only possible charge of discrimination in the McCarran-Walter Act is that it discriminates in favor of the people who made the greatest contribution to America, and this [new] bill puts them on the same plane as everybody else on earth."[44]

What is wrong, Sam Ervin was asking, with the national origins of the American people? What is wrong with maintaining them? What is wrong with preferring as immigrants one's own kinsmen?

On October 3, 1965, at the foot of the Statue of Liberty, Lyndon Johnson signed the Immigration Act of 1965. We live today with its consequences. But most Americans have never reconciled themselves to it, and many have actively resisted.

"Cesar Chavez, Minuteman"

As immigration specialist Steve Sailer writes in his article in *The American Conservative* in 2006, only three figures have holidays declared for their birthdays by the state of California: Jesus Christ, Martin Luther King, Jr., and Cesar Chavez. Chavez was canonized for his role in building the United Farm Workers Union, though the UFW today represents only 2 percent of the agricultural labor force in the state.[45] What enabled the UFW to flourish in the 1960s and 1970s was Congress's abolition of the *bracero* program, under which Mexican workers were seasonally invited in, but returned home after the harvest. In 1964, liberals, inspired by CBS's Edward R. Murrow *Harvest of Shame* documentary in 1960, killed the program.

With no *braceros* to do stoop labor, agribusiness was forced to raise the wages of Mexican-Americans, negotiate with Chavez, and recognize his union. Like Sam Gompers and Booker T. Washington and A. Philip Randolph, Chavez knew that illegal aliens would drive down the higher wages he had won for his workers—and kill his union.

To undercut Chavez, the growers bused workers up from Mexico, but the left stood with Chavez. "In 1969," writes Sailer, "Chavez led a march to the Mexican border to protest illegal immigration. Joining him were Senator Walter Mondale and Martin Luther King's successor as head of the Southern Christian Leadership Conference, Ralph Abernathy." In 1979, Chavez testified to Congress,

> when the farm workers strike and their strike is successful, the employers go to Mexico and have unlimited, unrestricted use of illegal alien strikebreakers to break the strike. And, for over 30 years, the Immigration and Naturalization Service has looked the other way and assisted in the strikebreaking. . . . The employers use professional smugglers to recruit and

transport human contraband across the Mexican border for the specific act of strikebreaking.[46]

Chavez, Sailer charges, routinely "finked on illegal scabs to *la migra*."[47] Columnist Ruben Navarette, Jr., reported in the *Arizona Republic* that Chavez, "a labor leader intent on protecting union membership, was as effective a surrogate for the INS as ever existed. Indeed, Chavez and the United Farm Workers Union he headed routinely reported, to the INS, for deportation, suspected illegal immigrants who served as strikebreakers or refused to unionize."[48]

How the world has changed. Today, liberal Democrats stand beside establishment Republicans like Bush and McCain for open borders and amnesty for 12 million illegal aliens, selling out the vital interests of semiskilled and unskilled Americans—black, Hispanic, and white—in better pay for the tough jobs they do. Corporate America owns the country. Like Lola, what it wants, it gets.

Numbers: Then and Now

To understand why Americans who never opposed immigration in the past are alarmed to the point of panic, consider the countries of origin, and the total number of immigrants who ever came to America from 1607 to 1958—as reported by JFK:

Nation of Origin	Total No. of Immigrants 1607–1958
Germany	6,798,313
Italy	5,017,625
Great Britain	4,642,096
Ireland	4,693,009
Austria-Hungary	4,280,863
Russia	3,344,998

Sweden	1,255,296
Norway	843,867
France	698,188
Greece	499,465
Poland	451,010
China	411,585
Denmark	354,331
Japan	338,087
Rumania	159,497
Finland	28,358[49]

Through those 350 years, JFK writes, America took in 42 million immigrants. Now compare those numbers with today's.

In 2006, we have as many *illegal* aliens inside our borders, 12 to 20 million, as all the Germans and Italians, our two largest immigrant groups, who ever came in two centuries. Our illegal population alone exceeds all the Irish, Jewish, and British immigrants who came. *Each year,* we catch more people breaking in at the border than all the Swedes or Norwegians who came to America in two hundred years. Half a million illegal aliens succeed in breaking in every year, more than all the Greeks or Poles who came legally from the American Revolution to 1960. More Salvadorans are in the Washington, D.C., metropolitan area alone than all the Greeks or Poles who ever came to America in the nineteenth and twentieth centuries. As Peter Brimelow wrote in his seminal article in *National Review* in 1992:

Amazingly, only about 500,000 legal immigrants entered the U.S. in the whole of the 1930s. (In those days there was virtually no illegal immigration.) And only about a million entered in the 1940s—including World War II refugees. By contrast . . . the U.S. accepted over 1.5 million immigrants, counting only legals, in the single year of 1990 alone.[50]

There are almost as many immigrants and their children in the United States in 2006—36 million—as all the immigrants who came in 350 previous years of American history. JFK, who thought the 156,700 annual limit on immigrants was fine but the nationalities mix might change a bit, could not comprehend a nation that, for twenty years, has taken in between 1 to 2 million, legal and illegal, every year, 90 percent of them from the Third World. In 1991, according to the final figures, the United States took in 1.8 million, twelve times as many people as John F. Kennedy thought was an acceptable figure.

13

Last Chance

Civilizations die when they fail to resolve the crisis of the age. So said Toynbee.

The existential crisis of Western civilization does not come from Islamic terrorism. Even with an atom bomb, terrorists could do but a fraction of the damage we inflicted on our civilization between 1914 and 1945, when scores of millions of our best and bravest perished as Europe was devastated by the Nazi and Red armies and round-the-clock bombing by the British and Americans.

The crisis of the West is of a collapsing culture and vanishing peoples, as a Third World that grows by 100 million people—the equivalent of a new Mexico—every eighteen months mounts the greatest invasion in the history of the world. If we do not shake off our paralysis, the West comes to an end.

By 2050, a depopulated Europe will have been overrun by African and Arab peoples and resemble the Bosnia and Beirut of today more than the Europe of Churchill and de Gaulle. By 2050, America will have become a multiracial, multiethnic, multilingual, multicultural conglomerate—a Balkanized Brazil of 420 million, a Tower of Babel, a replica of the Roman Empire after the Goths and Vandals had passed over.

In every way, whether by opinion survey or referendum, Americans have said they do not want to "go gentle into that good night." Yet candor compels us to concede this is almost certainly America's fate. For our 2,000-mile-long border with Mexico, the land bridge from the Third World into America, is being overrun. And the process may be irreversible, for the correlation of forces is not in favor of those who would preserve the nation.

Consider the feebleness of the U.S. government. Andrew Jackson, Theodore Roosevelt, or Dwight Eisenhower would have halted this invasion cold. Without apology. George Bush has persuaded himself the invasion is benign and the progressive thing to do is to welcome it. On this, there is not a dime's worth of difference between George Bush and Teddy Kennedy.

Concerned about his legacy, President Bush may yet live to see his name entered into the history of his country as the president who lost the American Southwest that James K. Polk won for the United States. As a patriot, how can President Bush allow this? Even the most primitive species reacts when its habitat is so massively and rudely violated.

Let us imagine a comparable situation. Ten million Americans, to escape poverty and find work during the Great Depression, migrate from the Dust Bowl down to Mexico. Settled there, they demand that Mexico provide them cash payments, subsidize their food, provide them free medical care, educate their children in English, teach them U.S. history, and start celebrating U.S. holidays. Suppose the Americans then began to commit crimes of assault, rape, and murder at three and four times the rate of the Mexican people and that the American young started joining criminal gangs at nineteen times the rate of Mexican kids. Suppose, then, that 10,000 Americans joined in the burning and looting of the second largest city in Mexico and millions marched under the Stars and Stripes to demand all the rights and privileges of Mexican citizens.

Mexico would have sent its army to drive these Americans back over the Rio Grande. Contrast this with America's cringing response when faced with a duty to defend our borders and remove intruders from our home. In America's border crisis, George Bush is a ninety-seven-pound weakling.

In almost every opinion survey, majorities of Americans say they want to stop illegal immigration, even if it means troops on the Rio Grande and a barrier fence from Brownsville to San Diego. But the majority no longer rules in America, when its interests collide with the globalist ideology of our transnational elites.

Consider the forces against reform. Corporate America wants an endless supply of cheap labor and the freedom to hire foreign workers and bring them to the United States. The major media, the unions, the churches favor amnesty. The Democratic Party sees in mass immigration the future voters who can end Republican hegemony. The GOP is terrified of offending 43 million Hispanics and of a cutoff in campaign cash if it imposes sanctions on corporate scofflaws who regularly hire illegal aliens.

The 36 million foreign-born already here want the guaranteed right to bring in their relatives. The survival of Hispanic media depends on a constant resupply of Spanish speakers. Internationalists see nations as relics of a forgettable past, world government as the future, and want to erase all borders. Critically, Hispanic voters in Texas, Arizona, New Mexico, and California, and the swing states of Colorado and Nevada, are approaching numbers where they may be decisive in all future presidential elections. If the border is not secured before we reach the tipping point, the border will never be secure. And that will be the end of the America we knew and loved.

Have We the Will to Act?

Liberalism is the ideology of Western suicide. Its ideas, pursued to their logical end, James Burnham argued, will prove fatal to the West. Conservatives, beguiled by serpents in their garden, have eaten of the forbidden fruit of liberal ideology and are about to lose Paradise. If America is not to be lost, we must speak the truth.

It is not true that all creeds and cultures are equally assimilable in a First World nation born of England, Christianity, and Western civilization. Race, faith, ethnicity, and history leave genetic fingerprints no "proposition nation" can erase. Ignoring this truth, we sent an army to Baghdad to democratize Iraq, only to discover that Iraqis were Shiites, Turkomen, Christians, Kurds, and Sunnis, for whom religion, history, and tribe were all-important. They wish to be ruled by the majority only when and where they are the majority.

Race matters. Ethnicity matters. History matters. Faith matters. Nationality matters. While they are not everything, they are not nothing. Multiculturalist ideology be damned, this is what history teaches. That is why Europeans do not want Turks in the European Union. That is why Serbs will ever resent the loss of Kosovo to Albanians. That is why African tribes still slaughter one another. That is why Israelis do not want a democratic state of Palestinians and Jews from the Jordan to the sea. That is why Muslims fight Christians in Indonesia, Nigeria, and Sudan, Buddhists in Thailand, Hindus in India, Jews in Palestine, Russians in the Caucasus.

Ideology and ignorance of history led Woodrow Wilson to consign millions of Germans to alien rule, leading straight to the revanchism of Hitler's Third Reich. Did they not know at Versailles that Germans would want their land and kinsmen back? It is fatal to ignore realities rooted in race, religion, and history. In Rhodesia and South Africa, whites are attacked for reasons of race and history. It is suicidal not to realize that Mexicans harbor a deep grievance against America and nurture a nationalist belief that we robbed them of half their country. Why would America open her door to scores of millions who harbor such beliefs deep in their psyche? It is self-delusion to blind oneself to the ethnic chauvinism of the indigenous peoples of Latin America, or the Han Chinese who stomp upon Tibetans, Uighurs, Mongols, Christians, and the Faithful of the Falun Gong as they move inexorably toward world power.

We need to awaken from the Panglossian fantasy that America has become the first universal nation and model for all mankind.

In our diversity is our strength, we are daily indoctrinated. But this has it upside down. Al Gore notwithstanding, *E pluribus unum* does not mean "Out of one, many," but "Out of many, one." In our unity is our strength. If we do not again become one nation and one people, we will lose our country. And, as Euripides wrote, there is no greater sorrow on earth than the loss of one's native land.

What Is to Be Done?

What Is to Be Done? was the title of Lenin's famous 1902 pamphlet, and we Americans today know in our hearts what must be done.

When the Seventeenth Street levee broke and the waters of Lake Pontchartrain inundated New Orleans, the imperative was clear: Fix the levee! Stop the flood! Before the cleanup could begin, before the refugees could return, the breach in the levee had to be closed so the lake waters ceased to drown the city.

And so it is with America's state of emergency. The immediate imperative is: Fix the border. Stop the flood. "America must not be overwhelmed," Sam Gompers wrote in his letter to Congress in support of the Immigration Act of 1924.[3]

The Bush guest worker program will only perpetuate and deepen the crisis. Once amnesty is granted, once those who broke in are told they need not go back, once all businesses are blanket-pardoned for past illegal hirings and permitted to go abroad to hire more foreign workers, the morale of the resistance will be shattered and the nation will lose control of the border forever.

Current projections are that by 2050, we will have a population of more than 420 million people, with 102 million Hispanics concentrated in the Southwest. African-Americans and Hispanics will be hugely overrepresented among our poor and working classes. Our affluent and professional classes will be dominated by Asians and whites. Our country will look like Latin America, with its chasm between rich and poor. Politically, this will produce a lunge toward statism. Demands for new social spending for health, education, and welfare for the scores of millions of poor and working-class people of color, and for quotas, racial and ethnic set-asides, affirmative action, and proportional representation for all minorities will be irresistible. We will never escape the prison of race. Our politics will be forever poisoned by it.

Do we want this future? If we do not, we must recapture control of immigration policy from politicians paralyzed by fear of ethnic lobbies and corporate contributors, or immobilized by ideology.

A Time-Out on All Immigration

The first imperative is an immediate moratorium on all immigration, such as the one we imposed from 1924 to 1965. That forty-year pause allowed the melting pot to work its magic and create the one people and one nation we were in the Eisenhower-Kennedy era. A breathing space is desperately needed again.

A ten-year time-out on immigration, reducing it to the levels of the Coolidge-Hoover-FDR-Truman-Eisenhower-Kennedy decades—

the levels JFK supported in 1958—will give us time to assimilate and Americanize the millions who have come legally since 1965. Without a pause, a time-out on mass immigration, assimilation will become impossible. But even with a moratorium, success is not assured.

For the 36 million immigrants here now are not only the highest number in any country in history, but, unlike the Great Wave of 1890–1920, almost all come from continents and countries whose peoples have never before been assimilated into a First World nation. Moreover, we no longer seem to possess the moral authority to demand that they assimilate. Our elites have converted to multiculturalism and regard such demands as cultural chauvinism. Middle America no longer seems to care whether the newcomers assimilate or not. Americans seem to be losing interest in an integrated society, so long as they are left alone. But though there is no guarantee we can recreate the sense of national unity and common identity America had in 1960, we cannot succeed if we will not try.

While the moratorium lasts, we should debate and decide whom we wish to come and whether we wish to alter, or preserve, the ethnic-religious composition of America. After all, America belongs to us, not the world.

To discriminate is to choose. All of us discriminate in choosing the people with whom we associate—and with whom we choose to live our lives. There is nothing wrong about giving the decision as to who comes to America, to be our adoptive sons and daughters, to American citizens, the adopting people.

To the father of the Constitution, James Madison, one consideration was paramount in deciding who should come and who should not: "I do not wish that any man should acquire the privilege of citizenship, but such as would be a real addition to the wealth or strength of the United States."[4]

If we follow his guidance, preferences should go to individuals who speak our English language, can contribute significantly to our society, have an education, come from countries with a history of assimilation in America, will not become public charges, and wish to become Americans. And as we remain a predominantly Christian country, why should not a preference go to Christians?

No Amnesty

After five years of ignoring the border, President Bush declared in Tucson, "we will not be able to effectively enforce our immigration laws until we create a temporary worker program."[5] This is naked extortion.

The president was saying he cannot do his constitutional duty to protect the country from invasion unless we first agree not to deport the 12 million invaders already here and allow U.S. businesses to go overseas and hire foreign workers for jobs Americans won't take at the wages offered.

President Bush needs to be told politely but pointedly, "No deal, Mr. President. No amnesty!" His guest worker program is a U.S. Chamber of Commerce–MALDEF scheme that means open borders forever. Though President Bush may declare, "I oppose amnesty!" every time he speaks, his guest worker program *is* amnesty, both for the illegals and for the businesses that hired them. Under the plan, Bush announced, no one is punished. Those who hired the illegals get blanket pardons. Those who broke in are allowed to stay, work six years, return home on sabbatical, come back to their jobs, and be put on a path to U.S. citizenship. Those who cheated win. That is amnesty.

Amnesties following civil wars are often necessary to heal a nation. But as people go unpunished for crimes committed, amnesties undermine the rule of law—for they say to the scofflaw: Don't be a fool, cross the border, break their laws, and in time, you too will receive amnesty.

Bush's amnesty would make fools of the millions who have waited in line for years for the privilege of coming to America. It would demoralize a U.S. Border Patrol whose agents daily risk their lives to defend our borders. Should those agents decide not to do their duty, how could we then blame them when the president of the United States refuses to do his duty?

When amnesty is granted, who will look into the criminal records of the illegal aliens who remain? The same officials who approved a student visa for Muhammad Atta to begin pilot training six months after he had crashed a 767 into the World Trade Center? Bush conceded in Tucson that one in twelve aliens caught at the border had a criminal record. If that is true of the 12 million here, amnesty would bring permanently into our midst 1 million criminals.

Twenty years ago, Ronald Reagan was persuaded to grant amnesty to 3 million illegal aliens. In the White House, this writer supported the decision, just as I had favorably reviewed JFK's *A Nation of Immigrants* and editorialized in favor of the Immigration Act of 1965. But following that amnesty, 1.5 million aliens were soon being apprehended every year at the border and half a million were crossing it successfully. This was not immigration as Americans once knew it. This was not Ellis Island. This was new, this was different, this was mass lawbreaking, the beginning of what has become an invasion that has left at least 12 million aliens in our midst, with 100,000 more being caught every month at the border, and hundreds of millions of Third World poor waiting and watching to see if the Americans will seal their border, or if the land bridge to the United States will remain open.

When Bush first broached his guest worker plan, there was a

surge to the southern border. If Congress votes the Bush amnesty, the flood never ends. The world will see America as a morally befuddled and flabby nation that lacks the toughness to order out of its house those who have walked in and demanded all the rights of family.

It needs to be said again: The more than a million people breaching our border every year for decades are not bad people. By and large, they are good people, desperate only to find the good-paying jobs they cannot find in their misgoverned nations back home. Most are hardworking, decent people. But they are not Americans and they do not belong in our home. And if we do not stop this invasion and start repatriating them to the lands whence they came, we will lose our country, and we will be unworthy of our fathers who gave this country to us—and unworthy of our children, for we will have, through our softness, squandered their priceless patrimony.

The Border Fence

Though the clock is running, America has one last chance to secure the borders and preserve the republic. Six critical steps need to be taken. The first is to build a permanent fence along the entire 2,000-mile border with Mexico, defining, sealing, and securing it forever.

Twin fences, fifteen feet high, would enclose a two-lane road to permit the Border Patrol to move in both directions. Motion sensors would be buried in the roadway to detect people who had breached the outer fence. Beyond each fence would be coiled wire eight feet high. Beyond the wire would be ditches to stop the trucks and SUVs of the narcotics traffickers and their renegade Mexican army and police allies. This would halt the mass illegal immigration across our southern border cold. The Border Patrol could handle the rest.

Is this a Berlin Wall, as Mexican politicians wail? That is absurd. The Berlin Wall was a prison wall to lock a captive nation in. Like a fence around a school, a home, or the White House, a border fence is to keep unauthorized people out. Nor is it some isolationist plot to cut us off from Mexico. There would be two hundred openings for rail and road traffic to facilitate trade, travel, and tourism. The lives of hundreds who perish in the desert and mountainous regions of our border every year would be spared. Seeing the fence, which this writer first proposed in 1991, huge numbers would no longer attempt to cross the desert and our borderland would no longer be a landfill for trash left by thousands sneaking across in the dark every night. In a Rasmussen telephone survey of 1,500 Americans, a border fence was backed by 60 percent. Support for it should be a condition of support for all candidates for Congress and the White House.

The $8 billion cost would be easily offset by the savings in the cost of welfare, health care, education, and incarceration of illegal aliens. And as we have tolls on U.S. highways and bridges, a two-dollar fee to enter the United States would finance it.

Once the fence rises, it would be as welcome to Mexicans as to us. Experience says so. So lawless was the San Diego–Tijuana corridor that Joseph Wambaugh made it the setting for his violent novel *Lines and Shadows*. In that no-man's-land that was the main corridor for entering California after dark, rapes were common. But after the 14-mile fence went up under "Operation Gatekeeper" mounted in 1994, the number of illegals caught being smuggled through fell by 98 percent. The smugglers moved to Arizona. The character of the U.S. border for fourteen miles inland from Imperial Beach changed. Land values rose. The same success can be achieved along all 2,000 miles.

As Duncan Hunter, whose San Diego district encompasses the fence, testifies, even the neighborhoods on the Mexican side now accept it. For these people, too, were abused by gangs that congregated, robbed, raped, and murdered. Says Hunter, the fence "brought down the border murders from an average of 10 every year to zero. It brought down the number of drug trucks from 300 a month to zero. It brought down the smuggling of narcotics and people to almost zero."[6]

What other anticrime measure ever produced results like this?

These results can be replicated all the way to Brownsville. As the fence rises, property values of residences and ranches will rise. Parks and Indian reservations will become secure again. The polluted and poisoned environment can be restored. America's side of the border will be America again, not some dark and bloody ground for drug and human traffickers where even the Border Patrol feels threatened. The fence is no longer an immigration issue. It is a national security and a national survival issue.

"Shameful," wailed President Vicente Fox when he heard 700 miles of border fence had been approved by the U.S. House. "Stupid! Underhanded!" yowled Foreign Secretary Luis Ernesto Debrez. "Mexico is not going to bear, it is not going to permit, and it will not allow a stupid thing like this wall!"[7] This fence, roared Debrez, is the product of "a true myopia and blindness of a group of xenophobic persons in the United States."[8]

The Mexican press went berserk and Bush was cast as the villain, writes Iraq war veteran Allan Wall, who lives in Mexico. "The Bush Wall," "Bush the Rapist," and "An Out and Out Racist" were the headlines to a few of the editorials. *El Universal* columnist Enriqueta Cabrera wrote of the fence, "what it attempts to do is seal the border, but more importantly, to send a message—a hard, xenophobic, and racist message."[9]

What hypocrisy. To defend her border with Guatemala, Mexico uses her military, treats illegals as felons, and often brutalizes and imprisons them. Jose Luis Soberanes, president of Mexico's National Commission on Human Rights, charges that the Mexican government "mistreats 'indocumentados' that cross its territory, it keeps them in jails, in overcrowded conditions, many times without food, without medical attention, and ... violating their human rights."[10] Adds Heather Mac Donald, "Mexico's border police have reportedly engaged in rapes, robberies, and beatings of illegal aliens from Central and South America on their way to the U.S. Yet compared with the extensive immigrant-advocacy network in the United States, few pressure groups exist in Mexico to protest such treatment."[11]

Reporting from Tultitlan, Mexico, in April 2006, the Associated Press's Mark Stevenson seconds Mac Donald, writing of shakedowns and even murder by Mexican police and soldiers.

[U]ndocumented Central Americans in Mexico suffer in silence.

Considered felons by the government, these migrants fear detention, rape and robbery. Police and soldiers hunt them down at railroads, bus stations and fleabag hotels. Sometimes they are deported; more often officers simply take their money. . . .

Maria Elena Gonzales, who lives near the tracks, said women often complain about abusive police. "They force them to strip, supposedly to search them, but the purpose is to sexually abuse them," she said.

Others said they had seen migrants beaten to death by police, their bodies left near the railway tracks to make it look as if they had fallen from a train.[12]

The Mexican regime that tolerates such abuse slanders as racist and xenophobic an America that, above all nations, has welcomed immigrants.

America is in no need of lectures on how to treat immigrants from a regime that is pushing a mass invasion of our country. In answering

Señor Debrez, as we build our security fence, we should listen to the counsel of Benjamin Jowett to his charges at Balliol, who were one day to run the empire: "Never retreat. Never explain. Get it done and let them howl."

In a Pew Hispanic Poll, 46 percent of all Mexicans said they would like to live in the United States; 20 percent said they were willing to break the law to get in. When Vicente Fox denounces us for securing our border, President Bush should ask him why half his countrymen are ready to leave Mexico to live here. It is not America's duty to serve as a safety valve for an endless series of failed Mexican regimes.

"Anchor Babies"

Under the Fourteenth Amendment, citizenship is granted to "All persons born or naturalized in the United States and subject to the jurisdiction thereof." That amendment overturned the most infamous act of judicial supremacy in U.S. history, the 1857 *Dred Scott* decision, which declared that the slaves could never be American citizens. The Fourteenth Amendment brought into our national family all the former slaves liberated by the Thirteenth.

But that phrase, "subject to the jurisdiction thereof," is critical. For citizenship was not extended by the Fourteenth Amendment to Indians living on reservations. Not until the end of the Indian wars and acts of Congress in 1887, 1901, and 1924 was U.S. citizenship conferred on the Indians.[13] Nor did the Fourteenth Amendment apply to children of foreign diplomats. Though they might be born in the United States, they were not citizens because they were not "subject to the jurisdiction thereof."

Yet the White House, the Congress, and the U.S. courts have tolerated the wholesale abuse of the spirit and letter of the Fourteenth Amendment. They have allowed citizenship to be conferred on every child born in the United States to an illegal alien. Pregnant women who sneak in or overstay their visas automatically entitle their babies to a lifetime of benefits at the expense of U.S. taxpayers, including twelve years of free schooling. The parents stay to collect the benefits. When the child reaches eighteen, he or she can sponsor relatives coming in.

How widespread is this racket? Immense, writes Phyllis Schlafly.

At least 383,000 babies are born in the United States, every year, to illegal immigrants; that's 10 percent of all U.S. births and about 40 percent of indigent births. The cost to U.S. taxpayers is tremendous, because all those babies, called anchor babies, claim birthright citizenship. Their mothers and other relatives then sign up for a vast stream of taxpayer benefits.[14]

According to the Center for Immigration Studies, 22 percent of all births in California are to illegal aliens. As these "anchor babies" are citizens at birth, they instantly begin to draw a lifetime of the benefits we provide all American children and their parents. Thus, social welfare costs continue to soar, though our native-born population has been close to stable for years. The remedy to the "anchor baby" racket is simple, but it requires courage from Congress.

Under Article I, Section 8 of the U.S. Constitution and the Fourteenth Amendment, all authority over citizenship and naturalization is given to Congress, not the federal courts. "Congress should end its silence and pass a law stating that a child born to an illegal immigrant is not a U.S. citizen because his parent has not made herself 'subject to [U.S.] jurisdiction.' "[15]

Such a law would end the rampant abuse of the letter and spirit of the Constitution, remove a primary magnet for women to sneak into the United States, and save citizens hundreds of billions of tax dollars over decades.

"Chain Migration"

Today, immigrants are allowed to bring family members to the United States, including children, spouses, siblings, and parents. These relatives then bring in their relatives in an unending process known as "chain migration."

This policy of family reunification first stands immigration policy on its head, for it makes immigrants—not Americans—the ultimate arbiters of who comes to America. Thus, whole villages from El Salvador are here, thanks to chain migration, while citizens from countries whose kinfolk built America wait in line. Ending this absurdity requires a simple reform.

Immigrants should be permitted to bring wives and minor children only. Other relatives should get in line with those already there. When an immigrant wins a green card, it should entitle him to work, and eventually bring his wife and minor children, not empower him to bring an extended family of dozens to the United States. If reuniting with parents, brothers, and sisters is an absolute imperative for a foreign worker, let him go home and visit them as long as he likes.

Ending Dual Citizenship

How many countries permit citizens to become citizens of foreign nations, swear allegiance to foreign powers, vote in foreign elections, run for office and accept high appointment in foreign regimes, and serve in the armed forces and fight in the wars of foreign nations, even nations hostile to their own?

Only one country permits this: the United States of America. So writes Stanley Renshon, the author of *The 50 percent American: Immigration and National Identity in an Age of Terror.*[16]

Why do Americans who once considered U.S. citizenship an honor and sacred trust tolerate this? The Bible teaches: "No man can serve two masters." A man can no more give loyalty to two countries than he can give fidelity to two women. One will always be first in his heart.

Moreover, the new citizen's Oath of Renunciation and Allegiance to the United States expressly forbids dual citizenship: "I hereby declare, on oath, that I absolutely and entirely renounce and abjure all allegiance and fidelity to any foreign prince, potentate, state or sovereignty of whom or which I have heretofore been a subject or citizen . . . and that I take this obligation freely without any mental reservation or purpose of evasion; so help me God." Does this oath mean nothing anymore?

"Citizenship which is not earned, cherished, and tied to obligations is not the real thing," writes Clyde Wilson, and U.S. citizenship has become a depreciated commodity.[17] Former editor William Dickinson traces the depreciation to "the disparagement of national sovereignty and the glorification of globalization." Before 9/11, he writes, "college students thought it fashionable to demean nationalistic feelings and seek a broader definition of their duties. 'I don't consider myself a citizen of the United States,' one student told me, 'I consider myself a citizen of the world.' "[18]

Eugene McCarthy once said there were three duties that every male citizen should perform: Pay taxes, vote, and bear arms for the nation. But today, a third of our population pays almost no income taxes. The share of our citizenry that votes is among the lowest of any democracy. Among our eighteen- to twenty-one-year-olds, voting participation is pathetic.

As Dickinson adds, the war in Iraq is "waged with money borrowed from future generations. . . . Meantime, troop strength is shakily maintained by volunteers, many of them from disadvantaged backgrounds, and lured by costly bonuses and benefits. Foreign nationals are recruited with promises of fast-track citizenship."[19]

Max Boot of the Council on Foreign Relations urges recruitment of illegal aliens and foreigners to fight America's wars, as the British Empire used Hessians and Gurkhas. A promise of "U.S. citizenship would be part of the pay," says Boot. American politicians, "so wary (and rightly so) of casualties among U.S. citizens might take a more lenient attitude" toward sending soldiers to fight and die if they were foreigners, not Americans.[20]

Americans who once cherished citizenship no longer seem to care that millions of their fellow citizens have sworn allegiance to foreign nations. Consider, Stanley Renshon notes, how far dual loyalty has now gone:

- Muhammad Sacirby, a U.S. citizen and dual national, became the foreign minister of Bosnia-Herzegovina in 1995–96.
- Aleksander Einseln, the chief of the Estonian army from 1991 to 1995, was a U.S. citizen.
- Valdas Adamkas was an EPA administrator in Chicago before he became president of Lithuania.
- Hussein Mohamed Aidid, a U.S. Marine Corps veteran, was a naturalized U.S. citizen who became Somalia's most powerful warlord on the death of his father, Mohamed Farah Aidid, America's most wanted man in Somalia after the "Black Hawk Down" killings of Delta Force troopers.
- John Walker Lindh went to Afghanistan to fight for the Taliban and was captured in a battle in which an American officer was killed.
- Rahm Emanuel, a U.S. congressmen, went to Israel at the time of America's Gulf War against Iraq—to join the Israeli army.

In January 2006, the Mexican pop singer, actress, and superstar Thalia became a U.S. citizen, taking the oath of allegiance in New

York. Asked if she would retain her Mexican citizenship, Thalia let reporters know where her true loyalty remains:

> This morning I acquired United States citizenship. Nevertheless, under the laws of my country, I can also have Mexican citizenship. . . . Just like some of my Latino friends such as . . . Gloria and Emilio Estefan. . . . I feel that this step will give me the opportunity to contribute to and support even more the Latin community in the United States. I am of Mexican nationality and I will always be a proud Mexican in heart and soul.[21]

To Thalia, U.S. citizenship is something she had just "acquired," like a driver's license or a new Mercedes. Though she had raised her hand and sworn an oath to the United States, renouncing "all allegiance and fidelity to any foreign . . . state, or sovereignty," she declared that Mexico remains "my country," that "I am of Mexican nationality and I will always be a proud Mexican in heart and soul."

Thalia may be a U.S. citizen. Can anyone reading her response to the press think for a moment she is an American?

How many Americans hold dual citizenship? No one knows. Some 151 nations allow it, many in the hope that their people who migrate to the United States will become citizens and advance the interests of the home country in America. One such nation is Mexico, which accounts for 30 percent of all immigrants and perhaps 60 percent of all illegal aliens, and which openly encourages U.S. citizens of Mexican ancestry to put Mexico first.

America's tolerance of dual citizenship may be traced to the Warren Court and its 1967 decision in *Afroyim v. Rusk*.

Beys Afroyim, a 1912 emigrant from Poland, became a naturalized American citizen in 1926. In 1950, he moved to Israel. When he tried to renew his U.S. passport in 1960, Afroyim was refused on the grounds he had voted in Israeli elections in 1951 and forfeited his citizenship. The Immigration and Nationality Act of 1940 stipulated that U.S. citizens shall "lose" their citizenship upon voting in any foreign state's election.

Afroyim argued that this provision, though it had been upheld in the 1958 *Perez v. Brownell* decision, was unconstitutional. The U.S. Appellate Court for the Second Circuit upheld the State Department's revocation of Afroyim's citizenship. But the Warren Court, 5–4, declared that Congress lacked the power to revoke Afroyim's citizenship, that a U.S. citizen must voluntarily relinquish his citizenship in order to lose it. The court further declared that even active-duty service in a foreign army or swearing allegiance to a foreign power was insufficient to deprive a citizen of his U.S. citizenship. Arnaud de Borchgrave claims that "there are . . . more than 500,000 Israelis with dual citizenship. . . ."[22] According to Renshon, 40 million U.S. citizens may now be able to claim dual citizenship.

Renshon makes a crucial point: Citizenship is not nationality. A man or woman may be a U.S. citizen without truly being an American. While citizenship confers rights and duties, nationality "refers to the emotional ties and core understandings about the world and common experience that binds members of a group together."

"Nationality" writes Renshon, "is the foundation of citizenship."[23]

If the oath of allegiance is to mean what it says, Congress should enact a law declaring that anyone who votes in a foreign election commits a crime. Anyone who serves in a foreign government or enlists in its armed forces renounces his or her U.S. citizenship and shall henceforth be denied a U.S. passport and the rights of an American. "*Citizenship without emotional attachment,*" says Renshon, "*is the civic equivalent of a one-night stand.*"[24]

Remove the Magnets

It is a Republican truism that if you subsidize something, you get more of it; if you tax something, you get less of it.

America runs the largest trade deficits in history because we do not tax imports—they enter duty-free—while exports carry in their price the cost of all the taxes we impose on managers, workers, and companies that remain in the United States. By reversing this penalty-reward formula, the United States could eliminate its trade deficit in a decade.

We could reduce and eventually eliminate our surplus of illegal and indigent aliens the same way: End the incentives that bring and hold them here, and increase the penalties for hiring and keeping them here.

As immigrants work for less than Americans, they drive down the wages of our working people. And they represent a wealth transfer from the poorest Americans to the richest. Businesses profit from lower labor costs, while the costs of welfare, rent supplements, emergency-room treatment, clinics, Medicaid, food stamps, earned income tax credits, legal services, courts, and prisons, where a disproportionate number of illegal aliens end up, is passed on to taxpayers. Many illegal immigrants work off the books, which makes them even more attractive to unscrupulous employers. As long as this penalty-reward formula persists, the invasion will continue.

What must be done? Instead of being rewarded, businesspeople who break the law by hiring illegal aliens for lower wages than U.S. citizens should be punished severely. Instead of providing social welfare to illegal aliens, including free education from preschool through high school, state and federal governments should provide only emergency services.

Why should taxpayers have to subsidize twelve years of education for the children of parents who entered illegally or are breaking our laws by being here? The reason: again, the Supreme Court. Under *Plyler v. Doe,* a 5–4 decision in 1982 by Justice William J. Brennan, an appointee Ike called one of his worst mistakes, Texas was ordered to provide illegal aliens the same education as American children. This has proven a magnet for foreigners to come to have their children educated for free, even if they have to break the law to get here or stay here. It is the population explosion among immigrants, legal and illegal, that is the primary and often the only reason new schools must be built and property taxes must go up.

How can the Congress turn off the magnets?

- Terminate birthright citizenship to children of illegal aliens.
- Permit states, counties, and communities to decide whether they wish to tax themselves to pay for the education of children of illegal aliens. In enacting a federal law to overturn *Plyler v. Doe,* Congress should invoke Article III, Section 2 of the Constitution to deny the right of review of the law to all federal courts, including the Supreme Court.
- All U.S. businesses should be required to match the Social Security numbers and names of all prospective employees by making a toll-free call to the Social Security Administration, just as retail clerks routinely call to check the credit cards of customers making expensive purchases.
- A fine should be imposed for every instance of hiring an illegal. Repeated hirings should bring jail terms. For businesses that hire illegals are triple cheaters. They cheat the government of taxes that must be made up by honest citizens. They cheat the community that has to pay the health, education, and welfare costs of illegal aliens and their children. And they cheat their competitors, who have to pay fair wages and honest taxes and are thus at a disadvantage.

- If a business is found to have hired illegals, all tax deductions for the wages of those workers should be disallowed and penalties and interest on the back taxes owed should be imposed. Companies found in chronic violation of U.S. immigration laws should lose their corporate charters.
- A national campaign should be undertaken to encourage states to enact versions of California's Proposition 187, which denied welfare benefits to illegal aliens, and Arizona's Proposition 200, which requires that, to be eligible for welfare benefits, citizens must provide proof of citizenship, or proof they are in the United States legally.
- Illegal aliens should be made ineligible for Social Security or the earned income tax credit. The EITC is meant to ensure U.S. workers a living wage, not to be used as a bonus for people who undercut the wages of working Americans while breaking our laws.

There are many steps that can end the abuses that have cropped up since passage of the Immigration Act of 1965. As Congress has the authority over citizenship under the Constitution, it should assert its right to preempt and override state and local laws during the state of emergency.

- America must offer asylum to the persecuted, but we should set a rule. If a refugee from tyranny, say, in Burma, arrives on free soil, say, Thailand, he or she is no longer a refugee entitled to asylum here. We cannot take in every political refugee on earth, for billions of people live in countries we designate as unfree.
- The Diversity Lottery under which 50,000 people are brought in each year should be abolished.
- State and local officials, especially law enforcement, should

be empowered by the U.S. government to inquire into the immigrant status of every suspect, and to arrest on sight known deportees who have committed felonies by sneaking back into the United States.

- Cities that enact "sanctuary" polices where police are forbidden to ask a suspect about his or her immigration status—i.e., are forbidden to assist in enforcing immigration laws—should have their federal funds reduced.
- U.S. funding for colleges and universities that grant in-state tuition rates to illegal aliens that they deny to out-of-state Americans should also be reduced.
- The OTMs, "other-than-Mexicans," caught at the border should be held in expanded Department of Homeland Security detention facilities and expeditiously deported. Any nation that refuses to take back citizens who entered our nation illegally should have all visa applications denied until it agrees to take them back. Nations that refuse to accept their own nationals who are illegally in the United States should have foreign aid terminated.

Like trade laws, immigration laws should be designed to protect the wages of Americans and the standard of living of their families. And that means an end to the flooding of the U.S. labor market with unskilled and semiskilled immigrant labor.

Remigration

"Massive deportation of the people here is unrealistic. It's just not going to work," an embattled President Bush railed in Irvine, California. "You can hear people out there [demonstrators] hollering it's going to work. It's not going to work."[25] John McCain repeatedly demands that opponents of his McCain-Kennedy bill explain how they propose to remove 12 million illegal aliens from the United States.

Bush is attacking a straw man. We do not need to create a Gestapo or send federal agents to round up and deport nannies or gardeners. And the answer to McCain, as Mark Krikorian has put it, may be summed up in a single word: attrition. Vigorous enforcement of U.S. laws will persuade millions to go home. If they cannot find jobs, if they are denied welfare, food stamps, and rent supplements, if their children are not all educated for free after they break in, they will not come, and many will go home, as earlier immigrants went home who did not find what they sought here.

In "Attrition Through Enforcement," Jessica Vaughn of the Center for Immigration Studies demonstrates how, with less than $2 billion worth of tougher enforcement, half the illegal aliens here could be persuaded to return home voluntarily within five years.[26]

Who should be deported at once? Anyone convicted of a felony, all gang members, any illegal alien arrested for drunken driving. Bail should be denied illegals charged with violent crimes. *Salus populi, suprema lex*—The safety of the people is the highest law. If witnesses to violent crimes in immigrant communities knew criminal predators would not be back on the street in hours, they would be far more willing to testify against them.

It can be done. If we will secure the border, deport the criminals, sanction employers who hire illegals, deny citizenship and social welfare except emergency aid to illegal aliens, in five to ten years our crisis will be at an end. But if we don't do this, the crisis will end America.

Because the world is watching. If we fail to secure our southern border, if we grant a second amnesty, the tipping point will have been passed. And there will then be no retrieving the country we inherited.

"Optimism is cowardice," said Spengler. To witness the sweep of

Western history since 1914 is to understand what Spengler meant. But a pessimism that induces despair can be as paralyzing as the guilt with which Western Man is afflicted.

What is required of us is the confidence and courage of our forefathers, who made no apologies for who and what they were as they believed—and rightly so—that theirs was the greatest civilization and culture the world had ever produced, and they meant to preserve and protect it.

It needs to be said again: If we do not solve our civilizational crisis—a disintegrating culture, dying populations, and invasions unresisted—the children born in 2006 will witness in their lifetimes the death of the West. In our hearts we know what must be done. We must stop the invasion.

But do our leaders have the vision and the will to do it?

Notes

1. How Civilizations Perish

1. Thomas Cahill, *How the Irish Saved Civilization: The Untold Story of Ireland's Heroic Role from the Fall of Rome to the Rise of Medieval Europe* (New York: Doubleday, 1995), p. 18.
2. Toynbee, as quoted by Mark Steyn, "It's the Demography, Stupid," Jan. 4, 2006, *Opinion Journal,* WSJ.com; www.opinionjournal.com.
3. Cahill, op. cit., p. 16.
4. Peter Heather, *The Fall of the Roman Empire: A New History of Rome and the Barbarians* (New York: Oxford University Press, 2006), p. xiii.
5. Ibid., p. 158.
6. Quoted in ibid.

2. The Invasion

1. Patrick J. Buchanan, *The Death of the West: How Dying Populations and Immigrant Invasions Imperil Our Country and Civilization* (New York: St. Martin's Press, 2002), p. 123.
2. Huntington quoted in Yeh Ling-Ling, "Mexican Immigration and Its Potential Impact on the Political Future of the United States," *Journal of Social, Political and Economic Studies,* vol. 29, no. 4 (Winter 2004); www.diversity alliance.org/docs/article/_2004winter.htm.
3. "Border Emergency Declared in New Mexico," *CNN.com,* Aug. 13, 2005; www.cnn.com/2005/US/08/12/newmexico.
4. Jacques Billeaud, "Ariz. Governor Orders Troops to Border," Associated Press, Mar. 8, 2006.
5. Donald L. Barlett and James B. Steele, "Who Left the Door Open?", *Time* magazine, Sept. 20, 2004; www.time-proxy.yaga.com/time/archive.
6. "President Discusses Border Security and Immigration Reform in America,"

271

Tucson, Arizona, Office of the Press Secretary, The White House, Nov. 28, 2005; www/whitehouse.gov/news/releases/2005/11.

7. James R. Edwards, Jr., "Two Sides of the Same Coin: The Connection Between Legal and Illegal Immigration," Center for Immigration Studies; www/cis.org/articles/2006/back106.html.

8. John F. Kennedy, *A Nation of Immigrants*. Revised and enlarged edition with an Introduction by Robert F. Kennedy (New York: Harper & Row, 1965), pp. 17, 51, 58.

9. Ibid., pp. 2, 3.

10. Barlett and Steele, op. cit.

11. Robert Justich and Betty Ng, "The Underground Labor Force Is Rising to the Surface," Bear Stearns Asset Management, Jan. 3, 2005.

12. John Judis, "Border War," *New Republic*, Jan. 16, 2006, p. 15.

13. J. D. Hayworth, with Joseph J. Eule, *Whatever It Takes: Illegal Immigration, Border Security, and the War on Terror* (Washington, DC: Regnery Publishing, 2006), p. 1 (italics in the original).

14. Glynn Custred, "Friends and Elites, Chickens and Coyotes," *American Spectator* (Nov. 2005), p. 28.

15. "Violent Clashes at Mexican Border Double," *Newsmax.com Wires*, Oct. 31, 2005.

16. D'Vera Cohn, "Area Soon to Be Mostly Minority," *Washington Post*, Mar. 25, 2006, p. A1.

17. "President Discusses Border Security," op. cit.

18. Jerry Seper, "Senator Fears U.S. Border Is 'Gateway' for Terrorists," *Washington Times*, Feb. 3, 2006.

19. John O'Sullivan, "Use 'Attrition' Strategy to Control Immigration," *Chicago Sun-Times.com*, April 25, 2006; www.suntimes.com/output/osullivan/cst-edt-osul25.html.

3. Coming to America

1. Peggy Noonan, "The American Way," *OpinionJournal*, WSJ.com, Dec. 8, 2005; www.opinionjournal.com.

2. Robert J. Samuelson, "Candor on Immigration," *The Washington Post*, June 8, 2005, p. A21; www.washingtonpost.com.

3. Mary Beth Sheridan, "In N. Va. Gang, a Brutal Sense of Belonging," *Washington Post*, June 28, 2004, p. A1; www.washingtonpost.com.

4. Arian Compo-Flores, "The Most Dangerous Gang in America," *Newsweek*, Mar. 28, 2005; www.msnbc.msn.com; Nicolas Zimmerman, "On the Docket: MS-13: Los Angeles' Unwelcome Export to Virginia," *Medill News Service*, posted Aug. 31, 2004; www.medill.northwestern.edu/archives.

5. Michelle Malkin, "M-13 Gang Activity Shows the Lethality of Immigration Schizophrenia," *Human Events Online,* posted Aug. 31, 2005; www.human eventsonline.com.

6. Compo-Flores, op. cit.

7. Ned Martel, "Taking a Long Look at a Latino Gang Named for Fire Ants," *New York Times,* Feb. 11, 2006.

8. D'Vera Cohn, "Area Soon to Be Mostly Minority," *Washington Post,* March 25, 2006, p. A9.

9. Compo-Flores, op. cit.

10. Zimmerman, op. cit.

11. "MS13's Growing Threat," *Pittsburgh Post-Tribune,* July 10, 2005; www.pittsburghlive.com.

12. Heather Mac Donald, "The Illegal Alien Crime Wave," *City Journal* (Winter 2004); www.cityjournal.org.

13. Ibid.

14. Ibid.

15. Roger McGrath, "End of the Rainbow," *The American Conservative,* Dec. 19, 2005, p. 9.

16. Jerry Seper, "Illegal Criminal Aliens Abound in U.S.," *Washington Times,* Jan. 26, 2004; www.washtimes.com.

17. *The Color of Crime: Race, Crime and Justice in America,* 2nd expanded ed. (Oakton, VA: New Century Foundation, 2005), p. 11.

18. "Criminal Aliens," Federation for American Immigration Reform (October 2002); www.fairus.org.

19. Bill O'Reilly, "Another Troubling Situation Involving Illegal Aliens," *Talking Points Memo,* FOX News, Jan. 6, 2003; www.foxnews.com.

20. Michelle Malkin, "Who Let Lee Malvo Loose?", *townhall.com,* Oct. 25, 2002; townhall.com/opinion/columns/michellemalkin/2002/10/25.

21. Patrick J. Buchanan, "Who Let in the Beltway Sniper?", *townhall.com,* Nov. 4, 2002; townhall.com/opinion/columns/patbuchanan/2002/11/04; "Suspect Probed in Alien Smuggling: Antigua Official Aid in Sniper Case," *Washington Times,* Oct. 31, 2002.

22. "Crime: The Open Borders Lobby's Dirty Little Secret," *FRONTPAGE MAG.COM,* Oct. 4, 2005, p. 2.

23. John W. Whitehead, "A Ticking Time Bomb: Diseases That Cross American Borders," Rutherford Institute, Dec. 11, 2004; www.rutherford.org.

24. Phyllis Schlafly, "American Citizenship Is Precious," *Phyllis Schlafly Report* (November 2005), p. 4.

25. Richard Pérez-Pena and Marc Santora, "Hepatitis Risk for East Asians in New York," *New York Times,* May 11, 2006, p. A29.

26. Report cited in Whitehead, op. cit.

27. *WorldNetDaily,* "Illegal Aliens Threaten U.S. Medical System," Mar. 13, 2005; www.worldnetdaily.com.

28. Edwin S. Rubenstein, "Give Me Your Tired, Your Poor . . . Your Infectious Diseases," *VDARE.com,* Sept. 30, 2004; www.vdare.com.

29. Sam Francis, "WSJ Edit Page: 'Cheap Domestic Servants Worth Disease, Terrorism Risk,' " *VDARE.com,* Mar. 21, 2002; www.vdare.com.

30. Whitehead, op. cit.

31. Ibid.

32. Rubenstein, op. cit.

33. *WorldNetDaily,* op. cit.

34. Joe Guzzardi, "Who Would Honor Geraldo ('There Would Not Be a Lawn Mowed or a Dish Washed but for Illegal Immigrants') Rivera?", *VDARE.com,* Dec. 9, 2005; www.vdare.com.

35. Deborah Simmons, "El Presidente on Illegals: Loco as a Fox," *Washington Times,* Mar. 31, 2006, p. A23.

36. John Hostettler and Lamar Smith, "Illegals Hurt Americans," *Washington Times,* Dec. 2, 2005, op-ed page; www.washtimes.com.

37. Edwin S. Rubenstein, "Looking (in vain) for 'Jobs Americans Won't Do,' " *VDARE.com,* Feb. 23, 2006; www.vdare.com.

38. Mark Krikorian, "Debating Immigration: An Analyst Defends Herself," *National Review,* Oct. 10, 2005; www.cis.org.

39. Hostettler and Smith, op. cit.

40. Paul Krugman, "North of the Border," *New York Times,* Mar. 27, 2006, p. A23.

41. Robert J. Samuelson, "We Don't Need 'Guest Workers,' " *Washington Post,* Mar. 22, 2006, p. A21.

42. Milton Friedman, Interview with Peter Brimelow, *Forbes,* Dec. 27, 1997.

43. Dr. Donald Huddle, "The Net Costs of Immigration: The Facts, the Trends and the Critics," Rice University, Oct. 22, 1996; wwwfairus.org. See also Patrick J. Buchanan, *The Death of the West* (New York: St. Martin's Press, 2002), p. 139.

4. The Face of America: 2050

1. Lewis quoted in Otis Graham, Jr., *Unguarded Gates: A History of America's Immigration Crisis* (Lanham, MD: Rowman & Littlefield, 2005), p. 50.

2. Cisneros quoted in Peter Brimelow, *Alien Nation: Common Sense About America's Immigration Disaster* (New York: Random House, 1995), p. 25.

3. Samuel Huntington, "Migration Flows Are the Central Issue of Our Times," *International Herald Tribune,* Feb. 2, 2001; www.iht.com.

4. Edwin S. Rubenstein, "The Stupid American? Look Again," *VDARE.com,* Dec. 22, 2005; http://www.vdare.com/rubenstein/015222_nd.htm.

5. Steven A. Camarota, "Immigrants at Mid-Decade: A Snapshot of America's Foreign-Born Population in 2005," *Backgrounder,* Center for Immigration Studies (Dec. 2005), p. 2.

6. Rubenstein, op. cit.

7. Ibid.

8. Steve Sailer, "No Excuse for *No Excuses," VDARE.com,* Oct. 26, 2003; www.vdare.com/sailer/no_excuses.htm (italics in the original).

9. Quoted in ibid.

10. "16,344 Per Student, But Only 12 Percent Read Proficiently," *Human Events,* week of Mar. 20, 2006, p. 3.

11. Joyce Howard Price, "Immigration, Poverty Linked," *Washington Times,* Nov. 6, 2005; www.washtimes.com/functions.

12. Sailer, op. cit.

13. Camarota, op. cit., pp. 9, 13.

14. "Dr. Martin Luther King, Jr., Quotes," Christian Association at the University of Pennsylvania, 2002, www.upennca.org/MLKquotes.html.

15. Camarota, op. cit., pp. 1–2.

16. Steve Sailer, "Americans First: What's Best for the Citizens We Already Have," *The American Conservative,* Feb. 13, 2006, p. 13.

17. Brimelow, p. 149.

18. "Counties Bordering Mexico Rank First in Federal Crime," news release, U.S./Mexico Border Counties Coalition, Mar. 8, 2006, www.border counties.org.

19. Patrick J. Buchanan, "To Live and Die in L.A.," *WorldNetDaily.com,* May 17, 2002; www.worldnetdaily.com.

20. Ibid.

21. Diana West, "Mexico North: Immigration Debate Ignores Reality," *Washington Times,* Mar. 31, 2006, p. A23.

22. Buchanan, "To Lie and Die in L.A."

23. Patrick J. Buchanan, *The Death of the West* (New York: St. Martin's Press, 2002), p. 139.

24. Ibid., pp. 139–40.

25. Ibid., p. 140.

5. Suicide of the GOP

1. John Stuart Mill, Letter to Sir John Pakington, MP, March 1866, www.spartacus.schoolnet.co.uk/PRmill.htm.

2. Steve Sailer, "Bushicide of the GOP—And of America," *VDARE.com,* Oct. 30, 2005; www.vdare.com.

3. Jonathan Aitken, *Nixon: A Life* (Washington, DC: Regnery Publishing, 1993), pp. 247–48; Patrick J. Buchanan, *The Death of the West* (New York: St. Martin's Press, 2002), p. 135.

4. Mike Allen, "RNC Chief to Say It Was 'Wrong' to Exploit Racial Conflict for Votes," *Washington Post,* July 4, 2005, p. A04; www.washingtonpost.com.

5. Ralph Z. Hallow, "GOP to Focus on Hispanics in New Strategy," *Washington Times,* Jan. 14, 2000; Anthony York, "The GOP's Latino Strategy," Salon.com Jan. 14, 2000; Sam Francis, *Ethnopolitics* (Raleigh, NC: Representative Government Press, 2003), p. 31.

6. Peter Brimelow, "Time to Rethink Immigration," *National Review,* June 22, 1992, p. 32; George F. Will, "Blaming the Voters," *Washington Post,* Sept. 24, 2000, p. B7.

7. William Frey, "The Silence Behind America's Immigration Impasse," *Financial Times,* May 3, 2006, p. 13.

8. Stephen Glover, "Are the Tories the Stupid Party Again?" *Daily Mail,* Dec. 5, 2000, p. 13; Buchanan, p. 136.

9. Sailer, op. cit.

10. Passel quoted in Laura Parker, "U.S. Hispanics Youth Assures More Growth," *USA Today,* May 10, 2001, p. 3A; Buchanan, p. 136.

11. Walter V. Robinson, "Immigrant Voter Surge Seen Aiding Gore," *Boston Globe,* Nov. 4, 2000, p. A1; Buchanan, p. 137.

12. Buchanan, Patrick J., *The Death of the West,* p. 137.

13. Carrick quoted in Robinson, op. cit.

14. Francis, p. 15.

15. Ron Unz, "California and the End of White America," *Commentary,* Nov. 1, 1999, p. 17; Buchanan, p. 138.

16. Steve Sailer, "Asian 'Natural Republicans' Vote 75 percent Democratic—Any More Bright Ideas?", *VDARE.com,* May 22, 2005; www.vdare.com.

17. Ibid.

18. William Kristol, "Y Is for Yahoo: Turning the GOP into an Anti-immigration Party Could Dash Republican Hopes of Becoming a Long-term Governing Party," *The Weekly Standard,* Apr. 10, 2006; http://www.weeklystandard.com.

19. Steve Sailer, "Michael Barone, Call Your Office! Hispanic Vote Gets . . . Smaller," *VDARE.com,* Aug. 15, 2004; www.vdare.com.

20. Steve Sailer, "NRO Debunks Bush's Hispanic Share Myth," *VDARE.com*, Dec. 9, 2004; www.vdare.com.

21. Sailer, "Michael Barone, Call Your Office!"; Steve Sailer, "Cesar Chavez, Minuteman," *The American Conservative*, Feb. 27, 2006, p. 13.

22. Mac Johnson, "A Major Victory Against Illegal Immigration—In Massachusetts?", *Human Events Online*, Jan. 16, 2006; www.humanevents online.com.

6. Roots of Paralysis

1. Donald Rumsfeld, news briefing, Nov. 29, 2005, www.defenselink.mil/transcripts/2005.

2. "Zogby Poll: Americans Fed Up with Illegal Aliens," *WorldNetDaily*, May 6, 2005; www.worldnetdaily.com.

3. "Poll: 3rd Party Scores with Border Backlash: Presidential Candidate Focused on Fence, Enforcement, Would Tie Dems, Beat GOP," *WorldNetDaily*, Apr. 27, 2006; www.worldnetdaily.com.

4. Victor Davis Hanson, "Mi Casa Es Su Casa: America's Porous Border Enables Mexico's Misrule," *Wall Street Journal*, Jan. 1, 2006, ed. page; www.opinionjournal.com.

5. Roy Beck and Steve Camarota, "Elite vs. Public Opinion: An Examination of Divergent Views on Immigration," *Backgrounder*, Center for Immigration Studies (Dec. 2002), www.cis.org. Steve Sailer, "Americans First: What's Best for the Citizens We Already Have?", *The American Conservative*, Feb. 13, 2006, p. 12.

6. Theodore Roosevelt, *Kansas City Star*, Dec. 1, 1917, in *Phyllis Schlafly Report*, vol. 39, no. 4 (Nov. 2005), p. 4.

7. Theodore Roosevelt, Letter to the American Defense Society, Jan. 13, 1919, in Schlafly, op. cit.; John Fonte, "Dual Allegiance: A Challenge to Immigration Reform and Patriotic Assimilation," *Backgrounder*, Center for Immigration Studies (Nov. 2005), p. 5.

8. President George W. Bush, "President Bush Proposes New Temporary Worker Program," The White House, Jan. 7, 2004, www.whitehouse.gov/news/releases//2004/01.

9. Peter Brimelow, *Alien Nation: Common Sense About America's Immigration Disaster* (New York: Random House, 1995), p. 211; Otis L. Graham, Jr., *Unguarded Gates: A History of America's Immigration Crisis* (Lanham, MD: Rowman & Littlefield, 2004), p. 53.

10. Thomas L. Friedman, "Port Controversy Could Widen Racial Chasm," *Deseret Morning News*, Feb. 25, 2006; www.deseretnews.com/d.

11. Roger Scruton, "The Dangers of Internationalism," *Intercollegiate Review* (Fall–Winter 2005), p. 35.

12. Robert J. Samuelson, "The Church of GDP," *Washington Post,* Jan. 12, 2006, p. A21.

13. John Judis, "Border War: The Fight Over Immigration Is a Fight Over Identity," *New Republic,* Jan. 10, 2006, pp. 16, 17.

14. John Attarian, *Economism and the National Prospect* (Monterey, VA: American Immigration Control Foundation, 2001), p. 5.

15. Ibid., p. 2.

16. Richard Cobden quoted in Alfred J. Eckes, Jr., *Opening America's Market: U.S. Foreign Trade Policy Since 1776* (Chapel Hill: University of North Carolina Press, 1995), p. 1; Patrick J. Buchanan, *The Great Betrayal* (New York: Little, Brown, 1998), p. 188.

17. Buchanan, pp. 188–89; John Bright and James E. Thorold Rogers, eds., *Speeches on Questions of Public Policy by Richard J. Cobden, M.P.* Vol. 1 (London: Macmillan & Co., 1870), pp. 362–63.

18. Attarian, p. 26.

19. Peter Brimelow, "Alien Nation: Round 2," *National Review,* April 22, 1996, pp. 43–45. Peter Brimelow, *VDARE.com,* http://www.vdare.com. Robert Bartley, "Open NAFTA Borders? Why Not?", *Wall Street Journal,* July 2, 2001; www.opinionjournal.com/columnists/bartley.

20. Bartley, op. cit.

21. Dan Whitcomb, "May 1 Immigrant Boycott Aims to 'Close' US Cities," Reuters, Apr. 23, 2006; http:reuters/myway.com. Lowell Ponte, "Uno de Mayo," *FrontPageMagazine.com,* May 1, 2008; www.frontpagemag .com.

22. Clyde Wilson, "As a City Upon a Hill," *Chronicles* (June 1985), in Tom Fleming, ed., *Immigration and the American Identity: Selections from Chronicles: A Magazine of American Culture, 1985–1995* (Rockford, IL: Rockford Institute, 1995), p. 30.

23. Jackson quoted in Walter A. McDougall, *Promised Land, Crusader State: The American Encounter with the World Since 1776* (New York: Houghton Mifflin, 1997), p. 78; see also Patrick J. Buchanan, *A Republic, Not an Empire* (Washington, DC: Regnery Publishing, 1999), p. 100.

24. Peter Brimelow, "Time to Rethink Immigration," *National Review,* June 22, 1992, p. 35.

25. Andrew Roberts, *Eminent Churchillians* (New York: Simon & Schuster, 1994), p. 214.

26. Leo McKinstry, "Dis-United Kingdom," *Weekly Standard,* Dec. 5, 2005, p. 14.

Notes

27. John Derbyshire, "The Luckiest Generation," *National Review Online*, Nov. 23, 2005.

28. Wilson, op. cit., p. 34.

29. Chilton Williamson, Jr., "Promises to Keep," *Chronicles* (July 1991) in Fleming, ed., *Immigration and the American Identity*, p. 111.

30. James Antle III, "Of Borders and Ballots," *The American Conservative*, Jan. 30, 2006, p. 20.

31. Brimelow, *Alien Nation: Common Sense About America's Immigration Disaster*, p. xv.

32. James Burnham, *Suicide of the West: The Meaning and Destiny of Liberalism* (New York: The John Day Company, 1964), p. 26.

33. Brimelow, *Alien Nation*, pp. 213–14.

7. A Grudge Against the Gringo

1. Buchanan quoted in Thomas A. Bailey, *A Diplomatic History of the American People*, 7th ed. (New York: Appleton-Century-Crofts, 1964), p. 250.

2. Díaz quoted in Herbert Mitgang, "War and the Tragic Mechanics of Manifest Destiny," *New York Times*, Apr. 5, 1989 (review of John S. D. Eisenhower's *So Far from God: The U.S. War with Mexico, 1846–48*).

3. Bailey, p. 238.

4. Alexander de Conde, *A History of American Foreign Policy* (New York: Charles Scribner's Sons, 1963), p. 181.

5. Robert Leckie, *From Sea to Shining Sea: From the War of 1812 to the Mexico War, the Saga of American Expansion* (New York: HarperPerennial, 1995), p. 503.

6. Bailey, p. 239.

7. Jaime Suchlicki, *Mexico: From Montezuma to NAFTA, Chiapas, and Beyond* (Washington, DC: Brassey's, 1996), p. 67.

8. Bailey, p. 239.

9. Leckie, p. 477.

10. Ibid, p. 480.

11. Bailey, p. 255.

12. Robert Ferrell, *American Diplomacy: A History* (New York: W. W. Norton & Co., 1959), p. 100; de Conde, p. 199.

13. James. D. Richardson, *A Compilation of the Messages and Papers of the Presidents* (New York Bureau of National Literature, 1897), vol. V, p. 2292; Bailey, pp. 256–57; de Conde, p. 199; Leckie, p. 521.

14. Leckie, p. 528.

15. Peter Brimelow, "A Modest (?) Proposal," *Forbes*, Mar. 27, 1995, p. 58.

16. Bailey, p. 350.

17. Ibid., p. 352.
18. Robert Ferrell, *American Diplomacy: A History*. Rev. and expanded ed. (New York: W. W. Norton & Co., 1969), p. 305.
19. Bailey, p. 351.
20. Ibid., p. 556; de Conde, p. 432.
21. Bailey, p. 555.
22. Ibid.
23. Ibid., p. 561.
24. Ibid, p. 557.
25. Ferrell, *American Diplomacy* (1959), p. 285.
26. "Mexicans Say Southwest Belongs to Them: Shouldn't Need Permission to Enter U.S.," press release, Americans for Immigration Control, Monterey, VA, June 11, 2002; Heather Mac Donald, "Mexico's Undiplomatic Diplomats," *City Journal* (Autumn 2005), p. 33.
27. William Frey and Jonathan Tilove, "Immigrants In, Native Whites Out," *New York Times Magazine*, Aug. 20, 1995, p. 50.
28. Carlos Loret de Mola, "The Great Invasion: Mexico Recovers Its Own," *Excelsior*, Mexico City, July 20, 1982; www.law.cornell.edu/uscode/17/107.shtm/.
29. Ferrell, *American Diplomacy* (1959), pp. 87–88.
30. Patrick J. Buchanan, *The Death of the West* (New York: St. Martin's Press, 2002), p. 130. Yeh Ling-Ling, "Mexican Immigration and Its Potential Impact on the Political Future of the United States, Appendix, El Plan de Aztlan," *Journal of Social, Political and Economic Studies*, vol. 29, no. 4 (Winter 2004): www.diversityalliance.org/docs/article_2002winter.html.
31. Buchanan, p. 130. See also Michelle Malkin, "Bustamante, MEChA and the Media," *townhall.com.*, Aug. 20, 2003; www.townhall.com/opinion/columns/michellemalkin/2003/08/20/16185.html.
32. Buchanan, p. 130; Ling-Ling, op. cit.
33. Buchanan, p. 130.
34. Ibid., p. 131.
35. Malkin, op. cit.
36. Buchanan, p. 131.
37. Hector Carreon, "Antonio Villaraigosa: Alcalde de Los Angeles?", *La Voz de Aztlan*; www.aztlan.net/alcalde_de_los_angeles.htm.
38. Buchanan, p. 129.
39. Michelle Malkin, "Racism Gets Whitewash from Press," *Conservative Chronicle*, Apr. 5, 2006, p. 1.
40. Allan Wall, "Mexico Gloats While Washington Cowers," *VDARE.com*, Apr. 11, 2006; www.vdare.com/awall/060411_gloat.htm.
41. Ibid.

42. Ernesto Cienfuegos, "Aztlan Arising: 700,000+ March in Los Angeles," *La Voz de Aztlan,* Mar. 26, 2006; www.aztlan.net/la_gran_marcha.htm.

43. Ibid.

44. Buchanan, p. 129.

45. Herbert L. London, "Can Sovereignty Be Preserved if Illegal Immigration Is Rewarded?", *Knight Ridder/Tribune,* Sept. 7, 2001; "Mexico Reconquering U.S. Territory? Writer Says Emigration Imposing Hispanic Culture on North America," *WorldNetDaily.com,* Aug. 15, 2001; "Leading Mexican Journalist: 'Mexico Is Recovering Lost Territories Via Immigration,'" *El Imparcial,* July 4, 2001, *FreeRepublic.com,* 8/11/2001.

46. "Remarks by the President to the Hispanic Chamber of Commerce," Albuquerque, NM, Aug. 15, 2001, press release, The White House.

47. Kelly Whiteside, "Notebook: Mexicans' Behavior Part of the Game," *USAToday,* Feb. 12, 2004; www.usatoday.com/sports/soccer/2004-02-12notebook-mexicans-crowd_x.htm.

48. Stephen Dinan, "Americans View Mexicans Well; Reverse Not True," *Washington Times,* Mar. 21, 2006, p. A10.

49. Buchanan, p. 128.

50. Ibid.

51. Jerry Seper, "Texas Sheriff Slams Lax Federal Border Security," *Washington Times,* Oct. 14, 2004, p. A11.

52. Ted Galen Carpenter, "Mexico Is Becoming the Next Colombia," *Foreign Policy Briefing,* no. 87, Cato Institute, Nov. 15, 2005, p. 3.

53. Dave Adams, "City's Crime Creeps to Twin," *St Petersburg Times Online,* May 9, 2005; www.sptimes.com/2005/05/09/news_pf/Worldandnation/City_s_crime_creeps_t.shtml.

54. Jerry Seper, "Drug Cartels' Battle Keeps Tourists Out of Border City," *Washington Times,* Oct. 18, 2005; www.washtimes.com.

55. James C. McKinley, Jr., "A War in Mexico: Drug Runners Gun Down Journalists," *New York Times,* Feb. 10, 2006; "Border Gunmen Storm Newspaper, Toss Grenade," Reuters, Feb. 7, 2006.

56. Seper, "Drug Cartels' Battle."

57. Carpenter, op. cit., p. 1.

58. Jerry Seper, "Mexican Military Incursions Reported: U.S. Border Patrol Alerts Arizona Agents," *Washington Times,* Jan. 17, 2006, p. A1; Jon Dougherty, "Border Patrol Fears Conflict with Mexican Military," *WorldNetDaily.com,* Dec. 19, 2005.

59. Seper, "Mexican Military Incursions," p. A16.

60. Alicia A. Caldwell, "Texas-Mexico Border Standoff Reported," Associated Press, Jan. 25, 2006.

61. Stephen Dinan, "Sheriff Insists Mexican Military Crossed Border," *Washington Times,* Feb. 8, 2006, p. 3.

62. Jerry Seper, "MS-13 Smugglers Deemed Threat to U.S. Field Agents," *Washington Times,* Jan. 13, 2006; www.washingtontimes.com.

8. The Aztlan Plot

1. Fr. Rigoni quoted in Lawrence Auster, *The Path to National Suicide* (Monterey, VA: American Immigration Control Foundation, 1990), p. 5.

2. Márquez quoted in Lawrence Auster, "America Is in Danger," *New York Newsday,* May 12, 1991, p. 26.

3. Appel quoted in Yeh Ling-Ling, "Mexican Immigration and Its Potential Impact on the Political Future of the United States," *Journal of Science, Political and Economic Studies,* vol. 29, no. 4 (Winter 2004); www.diversityalliance .org/docs/article/_2004winter.htm. Julie Weise, "Mexican Border Czar Ruffo: Economics Is Key to Solving Region's Woes—U.S. Firms Must Contribute More," *The News,* Mexico City, Mar. 8, 2001.

4. "Securing the North American Border Perimeter: Dismantling the U.S. Border, Bringing Canada and Mexico into Fortress America," June 10, 2005, CNN; 6/16/05 www.globalresearch.ca. William F. Jasper, "Abolishing the USA," *The New American,* Oct. 3, 2005, p. 24.

5. Dr. Robert A. Pastor, "A North American Community Approach to Security," Testimony Before a Hearing of the Subcommittee on the Western Hemisphere of the U.S. Senate Foreign Relations Committee, June 9, 2005, posted *Free Republic* by Travis McGee, June 13, 2005.

6. Ibid.

7. John Fonte, "Dual Allegiance: A Challenge to Immigration Reform and Patriotic Allegiance," *Backgrounder,* Center for Immigration Studies (November 2005), pp. 11–12; Allan Wall, "Does Dubya Know About Fox's Madrid Speech?" *VDARE.com,* May 29, 2002; www.vdare.com/awall/fox_madrid.htm.

8. Wall, op. cit.; Fonte, op. cit., p. 12.

9. Jasper, op. cit., p. 26.

10. Glynn Custred, "Friends and Elites, Chickens and Coyotes," *The American Spectator* (Nov. 2005), p. 30.

11. Fonte, op. cit., p. 12.

12. Custred, op. cit., p. 30; Ling-Ling, op. cit.

13. "In Mexico, Thousands Support Immigrants to U.S.," *Washington Post,* May 2, 2006, p. A8.

14. Custred, op. cit., p. 32; Fonte, op. cit., p. 9.

15. Fonte, op. cit., p. 10.

16. Ibid.

Notes

17. Georgie Anne Geyer, "Orchestration from Mexico," *Washington Times,* Apr. 6, 2006, p. A18.

18. Ling-Ling, op. cit.

19. Heather Mac Donald, "Mexico's Undiplomatic Diplomats," *City Journal* (Autumn 2005), pp. 36–37.

20. Ibid., p. 37.

21. Fonte, op. cit., p. 10.

22. Ibid, p. 10.

23. Stanley Renshon, "Reforming Dual Citizenship in the United States," *Center Paper 24*, Center for Immigration Studies (September 2005), p. 17; Fonte, op. cit., pp. 10, 14.

24. Bruce Fein, "Divided Loyalties," *Washington Times,* Dec. 13, 2005; Fonte, op. cit., p. 14.

25. Fein, op. cit.

26. Geyer, op. cit., p. A18.

27. Mac Donald, op. cit., p. 30.

28. Patrick J. Buchanan, *The Death of the West* (New York: St. Martin's Press, 2002), p. 132; Robert Collier, "NAFTA Gives Mexicans New Reasons to Leave Home," *San Francisco Chronicle,* Oct. 15, 1998, p. A11.

29. Buchanan, *Death of the West,* p. 132; "An Unlikely Mexican Foreign Minister," *New York Times,* May 12, 2001, p. A26; Jorge Castaneda, "Ferocious Differences: Differences Between Mexico and the U.S.," *Atlantic Monthly* (July 1995), p. 68; Custred, op. cit., p. 30.

30. Custred, op. cit., p. 30. Allan Wall, "Vicente Fox and the Braceros: Hypocrisy and Fraud," *VDARE.com,* March 23, 2004; www.vdare.com/awall/the_braceros.htm.

31. "Mexican Migrants to Get US Maps," BBC News, Jan. 25, 2006; www.newsvote.bbc.co.uk/go/pr/fr/-/2/hi/americas/4645782.stm.

32. Custred, op. cit., p. 30.

33. Mac Donald, op. cit., p. 32.

34. Lowell Ponte, "License to Kill," *FrontPageMagazine.com,* Sept. 10, 2003; http://www/frontpagemag.com.

35. Frey quoted in Peter Brimelow, *Alien Nation: Common Sense About America's Immigration Disaster* (New York: Random House, 1995), p. 68.

36. James Lubinskas, "Expressions of Ethnic Animosity," *FrontPageMag.com,* Nov. 24, 1999; www.frontpagemag.com/archives/racerelations/lubinskas 11-24-99.htm. Buchanan, *Death of the West,* p. 129.

37. Hal Rothman, "On How the Las Vegas Valley Will Inevitably Become a Predominantly Spanish-speaking Community," *Las Vegas Sun,* Dec. 25, 2005; www.lasvegassun.com/sunbin/stories/text/2005/dec/25;519871541.html.

38. Fonte, op. cit., p. 5.

39. Fein, op. cit.

40. Márquez quoted in Auster, "America Is in Danger," *New York Newsday,* May 12, 1991, p. 26.

41. Samuel P. Huntington, "Reconsidering Immigration: Is Mexico a Special Case?", *Backgrounder,* Center for Immigration Studies (November 2000), p. 5; Buchanan, *Death of the West,* p. 126.

42. Huntington, op. cit.

43. Glenn Garvin, "Loco, Completamente Loco: The Many Failures of Bilingual Education," *reasononline* (January 1998), p. 19; Buchanan, *Death of the West,* p. 126.

44. Huntington, op. cit.

9. What Is a Nation?

1. O'Sullivan quoted in Peter Brimelow, *Alien Nation: Common Sense About America's Immigration Disaster* (New York: Random House, 1995), p. 202.

2. Ben Wattenberg, "Melt. Melting. Melted," *Jewish World Review,* Mar. 19, 2001.

3. Strobe Talbott, "The Birth of the Global Nation," *Time* magazine (July 20, 1992), p. 70.

4. Abraham Lincoln, "The Perpetuation of Our Political Institutions," Address Before the Young Men's Lyceum of Springfield, Illinois, Jan. 27, 1838.

5. E. Christian Kopff, "The Future Belongs to Us," *Chronicles,* Oct. 5, 1995, p. 33; Patrick J. Buchanan, *The Great Betrayal* (New York: Little, Brown, 1998), p. 287.

6. Roger Scruton, "How I Became a Conservative," *The American Conservative,* Nov. 7, 2005, p. 23.

7. Buchanan, p. 286; Ernest Renan, *The Poetry of the Celtic Races and Other Studies* (Port Washington, NY: Kenikat Press, 1970), pp. 80–81. See also Lawrence Auster, *The Path to National Suicide: An Essay on Immigration and Multiculturalism* (Monterey, VA: American Immigration Control Foundation, 1990), p. 34.

8. Buchanan, p. 287; Renan, p. 79.

9. Peter Brimelow, "Time to Rethink Immigration," *National Review* (June 22, 1992), p. 34.

10. Vadim Borosov, "Personality and National Awareness" in Ellen Myers, "The Place of Nations in Biblical Creation," www.creationism.org; Alexander Solzhenitzyn, ed., *From Under the Rubble* (Boston: Little, Brown, 1975), pp. 208–09.

11. Myrdal quoted in Anatol Lieven, "Wolfish Wilsonians: Existential Dilemmas of the Liberal Internationalists," *Orbis* (Spring 2006), p. 250.

Notes

12. William J. Bennett and Jack Kemp, "A Statement on Immigration," Empower America, Washington, D.C., Oct. 19, 1994.

13. Peter Brimelow, "The National Question," *Chronicles* (June 1993), in Tom Fleming, ed., *Immigration and the American Identity: Selections from Chronicles: A Magazine of American Culture, 1985–1995* (Rockford, IL: Rockford Institute, 1995), p. 66.

14. Patrick J. Buchanan, *Where the Right Went Wrong: How Neoconservatives Subverted the Reagan Revolution and Hijacked the Bush Presidency* (New York: St. Martin's Press, 2004), p. 40.

15. Claes G. Ryn, "Cultural Diversity and Unity," in Fleming, ed., *Immigration and the American Identity*, pp. 175–76.

16. Ibid, p. 174.

17. Quoted in ibid, p. 176.

18. Arthur M. Schlesinger, Jr., *The Disuniting of America: Reflections on a Multicultural Society* (New York: W. W. Norton & Co., 1992), p. 37.

19. President Bill Clinton, "One America in the 21st Century," Address to the Graduating Class of the University of California at San Diego, June 14, 1997. See also Stanley Renshon, *The 50 percent American: Immigration and Identity in an Age of Terror* (Washington, DC: Georgetown University Press, 2005), p. 39.

20. Huntington quoted in Lieven, p. 251.

21. Schlesinger, pp. 134, 137.

22. "First Inaugural of George W. Bush," Jan. 20, 2001, http://www.law.ou.edu/hist/gwbush-inaugural-2001.shtml.

23. Sam Francis, "Tyranny Comes for Christmas," Dec. 24, 2004, *Creators Syndicate*; www.vdare.com/francis/041223_tyranny.htm.

24. "Our Revolution: Reagan's Farewell Address," *National Review Online*, June 5, 2004; www.nationalreview.com/document/reagan200406052132.asp.

25. James Pinkerton, "National Suicide: Jean Raspail Foretold the Breakdown Three Decades Ago," *The American Conservative*, Dec. 5, 2005; www.amconmag.com/2005.

26. Sam Francis, "Inventing Fake New Holidays Won't Help," *Creators Syndicate*, May 13, 2003; www.vdare.com/francis/fake/_holidays.htm.

27. Selwyn Duke, "Written by the Losers: Political Correctness Plays with the Past," *The American Conservative*, Mar. 13, 2006, p. 17.

28. Fleming, ed., *Immigration and the American Identity*, p. 14.

29. Schlesinger, pp. 47–48.

30. James R. Edwards, Jr., "Keeping Extremists Out: The History of Ideological Exclusion, and the Need for Its Revival," *Backgrounder*, Center for Immigration Studies (Sept. 2005).

31. See Timothy Keesee and Mark Sidwell, *United States History for Christian Schools*, 2nd ed. (Greenville, SC: Bob Jones University Press, 1991), pp. 108–09.

32. *The Papers of Thomas Jefferson*. Vol. 1: *1760–1776*, ed. Julian P. Boyd (Princeton: Princeton University Press, 1950), pp. 243–47; *The Writings of Thomas Jefferson*, Vol. 1 (Washington, DC: Thomas Jefferson Memorial Association, 1903), pp. 28–38. www.wsu.edu:8080/-dee/AMERICA/DECLAR.htm.

33. Crèvecoeur quoted in Schlesinger, p. 12 (italics in the original).

34. Washington quoted in John Fonte, "Dual Allegiance: A Challenge to Immigration Reform and Patriotic Assimilation," *Backgrounder*, Center for Immigration Studies (Nov. 2005), p. 5. See also Bruce Fein, "Divided Loyalties," *Washington Times*, Dec. 13, 2005, p. A19.

35. Fonte, op. cit., p. 5; Fein, op. cit., p. A19.

36. Quoted in Schlesinger, p. 25 (italics in the original).

37. Abraham Lincoln, first inaugural, Washington, D.C., Mar. 4, 1861.

38. Schlesinger, p. 35; Fonte, op. cit., pp. 5–6.

39. Schlesinger, p. 35.

40. Zangwill quoted in Wattenberg, op. cit.

41. Renshon, op. cit., p. xvii.

42. Ibid., p. xviii.

43. Thomas Jefferson, *Autobiography*, 1821.

44. Robert A. Rutland, *James Madison and the Search for Nationhood* (Washington, DC: Library of Congress, 1981), p. 128.

45. Abraham Lincoln, "Eulogy of Henry Clay," July 6, 1852, in Roy P. Basler, ed., *The Collected Works of Abraham Lincoln*. Vol. II (New Brunswick, NJ: Rutgers University Press, 1953), p. 132.

46. John Adams, Letter to John Taylor, Apr. 15, 1814. *The Works of John Adams*, ed. Charles Francis Adams, Vol. 6, p. 484 (1851).

47. Thomas Jefferson to Isaac H. Tiffany, 1816. ME 15:65.

48. Madison, *Federalist Papers*, p. 95.

49. Alexander Hamilton, *Works*, II, 4.40, as cited in *The Great Quotations*, George Seldes, comp. (New York: Pocket Books, 1972), p. 265.

50. Samuel Huntington, "The Erosion of American National Interests," *Foreign Affairs*, vol. 76, no. 5 (Sept.–Oct. 1997).

51. Claes Ryn, "Leo Strauss and History: The Philosopher as Conspirator," *Humanitas*, Vol. XVIII, Nos. 1 & 2, 2005, p. 55.

52. Huntington, "The Erosion of American National Interests," op. cit.

10. The Return of Tribalism

1. Arthur M. Schlesinger, Jr., *The Disuniting of America* (New York: W. W Norton & Co., 1992), p. 10.

2. Hacker quoted in Steven Goldberg, "Fads and Fallacies in the Name of 'Race Does Not Exist,'" *VDARE.com*, Feb. 21, 2006; www.vdare.com/misc/060221_goldberg.htm.

3. Sam Francis, as quoted by Patrick J. Buchanan in *Shots Fixed: Sam Francis on America's Culture War*, ed. Peter Gemma (Vienna, VA: Fran Griffin Foundation, 2006), p. xii.

4. Samuel Francis, "The Return of the Repressed," *Occidental Quarterly*, vol. 5, no. 3 (Fall 2005), p. 37.

5. Schlesinger, p. 10.

6. Steven Lee Myers, "Ethnic and Cultural Divisions Haunt Ukraine Before Vote," *New York Times*, Mar. 24, 2006, p. A10.

7. Renwick McLean, "Basque Nationalists See an Opening for Autonomy," *New York Times*, Mar. 24, 2006, p. A8.

8. Martin van Creveld, *The Rise and Decline of the State* (Cambridge: Cambridge University Press, 2005), p. 330.

9. Ibid., pp. 330–31.

10. Peter Brimelow, *Alien Nation: Common Sense About America's Immigration Disaster* (New York: Random House, 1995), p. 126.

11. Martin van Creveld, "The Fate of the State," *Parameters* (Spring 1996), p. 4; carlisle-www.army.mil/usawc/Parameters//96spring/creveld.htm.

12. Richard McGregor, "China Bans Screenings of 'Memoirs of a Geisha,'" *Financial Times*, Feb. 4, 2006, p. 5.

13. Juan Forero and Larry Rohter, "Bolivia Leader Tilting Region Further to Left," *New York Times*, Jan. 22, 2006, p. 1.

14. Isabel Sanchez, "President Names 'Cabinet of Change,'" *The Australian*, Jan. 24, 2006; www.theaustralian.news.com.au. "New Bolivian President Vows Justice for Indigenous People," *Agence France-Presse*, Jan. 23, 2006.

15. Monte Reel, "Race Is Wild Card in Peru Runoff," *The Washington Post*, June 3, 2006, p. A8.

16. Yeh Ling-Ling, "Mexican Immigration and Its Potential Impact on the Political Future of the United States," *Journal of Social, Political and Economic Studies*, vol. 29, no. 4 (Winter 2004); www.diversityalliance.org/docs/article_2004winter.html.

17. Ibid.

18. Shelby Steele, "Yo, Howard!: Why Did Dean Have to Embrace the Confederate Flag?", *Wall Street Journal*, Nov. 13, 2003; www.opinionjournal.com.

19. Nisbet quoted in Francis, pp. 43–44.

20. Cited in Schlesingér, pp. 110–11.

21. Theodore Roosevelt, "Speech to the Knights of Columbus," Carnegie Hall, Oct. 15, 1915, www.wikipedia.org/wiki/Hyphenated_American.

22. Steve Sailer, "The Color of Crime and the New Orleans Nightmare: George W. Bush vs. Jared Taylor," Sept. 18, 2005, *VDARE.com*; www.vdare. com/sailer/050918_crime.htm.

23. *The Color of Crime: Race, Crime and Justice in America.* 2nd expanded ed. (Oakton, VA: New Century Foundation, 2005), inside cover page.

24. Ibid.

25. Heather Mac Donald, "The Illegal-Alien Crime Wave: Why Can't Our Immigration Authorities Deport the Hordes of Illegal Felons in Our Cities?", *City Journal* (Winter 2004); www.city-journal.org.

26. John Pomfret, "Jail Riots Illustrate Racial Divide in California," *Washington Post,* Feb. 21, 2006, p. A1.

27. Ibid.

28. Roger D. McGrath, "Race War Behind Bars: In Los Angeles Prisons, Mexican Gangs Target Black Inmates," *The American Conservative,* Mar. 27, 2006, p. 20.

29. Randal C. Archibold, "More Injuries as Race Riots Disrupt Jails in Los Angeles," *New York Times,* Feb. 10, 2006, p. A14; www.nytimes.com/2006/02/10/national/10prison.html.

30. McGrath, op. cit., p. 20.

31. Pomfret, op. cit., p. A1.

32. Ibid.

33. Roger Kimball, "Charles Péguy," *The New Criterion,* vol. 20, no. 3 (November 2001); www.newcriterion.com/archive/20/nov01/peguy.htm.

34. Schlesinger, p. 16.

35. Claes G. Ryn, "Cultural Diversity and Unity," *Chronicles* (June 1993), in Tom Fleming, ed., *Immigration and the American Identity: Selections from Chronicles: A Magazine of American Culture, 1985–1995* (Rockford, IL: Rockford Institute, 1995), p. 173.

36. Patrick J. Buchanan, "The No-Whites-Need-Apply Caucus," *Creators Syndicate,* May 24, 2002; *TownHall.com,* May 27, 2002; www.townhall.com/opinion/columns/patbuchanan/2002/05/27/16338.8.html. Lynette Clemetson, "Minority Caucus Seeks Capitol Hill Bond," *New York Times,* May 19, 2002.

37. Clemetson, op. cit.

38. Ibid.

39. Goldberg, op. cit.

11. Eurabia

1. J. Enoch Powell, "Speech to West Midlands Conservatives, Apr. 20, 1968," www.vdare.com/misc/Powell-Speech.htm.

2. Jean Raspail, "The Fatherland Betrayed by the Republic," *Le Figaro*, June 17, 2004 (trans. Peter Wakefield Sault).

3. Bruce Bawer, *While Europe Slept: How Radical Islam Is Destroying the West from Within* (New York: Doubleday, 2006), quoted in *Book World*, Mar. 26, 2006, p. 5; Steven Simon, "Guess Who's Coming to Europe?" www.washingtonpost.com.

4. Powell, op. cit.

5. "Tory Leader Rules Powell Out of Shadow Cabinet," *Birmingham Post*, April 22, 1968; www.sterlingtimes.co.uk/powell_press.htm.

6. Tony Blankley, *The West's Last Chance: Will We Win the Battle of Civilizations?* (Washington, DC: Regnery, 2005), pp. 51, 55.

7. Leo McKinstry, "Dis-United Kingdom," *Weekly Standard*, Dec. 5, 2005, pp. 12–13.

8. Jason Bennetto, "Gang Held Over Smuggling 100,000 Turks into Britain," *The Independent*, Oct. 12, 2005; www.news.independent.co.uk /uk/crime/article 318866.ece. Daniel Pipes, "Europe Under Siege," *New York Sun*, Oct. 18, 2005; www.danielpipes.org/article/3043; Oct. 18, 2005; www. frontpagemag.com.

9. Raspail, op. cit.

10. Paul Craig Roberts, "Truth Follows Fiction: Camp of the Saints Begins in France," *VDARE.com*, Feb. 20, 2001; www.vdare.com/roberts/truth_follows_fiction.htm.

11. *Border Watch*, Newsletter of the American Immigration Control Foundation (May 1991), p. 8.

12. Sam Francis, "When the State Is the Enemy of the Nation," *VDARE.com*, July 19, 2004; www.vdare.com/francis/enemy_state.htm.

13. Francis, Raspail, op. cit.

14. Raspail, op. cit.

15. Ibid.

16. Ibid.

17. Jonathan Laurence, "U.S.-France Analysis, 2001," Center for European Studies, Harvard (Dec. 2001); www.brookings.eu/fp/cusf/analysis/ islam. htm.

18. Ibid.

19. Christopher Caldwell, "Allah Mode: France's Islam Problem," *Weekly Standard*, July 15, 2002; www.weeklystandard.com.

20. Peggy Hollinger, "Sarkozy Unveils Initiatives to Stop Urban Discontent That Fuelled Riots," *Financial Times*, Nov. 29, 2005.

21. David Pryce-Jones, "The Fear in France," *National Review/Digital*, Apr. 24, 2006. David Pryce-Jones, "David Pryce-Jones on the French: Ouch," *National Review*, Apr. 24, 2006, p. 25; *theaugeanstables.com*, Apr. 9, 2006.

22. Matthew Campbell, "Barbarians of Suburbs Target French Jews," *Sunday Times* (London), Apr. 2, 2006, p. 26; *TimesOnline*.

23. Molly Moore, "For the French Joie de Vivre Fades into Fear," *Washington Post*, Mar. 25, 2006, pp. 1, 13.

24. Elaine Ganley, "Historians Upset as France Burnishes Its Colonial Past," *Washington Times*, Oct. 23, 2005, p. A7. Jon Henley, "The Empire Strikes Back," *Guardian*, Dec. 16, 2005; www.guardian.co.uk./elsewhere/journalist/ story.

25. John Ward Anderson, "Law on Teaching Rosy View of Past Dividing France," *Washington Post*, Dec. 17, 2005, p. A18.

26. Ibid.

27. Ganley, op. cit., p. A7; Anderson, op. cit., p. A18.

28. Anderson, op. cit., p. A18.

29. Ganley, op. cit., p. A7; Anderson, op. cit., p. A18.

30. Anderson, op. cit., p. A18.

31. Ganley, op. cit., p. A7.

32. John Derbyshire, "The Luckiest Generation," *National Review Online*, Nov. 23, 2005; www.nationalreview.com/script.

33. Mark Burleigh, "Gang Terrorizes Train in France," *Washington Times*, Jan. 5, 2006, p. A1.

34. Craig S. Smith, "Party on Right Gains Support After Rioting Upsets France," *New York Times*, Apr. 23, 2006, p. A6.

35. Leslie Crawford, "Spaniards Want More Action on Moroccan Migrants," *Financial Times*, Oct. 18, 2005, p. 6.

36. Al Goodman, "Suspected Madrid Bombing Leader Killed," *CNN.com*, Apr. 4, 2004.

37. Crawford, op. cit., p. 6.

38. Pipes, op. cit.

39. Mark Mulligan and Raphael Minder, "Spain and Morocco Call for Joint Action Over Tide of Immigrants," *Financial Times*, Oct. 12, 2005, p. 3.

40. Pipes, op. cit.

41. Leslie Crawford, "African Migrants Risk All to Reach the Canaries," *Financial Times*, Mar. 18–19, 2006, p. 2.

42. Ibid.

43. The account that follows comes from Patrick J. Buchanan, "The Culture War

Comes to Holland," *Creators Syndicate*, Nov. 26, 2004; http://www.world
netdaily.com.

44. Blankley, p. 95.

45. James Bemis, "Europe: The Cost of Apostasy," *Latin Mass* (Spring 2006),
p. 17.

46. Quoted in Buchanan, "The Culture War Comes to Holland."

47. Francis Fukuyama, "A Year of Living Dangerously," *Wall Street Journal*,
Nov. 2, 2005, ed. page.

48. Ibid.

49. Francis Fukuyama, "Europe vs. Radical Islam," *Slate*, posted Feb. 27, 2006.

50. Ibid.

51. Robert Collier, "Germany Grapples with Turkish Immigration," *Washington
Times*, Dec. 4, 2005, p. A8.

52. Peter Schneider, "The New Berlin Wall," *New York Times Magazine*, Dec. 4,
2005, p. 68.

53. Ibid, p. 71.

54. Collier, op. cit., p. A8.

55. Schneider, op. cit., p. 70.

56. Robert Nisbet, *Prejudices: A Philosophical Dictionary* (Cambridge, MA:
Harvard University Press, 1982), p. 24.

57. Corbell-Essonnes and Evry, "An Underclass Rebellion," *Economist*, Nov. 10,
2005, p. 26.

58. Schneider, p. 70.

59. Ibid., p. 71.

60. Ibid.

61. Collier, op. cit., p. A8.

62. Tony Paterson, "Americans and Jews Villains in Blockbuster," *Washington
Times*, Mar. 1, 2006, p. 1.

63. Ibid.

64. "Party Off Ballot for Racist Ad," *Washington Times*, Nov. 27, 2005, p. 6.

65. Derek Turner, "The Empire Strikes Back: Reverse Colonization in Europe,"
Occidental Quarterly, vol. 5, no. 4 (Winter 2005–06), p. 48.

66. Tom Parfitt, "Population Gloom," *Guardian*, Dec. 29, 2005; www
.guardian.co.uk.

67. John Donne, "Devotions upon Emergent Occasions," Meditation XVII,
1624, in *John Bartlett, Familiar Quotations* (Boston: Little, Brown, 1955),
p. 218.

68. *World Population 2004*, Department of Economic and Social Affairs: Population Division, United Nations, August 2005, www.unpopulation.org.

69. Bemis, op. cit., p. 17.

70. Blankley, p. 25.

71. Mike Corder, Associated Press, "Racial Violence Shocks Australian City," *Breitbart.com,* Dec. 11, 2005; www.breitbart.com/news/2005/12/11/ D8EEF3JO0.html.

72. James Fulford, "Diversity vs. Freedom (contd.): Australians Fight on the Beaches," *VDARE.com*; www.vdare.com/misc/051221_fraser.htm.

73. Steyn quoted in ibid.

74. Caldwell, op. cit.

75. Corder, op. cit.

76. "Australian PM Condemns Race Riots," United Press International, Dec. 12, 2005; www.washingtontimes.com/newstrack/20051212-041252-9690r .htm.

77. Doug Struck, "Canada Thriving as New Leader Steps In," *Washington Post,* Feb. 6, 2006, p. A12.

12. "A Nation of Immigrants"?

1. Aldrich quoted in Otis J. Graham, Jr., *Unguarded Gates: A History of America's Immigration Crisis* (Lanham, MD: Rowman & Littlefield, 2004), p. xvi.

2. John F. Kennedy, *A Nation of Immigrants*. Revised and enlarged edn. with an Introduction by Robert F. Kennedy (New York: Harper & Row, 1965), pp. 2, 3, 64–65.

3. "That's Hospitality," *New Republic,* Apr. 17, 2006, p. 7.

4. Graham, p. xvi.

5. Ibid., p. 68.

6. Ibid., p. 69.

7. Arthur M. Schlesinger, Jr., *The Disuniting of America: Reflections on a Multicultural Society* (New York: W. W. Norton & Co., 1992), p. 32.

8. Kennedy, p. 3; James A Fulford, "Immigration Myths (A Series): FDR Never Addressed the DAR as 'Fellow Immigrants,'" *VDARE.com,* Mar. 21, 2001; www.vdare.com/fulford/fdr_dar.htm.

9. James R. Edwards, Jr., "Keeping Extremists Out: The History of Ideological Exclusion, and the Need for Its Revival," *Backgrounder,* Center for Immigration Studies (Sept. 2005), p. 2.

10. Ibid., p. 3.

11. Kennedy, p. 15.

12. Ibid., p. 64; Peter Brimelow, *Alien Nation: Common Sense About America's Immigration Disaster* (New York: Random House, 1995), p. 16.

13. Kennedy, pp. 69–70.

14. Ibid., p. 17.

15. Ibid., p. 70.
16. Peter Brimelow, Afterword, in Tom Fleming, ed., *Immigration and the American Identity: Selections from Chronicles: A Magazine of American Culture, 1985–1995* (Rockford, IL: Rockford Institute, 1995), pp. 225–26.
17. Kennedy, p. 71.
18. Brimelow, *Alien Nation,* p. 13.
19. Kennedy, p. 72.
20. Ibid., p. 73.
21. Louis R. Harlan, ed., *The Booker T. Washington Papers.* Vol. 1 (Urbana: University of Illinois Press, 1972), p. 331; Patrick J. Buchanan, *The Great Betrayal: How American Sovereignty and Social Justice Are Being Sacrificed to the Gods of the Global Economy* (New York: Little, Brown, 1998), p. 290.
22. Buchanan, *The Great Betrayal,* p. 291.
23. Graham, p. 46.
24. Frederick W. Marks III, *Wind Over Sand: The Diplomacy of Franklin Roosevelt* (Athens, GA: University of Georgia Press, 1988), p. 8.
25. Graham, p. 47.
26. Ibid., p. 50.
27. Vaile quoted in ibid., p. 49.
28. Wayne Lutton, "The Silent Invasion," in Fleming, ed., *Immigration and the American Identity,* p. 97.
29. Mae M. Ngai, "The Unlovely Residue of Outworn Prejudices," in Michael Kazin and Joseph A. McCartin, eds., *Americanism: New Perspectives on the History of an Ideal* (Chapel Hill: University of North Carolina Press, 2006), p. 109.
30. Kennedy, p. 74.
31. Ngai, op. cit., p. 117.
32. Kennedy, p. 78.
33. Brimelow, *Alien Nation,* p. 34; "Operation Wetback," *The Handbook of Texas Online,* www.tsha-vtex.edu/handbook/online/articles; "Today's Letter: A Reader Remembers Operation Wetback . . ." http:/vdare.com/letters/+1072701.
34. Graham, p. 81.
35. Kennedy, p. 80.
36. Ibid.
37. Ibid., p. 82.
38. Ibid., p. xi.
39. Lawrence Auster. *The Path to National Suicide: An Essay on Immigration and Multiculturalism* (Monterey, VA: American Immigration Control Foundation, 1990), p. 12. See also Peter Brimelow, "Time to Rethink Immigration,"

National Review, June 22, 1992, p. 31; Brimelow, *Alien Nation,* pp. 76–77; and Graham, p. 93.

40. Auster, pp. 12–13.

41. Georgie Anne Geyer, "Immigration: The Elephant in America's Room," Universal Press Syndicate (Oct. 2005); www.uexpress.com.

42. Lutton, "The Silent Invasion," p. 84.

43. Graham, p. 96.

44. Auster, p. 19.

45. Steve Sailer, "Cesar Chavez, Minuteman," *The American Conservative,* Feb. 27, 2006, pp. 11–13.

46. Sailer, "Cesar Chavez, Minuteman," p. 12.

47. Ibid.

48. Ibid.

49. Kennedy, pp. 84–85.

50. Brimelow, "Time to Rethink Immigration," p. 31.

13. Last Chance

1. Sam Gompers, "Letter to J. H. Reiter, Haverford College," Apr. 28, 1921, *The Social Contract Press;* www.thesocialcontract.com.

2. Peter Brimelow, "In Memoriam: Ronald W. Reagan," June 5, 2004, *VDARE.com;* www.vdare.com/pb/rwr/_memoriam.htm.

3. Gompers, "Letter to Congress," Mar. 19, 1924, *NumbersUSA;* www.numbersusa.com.

4. Lawrence Auster, *The Path to National Suicide* (Monterey, VA: American Immigration Control Foundation, 1990), p. 5.

5. President George W. Bush, "President Discusses Border Security and Immigration Reform in Arizona," press release, The White House, Nov. 28, 2005.

6. Amanda Carpenter, "(Duncan) Hunter Promotes Fence, (George) Allen Sits on It," *Human Events,* Dec. 16, 2005; freerepublic.com.

7. Victor Davis Hanson, "Mi Casa Es Su Casa," *Wall Street Journal,* Dec. 30, 2005; www.victorhanson.com.

8. Allan Wall, "Newsflash: HR4437 Rejected!—By Mexico's Meddling Government," *Memo from Mexico, VDARE.com,* Jan. 25, 2006; www.vdare.com/awall/060125_newsflash.htm.

9. Ibid.

10. Ibid.

11. Heather Mac Donald, "Mexico's Undiplomatic Diplomats," *City Journal* (Autumn 2005), pp. 40–41.

12. Mark Stevenson, "Few Protections for Migrants to Mexico," Associated Press, April 19, 2006; www.hosted.ap.org.

13. Phyllis Schlafly, "American Citizenship Is Precious," *Phyllis Schlafly Report,* vol. 39, no. 4 (Nov. 2005).

14. Phyllis Schlafly, "Congress Needs to Exercise Its Authority Over U.S. Citizenship," Copley News Service, Oct. 10, 2005; www.townhall.com. "Congress Must Control U.S. Citizenship," *Middle American News* (Nov. 2005), p. 21.

15. Ibid.

16. Stanley Renshon, "Reforming Dual Citizenship in the United States," *Center Paper 25,* Center for Immigration Studies (Sept. 2005), p. 5.

17. Clyde Wilson, "As a City Upon a Hill," in Tom Fleming, ed., *Immigration and the American Identity* (Rockford, IL: Rockford Institute, 1995), p. 35.

18. William B. Dickinson, cover memo, "A Letter to Fellow Citizens, Dec. 1, 2005," Biocentric Institute, International Academy for Preventive Medicine, Warrenton, VA: wdicki2@LSU.edu.

19. Ibid.

20. Max Boot, "Uncle Sam Wants Tu," *Los Angeles Times,* Feb. 24, 2005.

21. Allan Wall, "Your Fellow Citizen—Thalia!", *VDARE.com,* Mar. 1, 2006; www.vdare.com/awall/060301_thalia.htm.

22. Arnaud de Borchgrave, "Touching the Third Rail," *Washington Times,* Apr. 29, 2006, commentary page.

23. Renshon, op. cit., p. 7.

24. Ibid. (italics in the original).

25. Jim VandeHei and Jonathan Weisman, "Bush Begins Push for Immigration Deal with Congress," *Washington Post,* Apr. 25, 2006, p. A4.

26. Jessica Vaughn, "Attrition Through Enforcement: A Cost-Effective Strategy to Shrink the Illegal Population," Center for Immigration Studies (Apr. 2006); www.cis.org/articles/2006/back406.html.

Select Bibliography

Books

Attarian, John. *Economism and the National Prospect*. Monterey, VA: American Immigration Control Foundation, 2001.

Auster, Lawrence. *The Path to National Suicide: An Essay on Immigration and Multiculturalism*. Monterey, VA: American Immigration Control Foundation, 1990.

Bailey, Thomas A. *A Diplomatic History of the American People*. 7th ed. New York: Appleton-Century Crofts, 1964.

Brimelow, Peter. *Alien Nation: Common Sense About America's Immigration Disaster*. New York: Random House, 1995.

Buchanan, Patrick J. *The Death of the West: How Dying Populations and Immigrant Invasions Imperil Our Country and Civilization*. New York: St. Martin's Press, 2002.

———. *A Republic, Not an Empire*. Washington, DC: Regnery Publishing, 1999.

Fleming, Tom, ed. *Immigration and the American Identity: A Selection from Chronicles: A Magazine of Culture, 1985–1995*. Rockford, IL: Rockford Institute, 1995.

Francis, Sam. *America Extinguished: Mass Immigration and the Disintegration of American Culture*. Monterey, VA: American Immigration Control Foundation, 2002.

Graham, Otis J., Jr. *Unguarded Gates: A History of America's Immigration Crisis*. Lanham, MD: Rowman & Littlefield, 2004.

Kennedy, John F. *A Nation of Immigrants*. Rev. and enlarged ed. with an Introduction by Robert F. Kennedy. New York: Harper & Row, 1965.

Ngai, Mac. "The Unlovely Residue of Outworn Prejudices," in Michael Kazin and Joseph A. McCartin, eds., *Americanism: New Perspectives on the History of an Ideal*. Chapel Hill: University of North Carolina Press, 2006.

Select Bibliography

Renshon, Stanley. *The 50 percent American: Immigration and the National Identity in an Age of Terror.* Washington, DC: Georgetown University Press, 2005.

Schlesinger, Arthur, Jr. *The Disuniting of America: Reflections of a Multicultural Society.* New York: W. W. Norton & Co., 1992.

Published Articles and Reports

Camarota, Steve. "Immigrants at Mid-Decade: A Snapshot of America's Foreign Born Population in 2005," *Backgrounder,* Center for Immigration Studies (Dec. 2005).

Carpenter, Ted Galen. *Mexico Is Becoming the Next Colombia. Foreign Policy Briefing,* No. 87. Washington, DC: Cato Institute, 2005.

Custred, Glynn. "Friends and Elites, Chickens and Coyotes," *American Spectator* (Nov. 2005), p. 28.

Edwards, James R., Jr. "Keeping Extremists Out: The History of Ideological Exclusion and the Need for Its Revival," *Backgrounder,* Center for Immigration Studies (Sept. 2005).

Federation for American Immigration Reform. "Criminal Aliens." October 2002.

Fonte, John. "Dual Allegiance: A Challenge to Immigration Reform and Patriotic Assimilation," *Backgrounder.* Washington, DC: Center for Immigration Studies, 2005.

Judis, John. "Border War," *New Republic,* Jan. 16, 2006, p. 15.

Ling-Ling, Yeh. "Mexican Immigration and Its Potential Impact on the Political Future of the United States," *Journal of Social, Political and Economic Studies,* vol. 29, no. 4 (Winter 2004).

Mac Donald, Heather. "The Illegal Alien Crime Wave," *City Journal* (Winter 2004).

———. "Mexico's Undiplomatic Diplomats," *City Journal* (Autumn 2005).

McGrath, Roger. "End of the Rainbow," *The American Conservative,* Dec. 19, 2005.

Schlafly, Phyllis. "American Citizenship Is Precious," *Phyllis Schlafly Report* (Nov. 2005).

Whitehead, John W. "A Ticking Time Bomb: Diseases That Cross America Borders," Rutherford Institute, Dec. 11, 2004.

Index

Read more from America's leading populist conservative

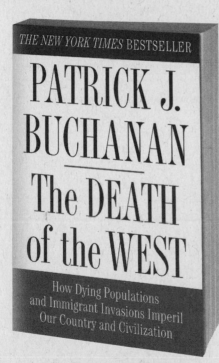

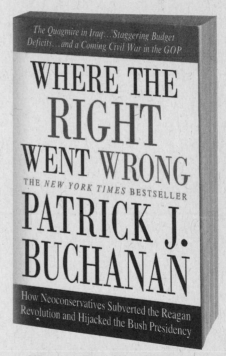

THE DEATH OF THE WEST
The *New York Times* bestseller that shocked the nation—an unflinching look at the increasing decline in Western culture and power.

WHERE THE RIGHT WENT WRONG
A searing indictment of the George W. Bush administration that chronicles the abandonment of true conservatism.

www.buchanan.org